*To Marla — ... ...
you capacity to color outside
the lines.*

*Cheers!
Phil*

LEAD
LIKE A
HERETIC

How to Challenge the Status Quo – and Thrive

DR. PHIL JOHNSON

PROMONTORY
PRESS

Promontory Press
www.promontorypress.com

ISBN:
978-1-987857-63-4 (paperback)
978-1-987857-93-1 (hardcover)

Typeset by Edge of Water Designs, edgeofwater.com
Cover design by Amy Cole of JPL Design Solutions

Printed in Canada
987654321

To

My Mother

Mary Ann Sawyer Johnson

December 5, 1908 – June 19, 1955

who instilled in me the heart, mind and soul
of a gracious, bold and compassionate heretic.
"The future," she daily reminded me,
"is as bright as the promises of God."

Blessing and love,
Philip Ernest

PRAISE FOR DR. PHIL JOHNSON

"Phil Johnson walks his talk, and has spent his life's journey smiling and serving more than any other human being I have come across, with humor, humility, generosity, personal sacrifice and a great measure of surprise and constructive disruption. (He once, literally, gave me the shirt off his back because I liked it!) For all the decades I have known him, his passion for servant leadership is unmistakable and unequaled. If you are looking to find inspiration in a message about what leadership could and should be, this is a must read!"

~ Edie Weiner, President & CEO, The Future Hunters

"I couldn't put Phil Johnson's book down. It is a full education on the problems of the world and the roles that caring people can play to improve the lives of other members of the human family. Phil is passionate and inspiring about helping others and shows you how to do it. As an author of Up and Out of Poverty, I couldn't help but think that Phil Johnson is the Good Samaritan role model for the spirit and passion needed to lift countless millions out of poverty."

~ Philip Kotler, Professor of International Marketing, Northwestern University

"Dr. Phil Johnson's tested seven-step guide to becoming a Compassionate Conspirator enables readers to transform the human family by the power of compassion."

~ Bob Danzig, former President, Hearst Newspapers

"That our world is seriously sick is a foregone conclusion. With timely insight, modeling, reflection and direction, Dr. Johnson points us to three things on the pathway toward healing – hope, health and harmony. Soulwise is a masterpiece – a must read for all who seek to make our world a better place."

~ Dr. Peter Okaalet, Africa Director, Medical Assistance Programs International

"Dr. Phil Johnson is an intellectual who truly speaks from the heart. If you want to change the world and don't know where to start, this book will show you how."

Barbara Pietrangelo, Executive Board Member, Million Dollar Round Table

"Phil Johnson wants to change the world, promoting hope to counteract the cynicism of our time. He believes spiritual renewal is essential for a harmonious world."

~ Tony Campolo, Professor of Sociology, Eastern University

"This warm, compassionate, compelling book is a paean to hope - to its power to both inspire and save. Phil Johnson shows by his own extraordinary life what people, individually and collectively, can do to make a better world."

~ Arnold Brown, Futurist, coauthor of FutureThink

"Soulwise is packed with hope and possibilities for those who desire to make a difference. It offers leaders around the world a road map to significance and life-changing results."

~ Ron Tschetter, former Director, United States Peace Corps

"Soulwise is a rich compendium of actions needed to alleviate the world's woes, written by a wise and loving man whose life has been devoted to helping others. This book will awaken you to the possibilities of human potential."

~ William E. Halal, Professor of Management, George Washington University

"Phil Johnson writes for the sake of action and change. Readers cannot just read, but must face up to doing, living and growing. Phil forces this confrontation: the world is not getting on so well, and you and I can do something about that."

Mark Fackler, Professor of Communication, Calvin College

LEAD

LIKE A

HERETIC

TABLE OF CONTENTS

FOREWORD

D r. Phil Johnson has written a book for our time.
With our world changing lightning fast because of technology,
we need leaders today to rethink routine, push the envelope, question the
status quo and help set our minds and hearts on fire with motivation.

So read "Lead Like A Heretic." Like oxygen to a flame, it can become
a beacon to help light your way. It engages, encourages and gives us hope
for a better tomorrow by showing us how many courageous souls have
challenged – and improved – the world around them.

And thus, they can help challenge us. They are, in Dr. Johnson's words,
heretics.

They are the heroes, models and mentors that I tell our students at
High Point University to emulate. I want our students to study, read and
walk hand-in-hand with such people so they can realize their full potential,
become who they want to be and make our world a better place.

I believe there is no more beautiful reason to live than that – to
use our talents to improve our community, our home, and plant seeds of
greatness in the lives of those around us.

Dr. Johnson believes that, too.

I know him from our speaking world. For Valentine's Day, I once sent
him a 10-pound chocolate bar to show my gratitude for his friendship,

and from "Lead Like A Heretic," I understand he shared a half-pound of that bar with twenty of his friends.

I understand they loved it.

But 10 pounds of chocolate was my way of showing appreciation. At High Point University, in the life-skills seminars I teach to seniors and first-year students, I tell them you need to leave what I call a "trail of tangibles" to show those around you that you appreciate them for who they are.

Plus, we all love chocolate, don't we? But we also love a good story. That's what you'll find in the pages of the book you now hold in your hands.

Dr. Johnson brings together popular culture and solid leadership theory to illustrate the importance of this African proverb: "For tomorrow belongs to the people who prepare for it today."

His book couldn't come at a better time.

We have leaders today who can answer questions, but don't know how to ask them. They can fulfill goals, but they don't know how to set them. They know how to get things done, but they don't know whether it's worth doing in the first place.

Meanwhile, our schools and universities nationwide don't teach what Dr. Johnson calls the "entrepreneurial spirit." They don't inspire students to be job creators and calculated risk-takers open to asking and answering the question, "What if?"

We do that at High Point University. We prepare our students for a world where change is constant, and once they graduate, they're ready to take on a world as it's going to be.

That makes us heretics, in Dr. Johnson's view. I'm okay with that.

In 2005, after a long career as an entrepreneur, a business owner, a consultant, an author, a leadership expert and professional speaker, I became president of High Point University. I'm an alum, Class of 1970, and a longtime member of the university's Board of Trustees.

But when I came in, I didn't want to maintain the status quo. I wanted to challenge it. I didn't want to think outside the box. I wanted to throw the box out the window.

In 12 years – and during one of the worst economic downturns in our country's history – we at High Point University have invested $2.1 billion and revamped our campus with new buildings, new programs and a new campus-wide, can-do culture grounded in HPU's solid liberal arts curricula.

Our faculty and staff have tripled, our enrollment has risen from 1,500 to 5,000 students and our campus has expanded from 90 to 430 acres.

It's like that roadside sign I wrote about in one of my books. The sign read: "We hear there is a recession. We chose not to participate."

We at High Point University have what I call "faithful courage." We dare to be different, we dare to throw the box out the window, and I'm ever so grateful for what our talented faculty and staff have done. They have prepared our students for a world that needs more innovation, more critical thinkers, more empathy and more love.

In "Lead Like A Heretic," Dr. Johnson writes about the need for that in a personal, smartly written way that feels more like a sermon. It's easy to understand why. Dr. Johnson is an ordained minister.

When he pastored a church decades ago, he used to prepare his Sunday sermon by going into the church's sanctuary. He'd sit in the chairs used by members he knew by first name, and he'd ask himself, "What do they need to hear from me this week?"

It feels he did the same thing with "Lead Like A Heretic." It's accessible, this ninth book he's written. He writes about the need for openness and respect as he tackles a topic that I believe is so important to the future of us and to the future of what needs to be.

More than 150 years ago, Charles Darwin said: "It is not the strongest of the species that will survive; nor the most intelligent that survive. It is the one that is most adaptable to change."

That is still true today.

We need to adapt. "Lead Like A Heretic" shows us how. That can lead to a better you.

It reminds me of the words John Wesley wrote to guide the people he called Methodists.

Do all the good you can,
By all the means you can,
In all the ways you can,
In all the places you can,
At all the times you can,
To all the people you can,
As long as ever you can.

Those words can guide all of us. Dr. Johnson believes that. So do I.

Dr. Nido Qubein
President of High Point University

INTRODUCTION

What do Pope Francis, Florence Nightingale, and Steve Jobs have in common?

They're all heretics—courageous souls who don't conform to an established attitude, doctrine, or principle.

We desperately need heretics to rise to the challenge of disengagement, especially in the workplace. The idea for this book emerged when I saw in my leadership coaching and consulting practice, over a period of several years, a dramatic increase in the disengagement of leaders and associates in the workplace. And when I researched the most recent data on this critical issue, I was stunned to learn that a whopping two thirds of American workers are disengaged. Furthermore, workplace disengagement distresses economies worldwide.

According to a Gallup report (State of the Global Workplace, 2013), disengagement costs the US workforce $450 to $550 billion annually. The article "Why Are So Many Employees Disengaged" in *Forbes Magazine* (January 18, 2013) indicates that The Bureau of National Affairs estimates US businesses lose $11 billion annually due to employee turnover alone. The decreased productivity of each disengaged employee costs each employer $3,400 to $10,000 in salary, and the cost of physical absenteeism is $902 per disengaged employee with a total cost over $75 billion per year. This workplace disengagement distresses economies worldwide.

To add insult to injury, *The Economist*, in its issue "The World in 2010," reports that 84 percent of senior leaders say that one of the three biggest threats facing their business is "disengaged employees," yet only 12 percent of them report regularly tackling the problem. In his book *Tribes: We Need You to Lead Us*, marketing guru Seth Godin writes, "Heretics are the new leaders. The ones who challenge the status quo, who get out in front of their tribes, who create movements ... Suddenly, heretics, troublemakers, and change agents aren't merely thorns in our side—they are the keys to our success."

Heretics lead from the inside out. "If a man loses pace with his companions," reflected American philosopher Henry David Thoreau, "perhaps it is because he hears a different drummer. Let him step to the music which he hears, however measured, or far away." *Lead Like a Heretic: How to Challenge the Status Quo—and Thrive* is a guidebook for leaders at all levels to hear their inner "drummer," and to fully engage, fully energize, and fully empower their followers. This book connects key strategies that historical and contemporary heretics use to enable leaders to engage, energize, and empower people at work, and may be applied to leaders of small to large businesses, non-profit organizations, as well as trade and professional associations.

Lead Like a Heretic will inspire, challenge, and encourage leaders to make a world of difference.

PART ONE

The Heretic: A Profile

CHAPTER 1

The Heretic: A Servant

The word 'heretic,' derived from the Greek *hairetikos*, which means "able to choose," refers to a person believing in or practicing religious heresy, or holding an opinion at odds with what is generally accepted. Common synonyms include dissenter, nonconformist, apostate, freethinker, and iconoclast. To start, we will observe the heretic as a servant, a dreamer, and a challenger. These are folks you'd want to get to know and spend time with. Let's begin with considering the heretic as a servant.

"I'm convinced the best secret of great leaders is they serve," commented Mark Miller, Vice-President of Organizational Effectiveness for Chick-fil-A. "Servant leaders do all the things you'd expect from other great leaders with an added dimension—their motive for leading in the first place. It's actually a matter of the heart."

The idea of a leader acting as a servant is a timeless concept. David, a prominent Biblical leader, provides in the book of 2 Samuel 23: 3-4 (*The Message*), an intriguing metaphor of a leader as servant: "God's Spirit spoke through me, his words took shape on my tongue ... Whoever governs fairly and well, who rules in the Fear-of-God, is like first light at daybreak without a cloud in the sky, like green grass carpeting earth, glistening under fresh rain."

Robert K. Greenleaf coined the phrase 'servant leadership' in "The Servant as Leader," an essay he first published in 1970. In that essay, Greenleaf articulated the essence of servant leadership: "The servant-leader is servant first … It begins with the natural feeling that one wants to serve, to serve first. Then conscious choice brings one to aspire to lead." Heretics embrace servant leadership, which may be practiced in a variety of organizations and institutions.

Heretics as servants identify with this story adapted from Loren Eiseley's 1969 essay, "The Star Thrower." A little boy was walking along a beach with his grandfather when they encountered a pile of starfish that had washed ashore. The little boy ran up to the pile, picked up a starfish, and threw it back into the ocean.

His grandfather caught up to him and gently inquired, "Son, the task is so enormous, what difference can we make?"

The boy responded, "A huge difference to that one!"

Let's build on this foundation of servant leadership to explore how heretics may be described as relentlessly renaissancical, remarkably resilient, and resolutely resourceful.

1.1 RELENTLESSLY RENAISSANCICAL

Heretics give birth to the new. They are essentially renaissancical, based on the derivation of 'renaissance,' from the Latin *renasci*, "be born again, rise again, reappear, be renewed." We study renaissance as a great period of revival of classical-based art and learning in Europe that began in the fourteenth century. By extension, a renaissance comprises a movement or period of robust creative and intellectual activity that is associated with a rebirth of civilization. My research indicates that heretics have played a major role ushering in these fruitful upsetting times.

"Our world today has reached a critical turning point," asserts Patricia Martin, in her book, *Renaissance Generation: The Rise of the Cultural*

Consumer—And What It Means to Your Business. "The passage into a better and brighter time will demand individuals and organizations that possess a force of creativity powerful enough to challenge the status quo, disrupt the marketplace, and transform society." My major challenge in life and leadership coaching of Chief Executive Officers today involves challenging them to embrace change with an exploratory perspective and to unleash their creativity with courage and grit.

"All progress," observed digital artist and singer-songwriter Michael John Bobak, "takes place outside the comfort zone." Steve Jobs, CEO of Apple, certainly lived outside the comfort zone. And from his permanent residence in the discomfort zone, he inspired and influenced others. Arrogant and stubborn, he often cast people into the discomfort zone without their permission. He staged his own kind of revolution relentlessly pursuing new opportunities. Jobs is one of the leading contenders for being the relentlessly renaissancical poster person.

Harvard business Professor Nancy F. Koehn writes about Jobs' legacy: "The more we learn about this brilliant, dogged, at times merciless, and yet supple entrepreneur, the more we realize that he believes he is out to change the world. And that's what seems to motivate him ... The revolution of which Jobs is so much a part is unfolding by virtue of the products he makes and how consumers use them. It is a mostly peaceful revolution that will, in Steve Jobs' eyes, liberate men and women around the world."

Perhaps Jobs' 2005 Convocation address at Stanford reveals best his relentlessly revolutionary perspective: "Your time is limited, so don't waste your time living someone else's life. Don't be trapped by dogma—which is living with the results of other people's thinking. Don't let the noise of others' opinions drown out your own voice. And most important, have the courage to follow your heart and intuition. They somehow already know what you truly want to become. Everything else is secondary."

Heretics use their relentlessly renaissancical capacity to explode possibility, defy conventional wisdom, and walk on the ledge.

Explode Possibility

Heretics never limit themselves. In fact, they do just the opposite. They explode possibility.

The central role and responsibility of heretics involves provoking the impossible by exploding the sense of the possible. They provoke with a purpose that begins with a premise. The word 'provoke' derives from the Latin *provocare*, which means to "call forward." Heretics call forward concerns and issues that need to be addressed openly. To provoke therefore implies the need to change. Provocation tests self- and institutional-confidence to take or recommend new and creative connections and actions, and enter into unknown territory. For the heretic, calling out concerns constitutes a wild adventure.

Leading like a heretic demands a thorough understanding of the nature of provocation and its far-reaching implications. One only has to scan history to recognize that agonizing resistance to change resulted in, among many images, heretics being burned at the stake. From my perspective as a life and leadership coach, remarkable leaders provoke with heart. They certainly provoke, and intentionally heat up the environment, not to offend, injure, or harm, but to make the world a better place for the whole human family. In other words, they provoke in love. Provocation for the heretic begins as a personal journey that provides a foundation for the inevitable risks and relative rewards of championing change. Provocation for leaders of a business, an institution, or a country constitutes an inside job. When leaders are comfortable in their own skin, they can, by their example, enable others to change.

Defy Conventional Wisdom

Relentlessly renaissancical heretics defy conventional wisdom. They know that conventional wisdom usually yields conventional results, so they purposefully go against the grain to expose new problems and seize new opportunities. It's not so much that they are against conventional wisdom (a generally accepted theory or belief that has worked in the past), but they recognize that the future demands fresh wisdom.

Ekaterina Walter, a marketing innovator, and author of *Sprinklr Evangelist*, contends that great leaders are a rare breed that couldn't care less about conventional wisdom. She points out that these leaders often play devil's advocate in order to spark creativity and commitment. I coached a CEO of a Fortune 100 company who mastered the role of devil's advocate. He used it sparingly and productively. His associates knew that whenever he 'played' that role, something very important was at stake. Psychologist Irving Janis pointed out in his seminal book on the topic of groupthink, *Victims of Groupthink*, that legitimizing the role of a contrarian in a group helps keep the group from mindless conformity.

I agree with management consultant Jay Deragon, whose recent article, "Smart Consultants Don't Follow Conventional Wisdom," strikes the nail on the head. In my leadership coaching and consulting practice, I've often found that defying conventional wisdom helps organizations strategically. In fact, progressive senior leaders today look specifically for unscripted coaching. In an interview to be his coach, a CEO of a Fortune 100 company asked me if I had an MBA. I thought I'd lost the opportunity when I told him that I didn't. His response surprised me: "Good. The last thing we need around here is another [insert religiously colorful language here] MBA." I started that day.

Let's now turn our attention to how heretics not only explode possibility and defy conventional wisdom, but also walk on the ledge.

Walk On The Ledge

"One night I couldn't sleep," joked comedian Stephen Wright. "So I got up and took a walk around the building—on the ledge."

Relentlessly renaissancical heretics find themselves 'on the ledge' following their ideals. They follow the advice of the heretic in exile, His

Holiness the Dalai Lama: "Know the rules well, so you can break them effectively." They also subscribe to the counsel of social psychologist Dr. Ellen Langer: "Rules are best to guide, not to dictate." Heretics act as rebels for their causes.

My ministerial colleague, The Rev. Mike Slaughter, lead pastor at Ginghamsburg Church in Dayton, Ohio, and author of *Renegade Gospel: The Rebel Jesus,* depicts Jesus as a ledge-walker: "The renegade gospel espoused by Jesus was a subversive movement. People who defy conventional wisdom are often the ones who contribute the most to human advancement." You may be familiar with the iconic image of the "Laughing Jesus" created in 1973 by my friend, the late Willis Wheatley, a colleague in The United Church of Canada. There are more than a million copies of the image in print today. Fortunately, I have, hanging in my office, a signed 24" x 36" copy of his sketch that was originally titled "Jesus Christ – Liberator." Willis actually drew four poignant portraits of Jesus. The three others include "Jesus Christ – God Become Man," "Jesus Christ – Sufferer," and "Jesus Christ – Revolutionary," which reveal so dramatically the heretical nature of Jesus.

1.2 REMARKABLY RESILIENT

"The secret of success," advises a Chinese proverb, "is to fall down seven times and get up eight."

The Torrens Resilience Institute offers valuable insight into the derivation of the word 'resilience.' Introduced into the English language in the early seventeenth century from the Latin verb *resilire*, the term resilience meant "to rebound or recoil." Over the past two decades, the term 'resilience' has evolved from the disciplines of materials science to become a concept used liberally and enthusiastically by policy makers, practitioners, and academics, to describe the capacity to bounce back, and to recover quickly from illness, change, or misfortune. Business schools have embraced the concept to explain why and how organizations must adapt their strategies to meet the requirements of an ever-changing business environment.

One may describe heretics as remarkably resilient. From my research on historical and contemporary heretics, it appears that resilience forms a significant part of their DNA. They don't think about bouncing back from the inevitable conflicts that arise from challenging the status quo. Automatically, they respond to setbacks purposefully and positively.

Heretics work to create a resilient society, a focus of Joshua Cooper Ramo in his book *The Age of the Unthinkable: Why the New World Disorder Constantly Surprises Us and What We Can Do About It*. "Construction of a resilient society need not be complex," Ramo contends. "The aim is simple enough: to withstand the surprises that await us; to absorb the worst nightmares and walk away with the core attributes of our freedom intact." Ramo predicts "resilience will be the defining concept of twenty-first-century security, as crucial for your fast-changing job as it is for the nation. We can think of resilience as a measure of how much disturbance a system can absorb before it breaks down so fundamentally that it can't easily return to the way it once was. Think of a plastic ruler. How far can you bend it before it snaps?"

I agree with Ramo's assessment and prediction regarding resilience. As a society, tragic events increasingly test our capacity to remain "unsnappable," willing and able to maintain our closely held beliefs and values. Recently, I watched on television only minutes after it occurred in Ankara, Turkey, the assassination of the Russian Ambassador Andrey Karlov. Modern technology gave us the visceral feeling of actually being there to witness this cold-blooded attack. To us, everything appears to happen almost in real time. Unfortunately, we may become numb to real danger in order to protect ourselves from falling apart. Wise leaders put organizational shock absorbers in place and provide their followers an example of thoughtful, calm, and patient resilience.

Let's continue exploring how heretics express their servant leadership by being remarkably resilient as they accept uncertainty, manage energy, and rise like a phoenix.

Accept Uncertainty

"In more than thirty years of research," observes Ellen J. Langer, in her book *Counter Clockwise: Mindful Health and the Power of Possibility*, "I've discovered a very important truth about human psychology: certainty is a cruel mindset." Langer's research provides this finding: "Of all the qualities in a manager conducive to innovation and initiative, a degree of uncertainty may be the most powerful. We found that those managers who were confident but relatively uncertain were evaluated by their employees as more likely to allow independent judgment and a general freedom of action."

Heretics accept uncertainty as a given in the life experiment. They understand that an appreciation of uncertainty pulls them and others out of themselves, and out of their comfort zones, to see, feel, and understand the world differently. The heretic concurs with American business magnate, investor, and philanthropist Warren Buffett's conviction that conservatism stems from the awareness that the future is profoundly uncertain. "In financial markets, almost anything that can happen does happen," he warns. "And it pays to conduct your affairs so that no matter how foolish other people get, you're still around to play the game the next day." At his company, Berkshire Hathaway, he keeps tens of billions in cash for a rainy day. And he never invests borrowed money, observing, "Whenever a really bright person who has a lot of money goes broke, it's because of leverage."

Heretics embrace uncertainty with all its attendant challenges, not because they fear the future, but because, in order to create a better future, they must make a shift from the conventional wisdom of being certain before acting, to recognizing uncertainty as an asset. Joshua Cooper Ramo articulates the case for accepting uncertainty: "A management approach based on resilience would emphasize the need to keep options open. Flowing from this would not be the presumption of sufficient knowledge, but the recognition of our ignorance; not the assumption that future events are expected, but that they will be unexpected."

Perhaps that's why we desperately need heretics to lead the way. An advertisement tag line for Mass Mutual Insurance Company, for whom I was an agent, presents a realistic stance: "You can't predict. But you can prepare."

Manage Energy

"Besides the noble art of getting things done," observes writer Lin Yutang, "there is a nobler art of leaving things undone."

Heretics follow the energy prescription of Jim Loehr and Tony Schwartz, in their book *The Power of Full Engagement: Managing Energy, Not Time, is the Key to High Performance and Personal Renewal.* Organizations unfortunately continue to spend a ton of money on time management, but pay little or no attention to energy management. Loehr and Schwartz identify the sources of energy: physical, defined by the quantity of energy; emotional, by the quality of energy; mental, by the focus of energy; and spiritual, by the force of energy. Energy management helps one become resilient: physically energized, emotionally connected, mentally focused, and spiritually aligned. Their book has dramatically influenced me personally and has helped in enabling my executive coaching business.

Dr. Mihaly Csikszentmihalyi (pronounced "chicks-sent-me-High-ee"), in his book *Flow: The Psychology of Optimal Experience*, describes flow as a "state of mind when consciousness is harmoniously ordered, and people want to pursue whatever they are doing for its own sake." Flow "happens when psychic energy—or attention—is invested in realistic goals, and when skills match the opportunities for action. The pursuit of a goal brings order in awareness because a person must concentrate attention on the task at hand and momentarily forget everything else."

Everybody needs a break for the health of it. Common wisdom says that authors write about what they need. That's true for me. Several years ago, I wrote a book, *Time-Out! How to Restore Your Passion for Life, Love and Work,* and learned how to take time out to refresh, renew, restore, recharge, rejuvenate, reboot, and rejoice. Full engagement requires systematic regular strategic periods of recovery when you can click the refresh button. Disengage to reengage. Retreat to advance. Nourish to flourish.

In his book *Leadership without Easy Answers,* Dr. Ronald Heifetz, a psychiatrist and professional cellist, reflects, "We need sanctuaries." He defines a sanctuary as "a place of reflection and renewal, where you can listen to yourself away from the dance floor and the blare of the music, where you can reaffirm your deeper sense of self and purpose ... one needs a sanctuary to restore one's sense of purpose, put issues in perspective, and regain courage and heart." I have several sanctuaries, my favorite of which is our family's cottage on the shores of Lake Michigan, just north of Ludington, Michigan, where I wrote most of this book. The cottage's name, Wah Win Ga, given by my wife's family, means a "place of vision" in the native language of the Chippewa, a Native American Indian tribe.

Heretics respect the good advice of Dr. Deepak Chopra, an Indian-American author and public speaker, regarding managing energy: "In the midst of movement and chaos, keep stillness inside of you."

Rise Like A Phoenix

"There is no easy walk to freedom anywhere," remarked Nelson Mandela, "and many of us will have to pass through the valley of the shadow of death again and again before we reach the mountaintop of our desires." Mandela, a heretic, presents us with an incredible example of a person's capacity to rise like a phoenix in spite of the odds, and of a servant leader who sacrificed deeply and nobly, and in the process, became a world icon for human rights.

Paul J. H. Schoemaker, research director of the Mack Institute for Innovation Management at the Wharton School of Business, travelled to South Africa where he met with government and business leaders to discuss Mandela's legacy. Schoemaker's article, "Lasting Legacy: Nelson Mandela's Evolution as a Strategic Leader," articulates Mandela's amazing resilience, highlighting the "importance of holding firm to a morally just vision and the ability to influence a sequence of key strategic decisions over time (decades, in his case) in order to bring truly remarkable results." Schoemaker points out, "The key to Mandela's leadership was to encourage racial harmony, forgiveness without forgetting, power sharing and a strong focus on the future, not the past."

The movie *Unbroken* captures the essence of "resilience thinking" as it follows the life of Olympian and war hero Louis "Louie" Zamperini, who survived in a raft for forty-seven days after a near-fatal plane crash in WWII—only to be caught by the Japanese navy and sent to a prisoner-of-war camp. It's a true story about the resilient power of the human spirit, and an epic drama of survival, resilience, and redemption. The movie's trailer sums up Zamperini's mantra: "If you can take it, you can make it." During the recession of 2008-9, superb leaders did not consider the turbulent disruption a negative setback but an opportunity to bounce back with resolve and lead their organizations into the future with confidence. Heretics seem to naturally possess resilience, and like the phoenix, face challenges not as an inconvenience but as a puzzle to be solved, and confidently rise from the ashes.

1.3 RESOLUTELY RESOURCEFUL

A Bornean Proverb catches the resolutely resourceful spirit of the heretic: "Where the heart is willing, it will find a thousand ways, but where it is unwilling, it will find a thousand excuses."

We continue our focus on the heretic as a servant, by considering how heretics are resolutely resourceful for their cause and for humanity. They practice what they preach. They use every possible avenue to achieve what they consider to be justice.

In my mind, the heretic who models so well this perspective on resourcefulness is His Holiness the fourteenth Dalai Lama, the spiritual leader of the Tibetan people. He frequently states that his life is guided by three major commitments: the promotion of basic human values or secular ethics in the interest of human happiness, the fostering of inter-religious harmony, and the preservation of Tibet's Buddhist culture, a culture of peace and non-violence.

I had the distinct honor of meeting him among fifty delegates at a United Nations-sponsored conference in Tiberius, Israel. In person, the Dalai Lama exudes humility, grace, and joy. The following statement expresses his commitment as a servant leader to the future of humankind:

May I become at all times, both now and forever
A protector for those without protection
A guide for those who have lost their way
A ship for those with oceans to cross
A bridge for those with rivers to cross
A sanctuary for those in danger
A lamp for those without light
A place of refuge for those who lack shelter
And a servant to all in need.

Let's dive in and see how heretics are resolutely resourceful. They seem to be born ready, ask not if but how, and possess network savvy.

Born Ready

An ad for the United States Coast Guard boldly declares: "I was born ready." From my research, heretics by and large seem to be born ready, too. Their DNA is wired to make a difference in the world, and compels them to fulfill their role with a natural capacity to excel.

Let me introduce you to Joey Alexander, a pianist who wowed the crowds at the Newport Jazz Festival in 2015. The headliner of the Festival, he displayed a mastery of technique and a deep, emotional connection with his music. Alexander, who has quickly cultivated a following of millions of fans, is considered one of, if not *the* best of, the new great jazz players to emerge in years. He taught himself to play by listening to his father's albums. Alexander is a Thelonius Monk devotee, and according to his biography posted on the Newport Jazz Festival website, he can "play the standards with astounding virtuosity and an advanced harmonic palette." He told the *New York Times*, "Jazz is a hard music and you have to work really hard and also have fun performing; that's the most important thing." What makes Alexander's music so fascinating is that he's just twelve years old. He was born ready.

Like Alexander, my granddaughter Elsa was born ready to play soccer. At age three, she demonstrated her natural coordination, skill, and agility. But you don't have to be young to discover your significant talent. Many find their groove later in life and contribute significantly to the welfare of humanity. Consider Grandma Moses, who took up painting in her late seventies to worldwide praise, and continued painting into her nineties. Ian Fleming, after succeeding as a journalist, banker, and stockbroker, went on to create James Bond when he was forty-five. Sir Alexander Fleming, a doctor and bacteriologist, at age forty-seven, discovered penicillin for which he received the Nobel Prize in 1945.

Everybody is born ready to develop themselves in their lifetimes. Sometimes the conditions under which we grow do not allow us to blossom immediately. But everyone has an opportunity in their lifetime to let their light shine. There are always opportunities for heretics with a keen awareness of their context to bring their 'born ready' talent to full bloom. "Only under certain circumstances of constructive stress or in certain states—great love, for example, or religious ardor, or the courage of battle—do we begin to tap the depth and richness of our creative resources, or the tremendous reserves of life energy that lie sleeping within us," intuitively reflects Ellen Langer. Nature or nurture? I'm not sure it matters a great deal. Both play a significant role. I do know, however, that when our natural talent and solid preparation intersect with opportunity, amazing things happen.

As my Scout motto urges: "Be prepared." Be ready, like servant-leader heretics, to spring into action for whomever, whenever, wherever, and however.

Not If But How

"I am not afraid," pronounced Joan of Arc, "I was born to do this." Nicknamed "The Maid of Orléans," France considers her a heroine for her role during the Lancastrian phase of the Hundred Years' War, and an enduring symbol of French unity and nationalism. Pope Benedict XV canonized her in 1920.

Joan of Arc believed that God had chosen her to lead France to victory in its long-running war with England and, with no military training, she convinced the embattled crown prince Charles of Valois to allow her to lead a French army to the besieged city of Orléans, where it achieved a momentous victory over the English and their French allies, the Burgundians. After seeing the prince crowned King Charles VII, Joan was captured by Anglo-Burgundian forces, tried for witchcraft and heresy, and at the age of nineteen, burned at the stake in 1431. Her fame only increased after her death, however, and twenty years later a new trial ordered by Charles VII cleared her name. She asked, not if but how, like many other heretics, and paid the ultimate price with her life.

Joan of Arc typifies heretics who faced incredible odds with dedication and persistence and changed the world. Resolutely resourceful, with the emphasis on resolutely, they asked a single question: How are we going to accomplish our goal? They didn't consider whether or not they could accomplish their goal. Their confident mindset announces: We will find a way! And as the saying goes, "Where there's a will, there's a way." They are, in a word, determined to find creative approaches to getting what's needed done.

I credit my mother for instilling in me the 'not if but how' attitude that has stood me in good stead in my officer training in the Canadian Armed

Forces, in my mission work to feed hungry children in Kibera Slum in Nairobi, in settling disputes in my mediation practice, and bringing civility to corporate boardrooms, where I recently 'channeled' my mother's tenacious compassionate spirit. A fierce genuine argument broke out among senior executives about their company's direction with lots of loud shouting and fist banging on the large oak table. As if I was on automatic pilot, I firmly stated what my mother said to my brother and me to resolve a dispute: "Sit!" To my amazement, and theirs, everybody stopped, sat down, and resolved their differences purposefully and profitably.

Have you seen something in the world that needs to be done and have the urge to do it? Maybe, just maybe, you're called to be a heretic.

Network Savvy

Adam Grant, the youngest tenured professor at the Wharton School of Business at the University of Pennsylvania, and the author of *Give and Take: A Revolutionary Approach to Success*, shows that "in our technological world, our relationships play an even more important role in an individual's success. We need to operate in a much more interdependent manner."

The emphasis on relationship interdependence is a foundational concept for heretics. Successful heretics recognize that they must foster relationships and constantly be network savvy to accomplish their goals. Grant notes three major trends in relationship interdependence: relationships and our personal reputations are ever more critical in shaping the opportunities that come our way, a shift to knowledge and service economy, and the rise of online social networks.

Grant provides what I have found to be a helpful tool in quickly assessing persons who heretics might want to work with or intentionally avoid. The three types of people he describes are the Takers, Matchers, and Givers. Takers strive to get as much as possible from others and Matchers aim to trade evenly. Givers are the rare breed of people who contribute to others without expecting anything in return.

This last type, Givers, accurately describes heretics. Grant's extensive research suggests three ways for heretics to behave like a Giver: Be willing to give more than you receive, find your 'helping' specialty, and figure out a way to make an unpopular task in your group or department more fun, interesting, or meaningful. Grant adds that the ones who put the interests of others first are the ones who will achieve long-term success.

Network-savvy heretics build a network around an idea that people believe in. They establish a solid foundation of trust with like-minded persons and then build on it together. Attending professional conferences provides an excellent opportunity to meet others in your own discipline and in a wide variety of others. For example, in May 2015, I attended the PubSense2015 Conference in Charleston, South Carolina. I chose this conference to meet other authors, literary agents, and publishers. Specifically, I wanted to secure a publisher for my two book proposals. Fortunately, I encountered Ben Coles, the CEO of Promontory Press, and we agreed to hybrid book contracts, and the book you have in front of you in print or digital form is the result.

We are only beginning to see the impact of the Internet on connecting globally. With social media, we have superlative opportunities to connect with others around the corner and around the world. This is particularly relevant to heretics who can, with a single click, find persons who share their concerns and passions.

CHAPTER 2

The Heretic: A Dreamer

"If your actions inspire others to dream more, learn more, do more and become more," believed John Quincy Adams, "you are a leader."

Author Grace Segran believes that one of the most under-appreciated business tools is dreaming. She relates how Marc le Menestrel encourages business people to integrate different parts of their identity into their professional outlook. He says the framework of dreaming can be a useful tool that allows people to activate the non-cognitive parts of themselves into their business lives. "Dreaming and visioning," he points out, "are techniques that connect the rational framework with the non-cognitive dimensions such as the spiritual, cultural and personal dimensions." One of my major responsibilities as a leadership coach involves enabling CEOs to integrate their particular gifts, especially their capacity to dream. One CEO shared that his primary dream was to become a novelist. When I pointed out that perhaps he was living a dream as CEO, his eyes lit up.

Heretics think without limits. Nothing restricts their thought patterns. They create the future without boundaries. They face the future as a *tabula rasa*, a Latin phrase often translated as "blank slate" in English and which originates from the Roman tabula or wax tablet used for notes, that was blanked by heating the wax and then smoothing it. And they are not restricted by time or space. Dan Pallotta, an American entrepreneur, author, and humanitarian activist, in his article, "What's the Point of Creativity?", articulates a refreshing perspective on the heretic as a dreamer. "The unspoken assumption is that our goal is to gain competitive advantage, to crush the competition, to win. But I believe the best creativity comes from a much deeper place than the desire to win. It comes from a desire to contribute to the lives of others, either by introducing something new that improves the quality of their lives or by showing people that something they thought to be impossible is in fact possible."

2.1 DISCERN AN IMPOSSIBLE DREAM

As a young man, Ed Catmull, co-founder with Steve Jobs and John Lasseter of Pixar Animation Studios, had an impossible dream: to make the first computer-animated movie. He nurtured that dream as a Ph.D. student at the University of Utah, where many computer science pioneers got their start, and then forged a partnership with George Lucas that led, indirectly, to founding Pixar with Steve Jobs and John Lasseter in 1986. Nine years later, changing animation forever, Pixar released *Toy Story*. Catmull used a gradual process of discernment, the ability to judge well, which triggered his impossible dream of an animated movie, and its ultimate fulfillment in films such as the *Toy Story* trilogy, *Monsters, Inc.*, *Finding Nemo*, *The Incredibles*, *Up*, and *WALL-E*, which have gone on to set box-office records and receive thirty Academy Awards.

Heretics go out of their minds to see the invisible. They have the natural capacity to embrace the mystery of life beyond time and space. It's as if they embrace the future and the future embraces them. They're wired to appreciate the present reality, but also to connect the dots for a compelling future for humanity. They respect their thoughts with wonder, reverence, and a particular practicality.

In my life and leadership coaching and consulting practice, I'm privileged to literally challenge senior leaders to go out of their minds to see the invisible—to conceive, articulate, and achieve their vision for the future of their entities. My business tag line reveals my coaching role: "Igniting Your Passion to Do the Impossible." I too have what most consider an impossible dream: I'm going to establish an independent Global Leadership Center in Nairobi for all of Africa.

I suspect that Google Inc. remains one of the most sought-after workplaces primarily because its founders, Larry Page and Sergey Brin, established the company with an underlying philosophy of 'think impossibility.' At the top of Fortune's list of the 100 Best Companies to Work For, Google's Chair, Eric Schmidt, reveals in *How Google Works* that, from the beginning, the company laid a foundation to systematize innovation. The company attracts a new breed of multifaceted employees known as the 'smart creatives.' Schmidt reveals: "It's a specific kind of person who wants to work in an environment that's always changing."

If you want to be a heretic, you need to put your imagination into high gear: build your castle in the air, build a foundation under your castle, and live in your castle. This is not some soft squishy activity. As Albert Einstein reflected: "When I examined myself, and my methods of thought, I came to the conclusion that the gift of fantasy has meant more to me than my talent for absorbing positive knowledge." Fantasy on!

"Creativity loves constraints," advises Marissa Mayer, CEO of Yahoo, "but they must be balanced with a healthy disregard for the impossible."

Surrender To Solitude

"Without great solitude," wrote Spanish painter and sculptor Pablo Picasso, "no serious work is possible."

Most would agree that leading at any level constitutes 'serious work.' For heretics particularly, being willing to surrender to solitude provides an opportunity to probe the depths of their being, draw on the wealth of their life experience, and discern their impossible dream.

In my executive coaching practice, I've witnessed the power of solitude to liberate the creative leadership capacity of leaders at the top in commerce, government, and sports, and enable them to invent their future and the future of the people they serve. I've never coached a leader who didn't have a dream. Many leaders unfortunately get caught up in the madness of urgency and fail to make time to be comfortable alone in their own skin. Paul Johannes Tillich, a German American Christian existentialist philosopher and Lutheran theologian, points out that language has created the word 'loneliness' to express the pain of being alone, and the word 'solitude' to express the glory of being alone.

Essayist, critic, and author William Deresiewicz delivered a provocatively heretical speech titled, "Solitude and Leadership: If you want others to follow, learn to be alone with your thoughts," to the plebe class at the United States Military Academy at West Point in October 2009. In the speech's opening, Deresiewicz submits to the cadets that "solitude is one of the most important necessities of true leadership." Then, he reminds them somewhat coincidentally, that when they get their commissions, they'll be joining a bureaucracy that may prevent them from getting what they need most in their leadership capacity: solitude.

"We have a crisis in leadership in America," claimed Deresiewicz, "because our overwhelming power and wealth, earned under generations of leaders, made us complacent, and for too long we have been training leaders who only know how to keep the routine going. Who can answer questions, but don't know how to ask them. Who can fulfil goals, but don't know how to set them. Who think about *how* to get things done, but not whether they're worth doing in the first place. What we have now are the greatest technocrats the world has ever seen, people who have been trained to be incredibly good at one specific thing, but who have no interest in anything beyond their area of expertise. What we *don't* have are leaders."

In summary, Deresiewicz declared, "What we don't have, in other words, are thinkers. People who can think for themselves. People who can formulate a new direction: for the country, for a corporation or a college, for the Army—a new way of doing things, a new way of looking at things. People in other words, with vision."

I wish I had been there to see the response of the senior officers, many of whom would agree privately with the speaker, but who recognize that they rose in the ranks and are where they are because of the military's regimentation. I wholeheartedly support Deresiewicz's thesis that solitude is the very essence of leadership.

A few years ago, I registered for a five-day spiritual experience at a Roman Catholic retreat center. My mentor, a priest, warmly welcomed me, reviewed the agenda, and asked, "Have you been on a silent retreat before?"

"Silent retreat?" I enquired.

"Yes," he responded matter-of-factly.

The only way I can describe the first couple of days of the retreat would be agonizingly unbearable, especially at meals. It got a little better toward the end. On reflection, I certainly appreciated the experience, especially a memorable lunch on the second last day. Sister Mary, who sat directly across from me, lost control of a single pea that slowly rolled across the table toward me, and provoked her to break the silence with a single word: "Dam!" To this day, Sister Mary remains the best dam sister I've ever met.

In order to surrender to solitude, be still, quiet, and receptive. "Great ideas come into the world as gently as doves," observed Albert Camus, a French philosopher and journalist. "Listen carefully and you will hear the flutter of their wings."

Clearing the noise from our multi-tasking circuits, allowing our minds to temporarily suspend active thought, and surrendering willingly to the present pays big dividends. I've witnessed CEOs facing extremely difficult decisions discipline themselves to enter an imaginary safe 'eye of the storm,' to be still, quiet, and reflective, and in the process, discover insights they would never have gained by racing ahead at full tilt on the corporate treadmill.

I like the way Annie Dillard, an American author best known for her narrative prose in both fiction and non-fiction, affirms the significance of surrendering to solitude:

You do not have to sit outside in the dark.
If, however, you want to look at the stars,
you will find that darkness is required.
The stars neither require it nor demand it.

Build Your Castle In The Air

While writing this book in my study at our cottage on the shores of Lake Michigan, I heard the happy voices of three young children enjoying building a sandcastle on the beach. As I observed them playing quite earnestly, I recognized the insight of George Nelson, author of *How to See*, who commented: "A child making a sandcastle has some kind of picture in his head telling him what to do next." The artist Pablo Picasso adds another relevant dimension: "Everything you can imagine is real."

As a heretic, you bring your unique being, personality, and constellation of gifts to the privilege of building your castle in the air. Most of all, you bring your imagination. "The world of reality has its limits," contends Jean-Jacques Rousseau, "the world of imagination is boundless."

Sometimes, it just takes a nudge for corporate leaders to put their imaginations into play. Jonah Lehrer, in his book, *Imagine: How Creativity Works*, devotes a chapter to the impact an outsider can have on creativity. I've often had the opportunity to coach and consult with entities that need a creative kick in the pants to get the creative juices bubbling. On one occasion, creativity occurred serendipitously. The hotel in Florida where I was "imagineering" called and asked if there was anything I needed. I flippantly responded: "A 24' x 30' sandbox on the beach would be great!" To my surprise, when I arrived, the hotel manager proudly showed me the sandbox complete with all the wood pieces left over from the construction. The executive team, while playing together with the pieces of wood, discovered a new structure for its company that paved the way for its recovery.

In my research, the majority of organizations use only a fraction of the incredible resource of their collective imagination. Gary Hamel, in his book *What Matters Now: How to Win in a World of Relentless Change, Ferocious Competition, and Unstoppable Innovation*, describes this unhealthy reality bluntly: "We suffer from an imagination deficit."

"We have to find new ways to explore possibilities," claims Ivy Ross, head of Google Glass at Google X. "In the past, companies could just look at the opportunities afforded by the market at that time. It was stable and predictable. Now, everything is changing. It is very dynamic. We need to focus on the possibilities of a world that does not yet even exist. We need to explore the 'what ifs.'" While attending the Hawaii Writers Conference in Maui, I attended a seminar on the craft of writing a novel. The presenter, who was himself a novel waiting to happen, conveyed that the most important question a novelist asks is, "What if?" But it's not only a question for novelists; it's also a primary question for heretics. Heretics are novelists who create the future by imagining impossible dreams. They plant the novelist's key question 'What If?' in their minds and hearts, and let their imaginations get in gear and create the future.

What if, Dr. William J. Mayo asked in 1931, I established an international medical clinic? What if, American swimmer Michael Phelps asked, I won eight gold medals at the summer Olympic Games in Beijing, China, in 2008? What if, Margaret Thatcher asked, I became Prime Minister of England? What if, Ted Turner asked, I founded a twenty-four-hour news network instead of the morning and evening news? Today, we know it as CNN.

What if, asked the United Nations Foundation, we applied gaming to support a good cause? And it did. The United Nations Foundation invited Bay Area tech founders and venture capitalists to make its charitable work more relevant to young people through the Global Good Challenge that encourages young people to take action on the world's most pressing problems and engage social networks.

What if, like 81 percent of Americans who feel they have a book in them, you wrote yours? What if you made a great speech? What if you started a new business? What if you challenged the status quo? What if you challenged your charitable organization to grow? What if you discovered a cure for lung cancer? What if you played your tuba in Carnegie Hall? What if you solved the problem of hunger in the world? What if you found the best job ever? What if the Chicago Cubs won the World Series? And the Cubs did in 2016!

Just imagine the possibilities. Millennials do. Stacey Ferreira and Jared Kleinert asked that question and chronicled their findings in their book *2 Billion under 20: How Millennials are Breaking Down Age Barriers and Changing the World.* The authors contend, "We have brought together seventy-five ambitious, successful, and forward-thinking young people from all walks of life in order to deliver this message to you and introduce you to the 2 Billion under Twenty movement. Why? Because if the 2 billion people in the world under twenty years old spent every day pursuing their passions and working together to solve the world's most pressing problems, just imagine what the world could be."

"Life is pure adventure," advises Maya Angelou, "and the sooner we realize that, the quicker we will be able to treat life as art."

Build A Foundation Under Your Castle

"If you have built castles in the air, your work need not be lost; that is where they should be," advised Henry David Thoreau. "Now put the foundations under them."

The heretic makes the transition from imagination to reality and builds a solid foundation under her or his castle in the air, a rock-solid foundation on which the dream may be developed and eventually achieved.

Rene Descartes, a French philosopher (1596-1650) who created a method of reasoning that could be used to test the logic of all scientific theories, rejected the belief that a probability was as acceptable as a certainty for proving a scientific theory. In his 1637 book, *Discours de la méthode* (Discourse on Method), he stated heretically that the existence of all things must be doubted until proven true. He did, however, claim one certainty: *Cogito ergo sum*, which means, "I think, therefore I am." A far more significant certainty in my life, regarding building a foundation under my castle of a Global Leadership Center in Africa, alters Descartes' statement to read, "I love, therefore I am." Leaders who build on love find that their dreams are more contagious.

"There are two equally dangerous extremes," Blaise Pascal, a French mathematician, physicist, and inventor reminds us, "to shut reason out and to let nothing else in." Whether it's true or not, I agree with Virginia Woolf, an English writer and one of the foremost modernists of the twentieth century, who deliciously claimed, "One cannot think well, love well, sleep well, if one has not dined well."

"If you love what you do and are willing to do what it takes, it's within your reach," reflects Steve Wozniak, co-founder of Apple. "And it'll be worth every minute you spend alone at night, thinking and thinking about what it is you want to design or build."

2.2 CLAIM YOUR IMPOSSIBLE DREAM

A Latin proverb, *nemo dat quod non habet,* which means, "nobody gives what he does not have," reminds us of the responsibility of heretics to claim their impossible dream.

When I served as an agent in the insurance business, I trained as a long-term care (LTC) specialist and conducted seminars for agents on the wisdom of encouraging their clients to have LTC in their portfolio. On one occasion, I met with a group of twenty-five relatively new agents who had experienced very limited success in selling the product. I began the session by asking how many of the participants personally had LTC in their portfolios. None claimed the concept or the product. It's difficult to sell what you don't have or persuade others to follow an impossible dream.

Heretics listen intently to the beat of their internal drum and claim what moves or influences them. Many people refer to this as their calling. And it's a personal choice. Heretics accept a call to lead that many times comes to them in an epiphany, a term that derives from the Greek word *epiphaneia*, which means 'appearance' or 'manifestation.' For heretics, the call, epiphany, or new beginning, may come at a moment of great or sudden revelation that involves an intuitive grasp of reality through something usually simple and striking, or an illuminating discovery, realization, or disclosure. It's an inner sense of discovering what one is intended to do with all their gifts, aptitudes, and skills. Heretics claim their calling with total commitment.

Early in my pastoral calling, a young charming couple came to me to be married. I met with them, and in the course of pre-marital counseling, learned that they wanted a five-year marriage. Unfortunately, their own families hadn't modeled a consistent marriage relationship and they didn't want to take a long-term chance themselves. I explained that the vows of the marriage covenant intended marriage to be for life and perhaps they should reconsider. They left my office disappointed and a little angry. However, almost a year later, they came back to see me and revealed they wanted to get married for life. I agreed to marry them and the rest is history. They're still married. It doesn't always work out that way, but for them, claiming their calling to completely love and honor each other, gave their five children a marvelous gift.

Heretics claim their impossible dreams graciously, humbly, and patiently.

Graciously

"The bottom line of a calling is measured by pain, learning, and grace," observed Michael Novak, an American Catholic philosopher, novelist, diplomat, and author. Claim your impossible dream graciously like a ballerina who performs with simple elegance and refined movement. I use this example because my daughter, who always knew she was called to dance, epitomized grace even when she danced as a child—plus the fact I willingly spent a fortune on pointe shoes!

In religious belief, grace may be defined as the free and unmerited divine favor as manifested in the salvation of sinners and the bestowal of blessings. Grace, although difficult to define, honors or credits someone or something by one's presence. I've had the good fortune of experiencing many people who lived and breathed graciously. When I was doing my undergraduate work in college, I attended an InterVarsity Christian Fellowship Missionary Conference held over the Christmas vacation period in Urbana/Champaign, Illinois. The sessions and the camaraderie were wonderful, but the encounter I remember most vividly happened on the bleachers at the University of Illinois outdoor stadium.

Early one morning, I went to the track for my daily morning run and found myself running beside a gentleman who kept about the same pace. We ran together, hoods covering our heads from the cold winter air, and then he slowed down and went to sit in the bleachers. I did one more lap and joined him. As soon as he spoke to me, I recognized his voice, a voice known to millions around the world as the evangelist Dr. Billy Graham. What I recall clearly was his graciousness and our conversation about my calling that he affirmed with a pat on my back, and of course, a prayer. He certainly honored me with his presence. Grace often occurs unexpectedly like a divine surprise that takes your breath away.

Andy Crouch, in his book *Culture Making: Recovering Our Creative Calling*, relates how, as Chaplain at Harvard University, he could roughly divide the students into three groups: "There were the 'strivers,' kids who had been prepared day and night since elementary school, or nursery school, to make it to Harvard. They were up late and up early.

"Then there were the 'legacies,' as they were inelegantly known, children of alumni, plus the heirs of other kinds of privilege, whether celebrity, power, or wealth. The strivers' dominant trait was anxiety—they were sure the admissions office had made some kind of mistake. The legacies' dominant trait was, well, dominance. They carried themselves with a sense of entitlement, at home in Harvard's world, since it had been their home all along.

"The third group, smaller than the first two groups, who when they arrived at Harvard seemed nothing but delighted and surprised that the letter had landed in their mailbox that spring day. They could have moments of anxiety, or they could be perfectly self-assured. But what you remembered about them was the lightness in their manner, a sense of fun and even play that accompanied them into the dining room, the classroom and the lab. Not the play of the entitled who were at Harvard more for the social capital than the schoolwork; just the enjoyment of the very good life of studying, learning and growing that can be found at any college at its best. I came to think of these students as children of grace. Of all the students I met who received the coveted *summa cum laude* for their senior thesis, nearly everyone was in this third group, neither a striver nor a legacy, but a quietly brilliant child of grace."

Heretics claim their impossible dream graciously as a gift, a treasure, a trust. They reverse the common belief, "I'll believe it when I see it" to become, "I'll see it when I believe it."

Humbly

Merwyn A. Hayes and Michael D. Comer, in their book *Start with Humility: Lessons from America's Quiet CEOs on How to Build Trust and Inspire Followers*, "have noticed that if you want to be an effective, successful leader, there is a good place to start. Start with humility."

Humility constitutes one of the most overlooked characteristics in authentic leadership. Heretics, by and large, claim their impossible dream humbly as their calling. The word humility derives from the Latin root, *humus*, meaning 'of the earth,' figuratively down-to-earth people. Historically, heretics have been known to be so heavenly minded that they're no earthly good. I've observed that genuine humility effectively connects leaders and their followers by a common bond of humanity.

Jim Collins, in his book *Good to Great: Why Some Companies Make the*

Leap ... and Others Don't, points out that leaders who built greatness had a "paradoxical blend of personal humility and professional will," and that leaders with "gargantuan personal egos" were more likely to contribute to the demise or mediocrity of companies in the long run. The high cost of arrogance can be a killer of spirited commitment to the vision of a movement. In the ancient Greek culture, hubris denoted insolence and even violence, and just acting in a superior manner and belittling others was considered a crime. There seems to be a clear connection between overconfidence and moral failure. In ancient Rome, for example, emperors had a man stand close to them at all times whose job was to remind them of their mortality.

Perhaps heretics need to practice courageous humility like Saint Teresa, who followed the Biblical principle: "But those who exalt themselves will be humbled, and those who humble themselves will be exalted" (Matthew 23:12). *The Letters: The Untold Story of Mother Teresa*, the movie, describes how humility framed her life where compassion gave her purpose, faith gave her inspiration, and courage gave her strength. "Humility is not thinking less of yourself," said Christian apologist C. S. Lewis. "It is thinking of yourself less."

"If you have willpower and reasonable courage, not blind courage but courage without pride," reflected His Holiness the Dalai Lama, "even things that seem impossible at a certain stage turn into being possible because of continuing effort inspired by that courage."

Patiently

According to *The Home Book of American Quotations*, the motto of the U.S. Army Corps of Engineers during World War II expressed the need for a degree of patience in achieving the impossible: "The difficult we do immediately. The impossible takes a little longer."

We live in an instant culture that values—above all else, it would seem—immediacy. And the faster the better. Most hate waiting, especially when flying. At O'Hare Airport in Chicago, I heard an impatient gentleman vigorously demand that the ticket agent address his concerns, and when she calmly told him that he'd have to wait in line like everybody else, he went ballistic.

"Do you know who I am?" he asked the agent.

She replied, "With all due respect, sir, if you don't know who you are, that's your problem."

He exclaimed, "I'm a vice-president of this airline!"

The ticket agent, still with a calm demeanor, responded, "Congratulations, sir. You'll still have to wait in line."

All of us in line applauded.

The world's leading expert on self-control, psychologist Walter Mischel, a former professor at Stanford University, in his famous "Marshmallow Test," demonstrated how delayed gratification may be critical for a successful life. Mischel offered children a choice between one small reward, a marshmallow provided immediately, or two small rewards if they waited for a short period, approximately fifteen minutes, during which the tester left the room and then returned. In follow-up studies, the researchers found that children who were able to wait longer for the preferred rewards tended to have better life outcomes, as measured by SAT scores, educational attainment, body mass index (BMI), and other life measures. Two marshmallows are better than one.

In the introduction of Daniel Goleman's book *A Force for Good: The Dalai Lama's Vision for Our World*, the Dalai Lama offers his wisdom about patience: "Change in ourselves and in the world in which we live may not take place in a hurry; it will take time. Real change will take place when individuals transform themselves guided by the values that lie at the core of all human ethical systems, scientific findings, and common sense."

"Good ideas are not adopted automatically," noted United States Navy Admiral Hyman Rickover who directed the original development of naval nuclear propulsion and controlled its operations for three decades as director of Naval Reactors. "They must be driven into practice with courageous patience." A good example of this is the exceptionally long time it took to persuade physicians in hospitals that it was essential for them to wash their hands to prevent becoming carriers of infection.

Significant achievements require patience. Heretics discern an impossible dream, claim it graciously, humbly, and patiently, and then express it clearly, concisely, and compellingly.

2.3 EXPRESS YOUR IMPOSSIBLE DREAM

"Leaders come in many forms, with many styles and diverse qualities," observed John W. Gardner, Secretary of Health, Education, and Welfare under President Lyndon Johnson. "There are quiet leaders and leaders one can hear in the next county. Some find strength in eloquence, some in judgment, some in courage." Heretics come in many forms as well. The one thing they have in common is an impossible dream that they have claimed and want to express persuasively to others.

"If there is a spark of genius in the leadership function at all," remarked Warren Bennis and Burt Nanus in their book *Leaders: Strategies for Taking Charge*, "it must lie in the transcending ability, a kind of magic, to assemble— out of all the variety of images, signals, forecasts and alternatives—a clearly articulated vision of the future that is at once simple, easily understood, clearly desirable, and energizing."

Heretics are in the storytelling business that requires them to find their unique voice to tell their own story about their impossible dream. James M. Kouzes and Barry Z. Posner, in their book *Encouraging the Heart: A Leader's Guide to Rewarding and Recognizing Others*, offer an artist's approach: "Finding one's voice is something that every artist understands and every artist knows that finding a voice is most definitely not a matter of technique. It's a matter of time and searching—soul searching."

"And the truth of your experience," writes Anne Lamott in *Bird by Bird*, "can only come through in your own voice." Three years ago my otolaryngology team at the Mayo Clinic diagnosed me with spasmodic dysphonia (SD), so I'm acutely aware of the critical nature of finding one's voice. SD, a focal form of dystonia, is a neurological voice disorder that involves "spasms" of the vocal cords causing interruptions of speech and affecting the voice quality. It can cause the voice to break up or to have a tight, strained, or strangled quality. I take some comfort because I'm in good company with others who have the disorder: Diane Rehm, an American public radio talk show host of *The Diane Rehm Show* distributed nationally and internationally by National Public Radio, and Scott Adams, an American cartoonist, creator of the *Dilbert* comic strip. I once indicated to my wife, Melody, that my voice sounds so scratchy. She replied with her usual spontaneity, "Honey, it's sexy." So I'm going with her assessment.

Clearly

In promulgating your esoteric cogitations or in articulating your superficial sentimentalities or amicable philosophical or psychological observations, beware of platitudinous ponderosity. Let your conversations and communications possess a clarified conciseness, a compact comprehensibleness, a collated, concatenated cogency. Eschew all conglomerations of flatulent garrulity, jejune babblement, and asinine affectations. Let your extemporizing and unpremeditated explanations have intelligibility and veracious vivacity without rodomontade or thesauronical bombasts. Sedulously avoid all polysyllable profundity, pompous prolixity, setaceous vacuity, ventriloquial verbosity, and grandiloquent vapidity. Shun double-entendres, prurient jocosity, or pestiferous profanity, whether obscurant or apparent.

"There is no greater impediment to the advancement of knowledge," commented Thomas Reid, the Scottish philosopher, "than the ambiguity of words." Communicate your impossible dream as if it were a precious diamond with extraordinary clarity, the degree to which a diamond is free of inclusions.

In an interview conducted by Adam Bryant, John Riccitiello, chief executive of Electronic Arts, the video game maker, remarked, "what distinguishes leaders oftentimes is whether they paint a picture. The word 'vision' can be horribly overused, but they paint a picture of the way it's supposed to work, and it resonates with people … you have to be absolutely genuine. You have to know what you truly believe and what you truly value, and it has to be undeniably consistent.

Here are a few examples of clear expressions:

- GE Avionics Mission: "We invent the future of flight, lift up people in the air, and bring them home safely."
- The International Space Development Hub: "A center for the development of space resources, the protection of the environment, and human civilization."
- Septic Tank Service: "One call. We take it all."
- Selective Search—Executive Search Meets Personal Matchmaking: "The World Has 3.5 Billion WOMEN. We Help You Weed Out 3,499,999,999."
- Arnold Palmer, professional golfer: "Golf is deceptively simple."
- Lamont Webster Johnson, my father: "No."

Concisely

Steve Jobs declared his dream concisely: "I want to put a ding in the universe."

Heretics get to the heart of their impossible dream and tell their story concisely. Here's how Martin Luther King Jr. shared his dream: "I have a dream that one day this nation will rise up and live out the true meaning of its creed. We hold these truths to be self-evident: that all men are created equal."

Walt Disney expressed his vision in just four words: "Dream. Believe. Dare. Do." Adrian Gostick and Chester Elton, in their book *All In: How the Best Managers Create a Culture of Belief and Drive Big Results*, claim that Disney's "four words defined a culture of creativity, intelligent risk-taking, and empowerment."

Warren Buffett gets a lot of media coverage because he's incredibly skilled at something the media loves: speaking in memorable sound bites with vivid comparisons. For example, when asked about investing in the stock market, Buffett noted, "If past history was all there was to the game, the richest people would be librarians." On another occasion, he said, "In the business world, the rearview mirror is always clearer than the windshield." Think bumper sticker and T-shirt when crafting your concise statement about your impossible dream commonly referred to as your elevator speech. If you can reduce your dream to one concise memorable sentence, you're good to go on any elevator.

Heretics could learn how to tell their story concisely from State Farm Insurance's "Never" commercial that tells its story in thirty-one seconds flat:

I'm never getting married. Guaranteed.
We're never having kids.
You're never moving to the suburbs.
We're never getting one of those.
We're never having another kid. I'm pregnant.
I'm never letting go.
For all the 'nevers' in life, State Farm is there.
End of story.

Compellingly

"There is no greater agony," claimed Maya Angelou, in her book *I Know Why the Caged Bird Sings*, "than bearing an untold story inside you." Heretics identify with Angelou and express their impossible dream clearly, concisely, and compellingly.

Tell your story so that it grabs people's attention, speaks to their wants, needs, and desires, and inspires them to buy into your dream. You might find it helpful to ask what you want potential members of your movement to think and feel and do after they hear your compelling pitch.

Communicate that your impossible dream is worth the effort and pain to change and follow you.

In my own experience, if you make emotional connections with your audience, the more likely you are to positively influence them and win them over. For example, in my speeches, I tell my "Little Joe" story. Ten years ago, two of my pastoral colleagues and I were walking in Kibera Slum late at night back to my residence at the university where I was teaching. We had just come from comforting three families, each grieving the death of a very young child due to malaria. We were hurrying because it can certainly be dangerous in the slum after dark. On our way, I recognized in a shallow ditch of contaminated waste by the path what I thought was a very small child. I immediately stopped, much to the consternation of my colleagues, retrieved the two-year-old child, and administered CPR. By God's grace, I was able to save "Little Joe." When I tell my story, persons in audiences make it their story and not only respond emotionally, but often financially. In the bottom left hand corner of their checks, they usually write three words, "For Little Joe," which indicates their positive response to my compelling story.

John Medina, a developmental molecular biologist and author of *Brain Rules: 12 Principles for Surviving and Thriving at Work, Home, and School*, explains why graphics are a powerful teaching tool. "Most of the things that could kill us are moving, to put it in evolutionary terms. That's why a third of the brain is devoted exclusively to visual processing. It is far and away the dominant sense. But it's not just vision—it's the moving visual image that appears to be the spark that the brain pays most attention to." Medina advises presenters, "Burn your PowerPoint slides, and lead with a visual and make it move if you can."

Here are a few clear, concise, and compelling expressions of impossible dreams:

- Dr. William Sprague, Rotarian: "Eradicate polio."
- President Jimmy Carter: "I would like the last Guinea worm to die before I do."

- Doctors without Borders: "We find out where conditions are the worst—the places where others are not going—and that's where we want to be."
- Shiloh United Church of Christ: "Radically Alive. Boldly Inclusive. Wildly Compassionate."
- #UNPLUG: My Life was Crazy. So I disconnected for 25 days. You Should Too.
- President Ronald Reagan: "Ask yourself, 'Are you better off than you were four years ago?'"

In order to be heard, one must get away from the herd. We've now considered how heretics discern, claim, and express their impossible dream. So far, we've introduced the heretic as servant and dreamer. Let's move on to consider the heretic as challenger.

CHAPTER 3

The Heretic: A Challenger

Apple expresses the inner spirit of the challenger: "In everything we do, we believe in challenging the status quo. We believe in thinking differently. The way we challenge the status quo is by making our products beautifully designed, simple to use and user-friendly. And we happen to make great computers. Wanna buy one?"

Heretics start with the premise that the status quo worked yesterday, but it must be challenged in order to meet the demands of today and tomorrow. They challenge the status quo and aim to create a new status quo. Sam Walton, founder of Walmart, agrees. "I've always been driven to buck the system to innovate, to take things beyond where they've been." Helen Keller offers an historical view of challenging the status quo when she observed, "The heresy of one age becomes the orthodoxy of the next."

Righteous discontent has ignited many hearts, minds, and souls of heretics through the ages, some of whom paid the ultimate price, including Jesus of Nazareth. Jesus constantly challenged the status quo of his day and many of his followers today continue the model he set for his disciples. Heretics play a key role in families, profit and not-for-profit organizations, as well as society. They stand out from the crowd because they go against the grain, practice nonconformity, disturb the peace, pursue uncommon sense, swim against the stream, put the cat among the pigeons, shake up the establishment, disrupt safe organizations, and set things in a state of disequilibrium. The common thread among heretics seems to be that they are rebels with a cause, who are committed to making a world of difference wherever they land.

Creativity expert Sir Kenneth Robinson, in his book *The Element: How Finding Your Passion Changes Everything*, proposes a rousing toast to heretics who challenge the status quo and defy conventional wisdom. "Here's to the crazy ones. The misfits. The rebels. The troublemakers. The round pegs in the square holes. The ones who see things differently. They're not fond of rules. And they have no respect for the status quo. You can quote them, disagree with them, glorify or vilify them. About the only thing you can't do is ignore them. Because they change things. They push the human race forward. While some may see them as the crazy ones, we see genius. Because the people who are crazy enough to think they can change the world, are the ones who do, changing the world for the better."

Heretics, armed with a well-defined and articulated 'impossible dream,' recognize the need to challenge the status quo primarily to survive, thrive, or high-five (a term I will explain later). Let's start by exploring how they challenge the status quo to survive.

3.1 CHALLENGE THE STATUS QUO TO SURVIVE

Let's begin by gaining the perspective from two giants in the field of leadership: Warren Bennis, American scholar and organizational consultant, and Burt Nanus, visionary leadership expert, who for many years served as the director of research at the University of Southern California's Leadership Institute. They state, in their book *Leaders: Strategies for Taking Charge*, "The absence or ineffectiveness of leadership implies the absence of vision, a dreamless society, and this will result, at best, in the maintenance of the status quo or, at worst, in the disintegration of our society because of lack of purpose and cohesion."

Most organizations suffer from a kind of tunnel vision that makes it hard to envision a more positive future. They want to tune the corporate piano rather than invest in a brand new instrument. In troubled organizations rich with tradition and success, history can be a source of a curse and a blessing. The challenge is to break from the past without disavowing it, and to celebrate the past as a foundation for the future.

"In a world of mind-flipping change," observes management consultant Gary Hamel, in his book *What Matters Now: How to Win in a World of Relentless Change, Ferocious Competition, and Unstoppable Innovation*, "what matters is not merely a company's competitive advantage at a point in time, but its evolutionary advantage over time." Hamel continues: "Large organizations of all types suffer from an assortment of congenital disabilities that no amount of therapy can cure." And Dave Packard, co-founder of HP, points out: "More companies die of indigestion than starvation."

Contemporary circumstances cry out for heretics who will have the courage to challenge the status quo in order to survive, face the music in an organization on life support, breathe new life into every aspect of its operation, and potentially thrive in the future. In my leadership coaching practice, I use an "Inspire, Challenge, and Encourage" (ICE) approach to enable leaders to make a world of difference. By far, the most critical dimension, and the most satisfying, involves challenging senior leaders to do what must be done in order to survive before it's too late.

Challenging a leader of a profit, non-profit, or government agency requires building significant mutual trust and an advanced set of diplomatic skills. Before I begin a leadership-coaching relationship, I make a concerted effort to clarify my role to come alongside the leader to question and probe in a spirit of affirmation. In my experience, if a leader is open to being coached, he or she is most likely open to being challenged appropriately.

I coached a president of a medium-sized company that had lost its competitive advantage and spiraled out of control. His direct reports told me that their leader had lost touch with them and their customers. Under calmer conditions, he was personable and collaborative, but with the company going through a very rough period, he panicked and reverted to a lone-ranger style where it was his way or the highway. So I invited the president to go for a walk to engage him in a calm conversation in a non-threatening way. He welcomed the opportunity to share that he feared for his company's future and I enquired whether he realized that in order for his company to survive he would have to examine his current leadership style that was killing his company. After a couple of minutes, he broke the silence by asking me if I thought he could bring his company back from the brink. I responded positively. With a renewed sense of purpose and confidence, he enabled his company not only to survive but also to thrive.

The Chilean poet and politician Pablo Neruda wrote the insightful poem, "You Start Dying Slowly," about making responsible choices in life and organizational survival.

> *You start dying slowly*
> *If you do not change your life*
> *when you are not satisfied*
> *with your job, or with your love,*
> *If you do not risk what is safe for the uncertain,*
> *If you do not go after a dream,*
> *If you do not allow yourself,*
> *At least once in your lifetime,*
> *To run away from sensible advice.*

Heretics challenge the status quo to help their organizations survive. They heed the wise words of activist Maya Angelou: "Life is not about waiting for the storm to pass. It's about learning how to dance in the rain." Heretics purposefully raise a ruckus, inspire hope, and confirm conviction.

Raise A Ruckus

Whenever a radical change of culture is required, experts advise that the first step toward change is to profoundly modify the organization's behavior by a variety of highly visible actions. Or, as Stanford Business School Professor Richard Pascale recommends, "Organizations need to be repeatedly shocked into change."

Heretics challenge the status quo by raising a ruckus. They know that people rarely listen when you hint. They sound the alarm with attention-getting headlines: It Ain't Workin'! Let the Status Quo Go! Revive to Survive! Tsunami Coming! Reinvent or Steep Descent! Revive or Nose Dive! Change or Die! The Party's Over! Caught between a Rock and a Hard Place! We're Screwed! Call 911!

How does an organization or a country get to this point of desperately needing urgent care? When the United States faced defaulting on its debts and a downgrading of its credit unless legislators and the President acted collaboratively in the next twenty-four hours, Alan Weiss, author of *Million Dollar Consulting*, offered poignant clues to an answer. "It may just be because we have politicians, but not statesmen; celebrities, but not exemplars; athletes, but not sportsmen and women; lawyers but not jurists; pop idols but not talent; executives but not leaders. Compromise, collaboration, and consensus require (ironically) strength and empathy, not weakness and antipathy; the selfless, not the selfish. We need to be willing and able to stand out in a crowd and say, 'This way!' without demanding it be only our way."

Heretics feel compelled to raise a ruckus because they realize the organization of which they are an integral part needs emergency care. Heretics instinctively understand the nature of urgency. When the Ebola epidemic broke out in West Africa in 2014, the United Nations, in partnership with other organizations, worked tirelessly to halt the spread of the disease. Ban Ki-moon, UN secretary-general, urged, "There is no time to lose. What began as a public health emergency is now a complex crisis with profound social, economic, humanitarian, political and security dimensions." Sometimes it takes a crisis for organizations to get moving and act quickly and responsibly.

Only decisive action will save the day. The Biblical heretic, Noah, took decisive action, built an ark, and warned the people of the impending danger of an apocalyptic flood. Martin Luther rejected several teachings and practices of the Late Medieval Catholic Church. He sounded the alarm about certain actions of the Roman Catholic Church in the sixteenth century and recommended a complete overhaul of church practices and led a movement known as the Protestant Reformation. Mary Barra faced a similar situation in her role as General Motors' first female CEO, and raised a ruckus to reinvent the company and reform the company's sclerotic culture, especially in the light of its massive recall scandal. She confidently declared: "I'm not asking people to do it. It's a requirement, not only that they hold themselves accountable to do it, but that they hold others accountable."

Because heretics view change as imperative in the process of organizational survival, they raise a ruckus and then inspire hope.

Inspire Hope

John W. Gardner, in his book *No Easy Victories*, described the task of leaders: "The first and last task of a leader is to keep hope alive—the hope that we can finally find our way through to a better world—despite the day's bitter discouragement, despite the perplexities of social action, despite our own shallowness and wavering resolve." American basketball player and coach John Wooden agrees with Gardner: "Adversity is the state in which man most easily becomes acquainted with himself." Or, as the Dalai Lama maintains, "It is under the greatest adversity that there exists the greatest potential for doing good, both for oneself and others."

The foundation for regaining the trust necessary for survival involves accepting at least some of the responsibility for the present state of the organization. Adrian Gostick and Chester Elton, in *All In: How the Best Managers Create a Culture of Belief and Drive Big Results*, provide this insight: "If leaders can acknowledge the fears of workers and regain their trust first, the cumulative power can accelerate the return to normalcy for clients, customers, and shareholders. Furthermore, the proper management of an emergency assures employees that their belief in leadership is well founded and often creates a level of trust that is higher than before the crisis." Whereas placing blame doesn't help the cause of survival and inspiring hope, confessing that you as the leader were responsible for your piece of the mess earns trust. Even making a simple statement like, "I didn't see the changes coming," can begin to build trust in a leader's character and competency.

Heretics seize the opportunity to present a new status quo, a way forward to a brighter future, with the confidence that together the organization can and will survive. They, hearing the beat of a different drummer, need to take the helm and call the strokes that will guide the organization through rough waters. They use the current situation as a springboard to launch a movement with a realistic picture of the future, and the resolve to rebuild a culture in crisis. Gostick and Elton observe, "Ironically, it is the very moment of crisis when the organization needs its people to believe the most and yet their faith is challenged."

That's what Martin Luther did in initiating the movement known as the Protestant Reformation. Eleanor Roosevelt recommended a similar strategy: "It is better to light a candle than to curse the darkness." Noah, who accepted his divine calling, inspired a dedicated few to get in the ark before the flood came and survive.

An interviewer asked GM's new CEO, Mary Barra, to express her career philosophy: "My parents were both born and raised in the Depression. They instilled great values about integrity and the importance of hard work, and I've taken that with me to every job. Another kind of core tenet is: I believe in the power of teamwork, and I think you will have superior results if you are aligned and win the hearts and minds of your employees if they understand where the company is going and they're all in." Already, she's inspiring the people in her global corporation. Warren Buffett, referring to the carmaker's most renowned CEO, says: "I hope that Mary Barra turns out to be the Alfred Sloan of the twenty-first century. From what

I've seen, she's got the goods."

Heretics inspire hope for survival and eventually *thrival*.

Confirm Conviction

"When you're finished changing," observed Benjamin Franklin, one of the Founding Fathers of the United States, "you're finished." So one of the major tasks for heretics is confirming the conviction of members of the organization to move forward together.

Howard Schultz did just that when he announced to Starbucks: "If you don't believe we can turn this company around, if you even have a smallest bit of doubt, come and see me privately. It will be easier to have this conversation now than if I have to come and find you three months from now. You have to really believe we can do this."

Noah repeatedly indicated to the people that the end was near, and only a few responded, got on the ark, and were saved from the flood. It's interesting to note that Noah was forthright about his belief and trusted others to commit without judgment or pressure. Martin Luther followed a similar approach in gathering people to follow him in the Protestant Reformation.

I felt a little like Luther when a church interviewed me to become its senior Pastor. Aware of the congregation's somewhat troubled history, I asked each one on the Search Committee to confirm their conviction to stand together with one voice as we went forward. Immediately, one member jumped to his feet and declared he would stand by my leadership no matter what. And one by one, they stood until all were standing in agreement.

The visible support of the Search Committee signaled its willingness to stand together with me in our mission as a congregation. Even if conflict did arise in the future, I felt confident that I was not alone in my pastoral leadership role. I accepted its invitation and we went forward with a united commitment to the congregation's vision and mission. That mutual support paid big dividends especially in the short term but not in the long run. Confirming conviction is an ongoing process with no guarantees.

By confirming conviction, heretics celebrate a new beginning toward survival. "If you do not change direction," warned Lao Tzu, an ancient Chinese philosopher and writer, "you may end up where you are heading."

3.2 CHALLENGE THE STATUS QUO TO THRIVE

"Organizations that destroy the status quo win," believes Seth Godin, author of *Tribes: We Need You to Lead Us*. "Individuals who push their organizations, who inspire other individuals to change the rules, thrive." Heretics make a conscious choice to challenge the status quo to thrive.

Ron Pevny, from The Center for Conscious Eldering, provides a helpful distinction between the mindset for survival and *thrival* consciousness: "I define survival consciousness as being primarily focused on safety, holding on to what we are and have against the fear-inducing onslaught of change, threat and uncertainty from the world around us, and from the reality of our aging. The survival mentality sees change as inherently dangerous and to be resisted, with stability as the most highly valued goal … The consciousness of thriving acknowledges the need for safety and takes appropriate steps to support our security, but looks beyond safety to what it means to be truly alive, growing, and expanding."

Most of my leadership-coaching clients would be included in the 'thrival' category. They are not particularly interested in merely surviving. They frame their main responsibility as CEO in terms of the future, in which I estimate they spend about 90 percent of their time. They calibrate actions in the present for a future perfect reality. They refuse to be seduced by the tyranny of the urgent and do not take on the role of putting out fires. They challenge the status quo to thrive even if it results in resistance to the organizational direction. Thrivers welcome increased expectations as a challenge.

On the other hand, survival-oriented leaders desperately hang on in fear they may lose even that which they have. They focus almost exclusively on the present and the future rarely appears on their radar. One CEO claimed that all he wanted to do was keep his organization breathing. Survivors slide into a crisis mode to avoid failure and perpetuate an illusion of safety.

It requires courage to challenge the status quo to thrive especially when leading in difficult times. And almost all organizations report that these are difficult times. A recent PricewaterhouseCoopers survey indicates CEOs' pessimism over the global economy is rising and political instability is also near top of executives' worries. Two out of three corporate CEOs around the world see a risky business environment and worry about growth prospects of their own companies. Dennis Nally, chairman of PricewaterhouseCoopers, the tax consulting group that did the study, released on the eve of the World Economic Forum in Davos, Switzerland, in January 2016, commented, "Without question chief executive confidence levels are down in a very significant way year-to-year. Whether due to the economic environment or geopolitical factors, there are clearly more threats faced by CEOs today than we have seen over the last few years."

Heretics know that in order to thrive, organizations have to adapt. Heretics may find, as I have, that one of the best resources to enable them to adapt effectively is *The Practice of Adaptive Leadership: Tools and Tactics for Changing Your Organization and the World* by Ronald A. Heifetz, Marty Linsky, and Alexander Grashow. The authors define adaptive leadership as the practice of mobilizing people to tackle tough challenges and thrive. Specifically, their book focuses on change that enables the capacity of organizations to thrive. Main thrusts of adaptive leadership include the following: builds on the past rather than jettisoning it, occurs through experimentation, relies on diversity, and generates loss. Two leaders I've had the privilege of coaching helped their organizations remarkably survive but didn't enable them to thrive. In both cases, they were about to retire and didn't have the enormous energy it takes to make the transition from survival to *thrival* thinking. In fact, I believe that they retired without telling.

Here's award-winning author Sonia Marsh's message of encouragement to heretics to thrive: "The organizations filled with bold, gutsy and confident leaders, those who are willing to shake things up and charge the hill, will find that the field is uncrowded. Success belongs to those organizations willing to invest in leadership."

Shake Up The Establishment

"Exemplary leadership," state James M. Kouzes and Barry Z. Posner in *Turning Adversity into Opportunity*, "disrupts the status quo." These are words of intention and action that often thrust the establishment into the discomfort zone. Heretics, tighten your seat belts and get ready for an adventurous bumpy road ahead.

In his commencement address, given to Stanford University in June 2005, Steve Jobs offered fellow heretics the ultimate perspective on shaking up the establishment: "Your time is limited, so don't waste it living someone else's life. Don't be trapped by dogmas—which is living with the results of other people's thinking. Don't let the noise of others' opinions drown out your inner voice. And most important, have the courage to follow your heart and intuition. They somehow know what you truly want to become. Everything else is secondary." Jobs' approach resonates with me. I followed my own heart and intuition and left my vocation as a pastor to pursue motivational speaking and leadership coaching opportunities. Many thought I was crazy but I already knew that.

Perhaps Pope Francis channeled the mind and heart of Steve Jobs because the Pontiff is not wasting any time in shaking up his religious establishment today. One journalist described the Pope's action as "disturbing the peace with a little revolution." Jesuit Cardinal Bergoglio, elected as Pope Francis on March 13, 2013, started shaking up the establishment of the Roman Catholic Church at the top, the Curia. Francis issued a blistering indictment of the Vatican bureaucracy, accusing the cardinals, bishops, and priests who serve him of using their Vatican careers to grab power and wealth, of living 'hypocritical' double lives and forgetting that they're supposed to be joyful men of God.

Francis turned the traditional, genteel exchange of Christmas greetings into a public dressing down of the Curia, the central administration of the Holy See, which governs the 1.2 billion strong Catholic Church. He made clear that his plans for a radical reform of the structures of church power must be accompanied by an even more radical spiritual reform of the men involved. Ticking off fifteen 'ailments of the Curia' one by one, Francis urged the prelates sitting stone-faced before him in the marbled Sala Clementina to use the Christmas season to repent and atone and make the church a healthier, holier place in 2015.

Perhaps, as Gerald Brenan expressed in *Thoughts in a Dry Season*, Pope Francis injected new life into the church: "Religions are kept alive by heresies, which are really sudden explosions of faith. Dead religions do not produce them." This heretical spirit of shaking up the establishment in the church can also be observed in politics.

Heretics shake up the establishment in order to thrive.

Rethink Everything

Thomas R. Horton, author of *The CEO Paradox: The Privilege and Accountability of Leadership*, offers this advice for leaders who want to challenge the status quo to thrive: "The real key, or tool, to cultural change is a commitment on the part of top management to be willing to change anything. And everything."

Pope Francis, elected with a mandate for reform, continues to challenge the Roman Catholic Church worldwide to rethink everything especially in the areas of stewardship for the earth, justice for the poor and victims of sexual abuse, and transparent financial management. Elizabeth Dias, Religion and Politics Correspondent for *TIME* Magazine, interviewed Pope Francis and found him to be street smart, savvy, cunning, and not afraid of making mistakes—all qualities necessary for shaking up the establishment to thrive.

Let me elaborate, for example, on the first of these issues, how the Pope has urged the Church to rethink everything about stewardship of the earth. He challenged the world to clean up its filth when he issued "*Laudato Si*," his encyclical on climate change that is a "melodic indictment," depicting a materialistic and wasteful society that is hurting the planet and its poorest people. He commented: "The exploitation of the planet has already exceeded acceptable limits and we still have not solved the problem of poverty."

At the heart of Francis' theological argument is the concept of "integral ecology," which gives a more central role for the environment in longstanding Catholic social teaching by linking destruction of nature with injustices such as poverty, hunger, inequality, and violations of human dignity. In his final "Prayer of our Earth," the Pope beseeches God: "Bring healing to our lives, that we may protect the world and not prey upon it, that we may sow beauty, not pollution and destruction. Touch the hearts of those who look only for gain at the expense of the poor of the Earth." Pope Francis' intentional shaking up of the establishment by rethinking everything has shaken the very foundation of the Church. And he's only just begun.

Innovate Proactively

According to Robert Leonard, chairman of Hofstra University's linguistics program, the word innovation derives from the Latin noun, *innovatus*, which means "renewal or change," and appeared in print as early as the fifteenth century.

Clayton Christensen, a professor at the Harvard Business School and the author of *The Innovator's Dilemma*, classifies innovations into three types: efficiency innovations, which produce the same product more cheaply, such as automating credit checks; sustaining innovations, which turn good products into better ones, such as the hybrid car; and disruptive innovations, which transform expensive, complex products into affordable, simple ones, such as the shift from mainframe to personal computers. He points out that a "company's biggest potential for growth lies in disruptive innovation, noting that the other types could just as well be called ordinary progress and normally don't create more jobs or business."

The title of an article in the August 2015 edition of *National Geographic* indicates an unwavering commitment of the Pope to innovate proactively: "Pope Francis: Remakes the Vatican." The Pontiff gave early signs that he was going to shake things up a bit, including his homily at the beatification of Pope Paul VI on October 19, 2014, when he stated his divine connection with a God of change: "God is not afraid of new things! That is why he is continually surprising us, opening our hearts and guiding us in unexpected ways."

At his first meeting with the press, the Pope declared his primary ambition, "How I would like a church that is poor and for the poor." Around the world, the media has described him as a reformer, a radical, and a revolutionary. True to his mandate, Pope Francis continues to remake and surprise the Vatican. The Pontiff declared that bishops who covered up sexual abuse by priests are guilty and should be dealt with accordingly. The Holy Reformer also declared that sound financial management was a pillar of his greatest mission: aiding the poor and underprivileged. He has already taken steps, but no giant leaps, toward a leaner, more efficient Vatican administration.

3.3 CHALLENGE THE STATUS QUO TO HIGH-FIVE

"We're not in this to test the waters," declared an unknown heretical entrepreneur. "We are in this to make waves." An entrepreneur simply means one who undertakes an enterprise, one who challenges the status quo by creating a new status quo in ideas, products, or services, and celebrates with high-fives: a gesture of greeting or elation or congratulation or good-fellowship or triumph, where one person's upraised palm slaps the upraised palm of another person.

"Entrepreneurs are never satisfied with the status quo," says Stephan Bourque, founder and CEO of Vancouver, British Columbia-based Incognito Software, who discovered he was not destined for the corporate world when his new and better ways of doing things were interpreted as unwanted criticism by his bosses. Now, he says, "I wish my employees would get into more trouble—because it shows they are on the lookout for opportunities to improve themselves or company operations."

The idea of the impossible attracts these high-fivers. "Where most others avoid risk, entrepreneurs see potential," says Robert Irvine, chef and host of Food Network's Restaurant, coincidentally named Impossible. Robert L. Schwartz, professor of law at the University of New Mexico School of Law, comments, "The entrepreneur is essentially a visualizer and an actualizer. He can visualize something, and when he visualizes it, he sees exactly how to make it happen." Entrepreneurs, in contrast to intrapreneurs, their innovative colleagues who work within organizations, don't seek permission. They're in charge with all its risks and responsibilities.

If you want a quick introduction to today's remarkable high-fivers, read the insightful article "This Is Generation Flux: Meet The Pioneers Of The New (And Chaotic) Frontier Of Business," which gives the reader some key clues about the mindset of these entrepreneurs. Future-focused, Generation Flux thrives on ambiguity, fluidity, and chaos. If there is a pattern to the next couple of decades, there probably is no discernable pattern. "What defines Generation Flux," the article points out, "is a mind-set that embraces instability, that tolerates—and even enjoys—recalibrating careers, business models and assumptions. Our institutions are out of date; the long career is dead; any quest for solid rules is pointless, since we will be constantly rethinking them; you can't rely on an established business model or a corporate ladder to point your way; silos between industries are breaking down; anything settled is vulnerable." Sounds like the essence of heresy, a "Flux Manifesto."

To flourish today requires a new kind of openness. More than 150 years ago, Charles Darwin foreshadowed this era in his description of natural selection: "It is not the strongest of the species that will survive; nor the most intelligent that survive. It is the one that is most adaptable to change."

High-fiving heretics thrive. They color outside the lines, push the envelope, and persevere. What an incredibly exciting time to be alive and thrive!

Color Outside The Lines

"Curiosity is the most powerful thing you own," says James Francis Cameron, a Canadian filmmaker, inventor, engineer, and deep-sea explorer. Disney affirms Cameron's belief: "We keep moving forward, opening new doors, and doing new things, because we're curious and curiosity keeps leading us down new paths." Albert Einstein claimed, "I have no special talents, I am only passionately curious." It's no wonder NASA's Mars Science Laboratory mission gave the name "Curiosity" to the car-sized robotic rover exploring the Gale Crater on Mars.

Entrepreneurs curiously color outside the lines, a fitting place for them since they consider themselves outsiders. The educational system generally drives them insane: here are the lines, color inside them—a nightmare of regimentation with little critical thinking. They gravitate naturally beyond the lines. They are never satisfied with the status quo. That's a good description of me too as a student in school and now as a professor of leadership, creativity, and innovation. In fact, one of my best failures was creating *The Anti-Coloring Book* that sold a whopping twenty-two copies.

The unknown, the not yet, fascinates entrepreneurs. They love a challenge, and the bigger the better. Maynard Webb, founder of Webb Investment Network, and author of *Rebooting Work: Transform How You Work in an Age of Entrepreneurship*, points out that for entrepreneurs, the idea is but the first step of the journey. For example, ezmoves® were invented in 1993 when a father and son, who were carpet installers, knew there had to be an easier way to move furniture. They were certain that there was something better than conventional wheeled dollies. Thus, they invented the ezmoves® Furniture Slides, freeing them from the daily backaches they suffered due to moving heavy furniture.

Entrepreneurs are passionate about discovery that results from random combinations, connections, and collisions. Tony Hsieh, CEO of Zappos, observed, "Innovation is often the result of random conversations—collisions—where ideas outside your industry are applied to your own. We want to accelerate these collisions among people." The movie *Crash* epitomizes what happens when people collide with one another. The movie's writer-director, Paul Haggis, interweaves several connected stories about race, class, family, and gender in Los Angeles in the aftermath of 9/11.

Entrepreneurs like John Barfield, founder of the Bartech Group, encourage young aspiring entrepreneurs. In his book *Starting from Scratch: The Humble Beginnings of a Two Billion-Dollar Enterprise*, he claims that "as an African American, I believe it's my responsibility to be an example to our young people … There's no end to what you can do if you use your imagination. This is what I like about entrepreneurism."

Two of the Millennials I know personally and work with demonstrate this entrepreneurial spirit of adventure that challenges the status quo to high-five. I engaged Kelly Hudson, a recent graduate in Social Media to assist me in enlivening and increasing my presence on the web. I also hired Troy Spoelma, a college student majoring in art and film, to shoot a series of promotional videos for my practice. Both are forward thinking, highly motivated, and eager to make their mark in the world.

Young entrepreneurs with bold imagination, especially those creating technological start-ups in Silicon Valley, follow a long line of historical and contemporary entrepreneurs that can inspire and guide them as they give birth to a new dream and start a new venture. Ray Kurzweil, an American author, computer scientist, inventor, and fellow futurist in the World Future Society, contends, "The past is over; the present is fleeting; we live in the future." Heretics, kindred spirits with Kurzweil, color outside the lines and push the envelope.

Push The Envelope

Peter Drucker, an Austrian-born American management consultant, educator, and author, describes the entrepreneurial process: "The entrepreneur always searches for change, responds to it, and exploits it as an opportunity."

Entrepreneurs push the envelope. Merle Tenney, a language technology consultant, reports that the term *pushing the envelope* originally comes from the field of aviation. It's a reference to the flyable portion of the atmosphere that envelopes the earth. Pilots would push the envelope when they were testing the speed or elevation limits of new aircraft. The term entered the mainstream by way of Tom Wolfe's novel *The Right Stuff*. "Push the envelope" is now used figuratively to mean "stretch the boundaries."

This term has since been applied metaphorically to any situation in which a person or a group is pushing the limits or doing something new in any area of activity, or to approach or extend the limits of what is possible. Entrepreneurs I know often apply the term in a self-congratulatory way to highlight the novelty and risk-taking dimension of their activity. In these interactions, there are repeated high-fives all around.

NASA astronaut and Expedition 46 Commander Scott Kelly, and his Russian counterpart, Mikhail Kornienko, certainly pushed the envelope. "Scott Kelly's one-year mission aboard the International Space Station has helped to advance deep space exploration and America's Journey to Mars," said NASA Administrator Charles Bolden. "Scott has become the first American astronaut to spend a year in space, and in so doing, helped us take one giant leap toward putting boots on Mars." Kelly and Kornienko returned to Earth on Tuesday, March 1, 2016.

The "New Space" entrepreneurs are definitely pushing the envelope in the booming space industry. In January 2016, Jeff Bezos's Blue Origin launched a rocket just past the boundary of space and then recovered it in a soft landing. The company said its New Shepard vehicle made history when it became the first rocket to pass the boundary of space, what's known as the Karman line, 100 km high, and then land vertically upon the Earth for the second time in a row. Entrepreneur Richard Branson's Virgin Galactic has returned to the space race and is selling rides on SpaceShipTwo for $250,000. So far, nearly 700 have signed up.

Stephen Hawking and Russian billionaire Yuri Milner announced on April 12, 2016, that they are really pushing the space envelope. They're teaming up in a $100 million hunt for alien life that will rely on a fleet of postage-stamp-sized spacecraft to explore the universe. Their project called Breakthrough Starshot hopes to launch thousands of the tiny light-propelled spacecraft—called nanocrafts—with the goal of reaching the star system in twenty years.

When someone asked Larry Page, an American computer scientist and Internet entrepreneur who co-founded Google Inc. with Sergey Brin, "What is the one sentence summary of how you change the world?" Page answered, "Always work hard on something uncomfortably exciting!" When heretics hear this, they break into their high-five happy dance!

Persevere

Steve Jobs, a classic high-fiver, observed: "I'm convinced that about half of what separates successful entrepreneurs from the non-successful ones is pure perseverance." I observed conscientious perseverance at the 2016 Iron Man competition in Chattanooga, Tennessee. The number 140.6 that I saw embroidered on their hats told the story of their unwavering commitment to swim 2.4 miles, bike 112.0 miles, and run 26.2 miles. I personally identify with these Iron Man competitors, especially in my running of the 400-meter hurdles.

One needs perseverance to channel the innovative energy into a successful outcome. I've witnessed irrational entrepreneurial exuberance in spite of an extremely high failure rate. According to *Bloomberg Businessweek*, a publication that delivers business and market news to the world, eight out of ten entrepreneurs who start businesses fail within the first eighteen months. One of the causes of failure, in addition to not really being in touch with customers through deep dialogue, is a leadership breakdown, a founder dysfunction.

Innovation guru Robert G. Cooper, author of the classic book *Winning at New Products*, confirms that only one of seven new product ideas is really a success in the market. For every seven new product ideas, about four enter development, 1.5 are launched, and only one succeeds. The rest have been stopped, failed, or forever stuck in the back end of the innovation funnel. The innovativeness of new products and services that do reach the market is becoming less and less, and new-to-the-world products, the first in their kind and creating an entirely new market, represent only ten percent of all new products. And research shows that this percentage is even shrinking.

Thomas Paine, one of the Founding Fathers of the United States, eloquently framed challenging the status quo for all entrepreneurs: "I love the man that can smile in trouble, that can gather strength from distress and grow brave by reflection. T'is the business of little minds to shrink, but he whose heart is firm, and whose conscience approves his conduct, will pursue his principles unto death."

Now, we will consider how heretics engage people to form a cohesive movement with the singular goal of achieving their impossible dream.

PART TWO

Lead Like A Heretic: Engage

CHAPTER 4

Cultivate A Climate Of Engagement

"The real role of leadership is climate control—creating a climate of possibility," noted author, educator, and creativity thinker Sir Ken Robinson. "If you do that, people will rise to it and achieve things that you completely did not anticipate and couldn't have expected." Heretics cultivate the conditions where creativity can take place—a culture where curiosity reigns and imagination is a legitimate purposeful activity that permeates every aspect of the organization.

Leaders accept the responsibility of controlling the climate of 'the organizational weather' that sets the conditions for growth, and invite followers to live and work in a climate where impossibility thinking is encouraged and rewarded. This engagement dimension of climate marks a dramatic shift in leadership priorities. Gary Hamel, in his book *What Matters Now: How to Win in a World of Relentless Change, Ferocious Competition, and Unstoppable Innovation*, explains the new role of contemporary leaders: "Leaders must no longer be seen as grand visionaries, all-wise decision-makers, and heroic deal-makers, but rather as 'social architects,' 'constitution writers,' and 'entrepreneurs of meaning.' They must see their primary responsibility as creating work environments that encourage their associates to collaborate, innovate, and excel." Heretics, as responsible leaders, create the conditions including emotional stability for others to work productively.

Defining Success, a global research study conducted by consulting firm Accenture, provides valuable insights into what 4,000 employees of three main generations, Baby Boomers and Generations X and Y, value from their employers. It found that, when asked to describe a 'good work environment,' the term 'rewarding' was cited by the most respondents (59 percent), while 'honest,' 'flexible,' and 'interesting' followed at 54 percent, 50 percent, and 49 percent, respectively.

Ed Catmull, in his book *Creativity, Inc.: Overcoming the Unseen Forces That Stand in the Way of True Inspiration*, chronicles how he established and sustained a culture of disciplined creativity during setbacks and success at Pixar. In large measure, the environment Catmull and his colleagues built enhanced the creative process and defied convention in producing the movie *Toy Story* and thirteen movies that followed. He believed that it's not the manager's job to prevent risks, but to make it safe for others to take them. Here's an example of his clear straightforward leadership philosophy: "Give a good idea to a mediocre team, and they will screw it up. But give a mediocre idea to a great team, and they will either fix it or come up with something better."

"The role of the leader is not to come up with all the great ideas," contends Simon Sinek in *Start with Why: How Great Leaders Inspire Everyone to Take Action*. "The role of the leader is to create an environment in which great ideas can happen." Heretics cultivate a FIT climate of impossibility, a climate of Freedom, Integrity, and Trust.

4.1 FREEDOM

"Liberty, when it begins to take root," claimed George Washington, "is a plant of rapid growth."

Heretics understand that freedom comes with responsibilities. I remember as a teenager going to a concert presented by young people in a popular organization, Up with People, an educational organization founded in 1965, whose stated mission is to bridge cultural barriers and create global understanding through service and a musical show. To this day, I remember the lyrics of the theme song: "Freedom isn't free. Freedom isn't free. You've got to pay a price. You've got to sacrifice for your liberty."

Radical Anglo-American political theorist and revolutionary Thomas Paine helped to advance the cause of liberty in both the United States and France. In 1772, he was dismissed from his job as a customs officer for agitating for higher salaries and emigrated to the United States. In 1776, he published a pamphlet entitled *Common Sense*, which forcefully argued for the independence of the thirteen Colonies. And then, in 1791, he wrote in defense of the French Revolution, *The Rights of Man*, where he argued that there are natural rights common to all people and that only democratic institutions could guarantee those rights. In 1792, Paine was prosecuted for treason.

Thomas Jefferson, an American Founding Father who was principal author of the Declaration of Independence, observed, "The boisterous sea of liberty is never without a wave."

French philosopher, author, and journalist, Albert Camus added, "Liberty is dangerous."

Investment in assuring other people's freedom gains substantial returns in both the short- and long-term. But, as Ronald Reagan warned, "Freedom is a fragile thing and is never more than one generation from extinction. It is not ours by inheritance; it must be fought for and defended constantly by each generation, for it comes only once to a people. Those who have known freedom, and then lost it, have never known it again."

Heretics cultivate a climate of engagement, an atmosphere of freedom where each person in their movements feels free to be uniquely oneself, to be radically practical, and to be outrageously audacious.

Freedom To Be Uniquely Oneself

"There is a vitality, a life force, an energy, a quickening that is translated through you into action, and because there is only one of you in all time, this expression is unique," remarked American modern dancer and choreographer Martha Graham. "And if you block it, it will never exist through any other medium and will be lost."

Freedom for the heretic begins by answering this personal foundational question: Who am I? "The two most important days of your life," wrote Mark Twain, "are the day you were born and the day you find out why." Heretics make every effort to know themselves, who they are, each with his or her 100 trillion cells in the human body that make up all our tissues, muscle, bone, and blood, which in turn make up our organs.

To be a heretic means you must be comfortable in your own skin in order to help others feel comfortable in their skin. You accept yourself as a person of worth and trust your capacity to be and become authentically the unique person you were created to be. You are careful not to merely fulfil a heretical role, but express in your leadership calling the essence of your identity. A CEO I coached had two distinctive personalities. When he spoke in public, he was dead serious and bored his associates to tears. In private, I experienced him as personable and a great storyteller with a dry sense of humor. When I chatted with him about this dichotomy, he indicated that he purposely used his CEO role and voice in public to appear in control of the affairs of his company. I suggested he think about adopting a hybrid model for speaking that combined his public serious nature with his private relaxed style. The result was jaw dropping. In his next public speech, I saw him inspire his audience. His associates shared with me that they were sure he was on a new miracle medication.

"If you seek to lead," advised Dee Hock, founder and CEO emeritus of Visa, "invest at least 50 percent of your time in leading yourself." There is a danger of defining ourselves solely in terms of our role as leaders. Heifetz, in *Leadership on the Line*, offers, "To anchor ourselves in the turbulent seas of the various roles we take in life, professionally and personally, we have found it profoundly important to distinguish between the self, which we can anchor, and our roles, which we cannot."

Heretics know their unique selves and offer freedom for others to be uniquely themselves. Identity can be such a slippery concept. Saint Augustine confessed, "I cannot grasp all that I am." On a lighter note, playwright Oscar Wilde recommended, "Be yourself. Everyone else is already taken." Or as American actress, comedian, and singer Lily Tomlin revealed, "I always wanted to be somebody. I wish I'd been more specific." Ike, a character in the movie *Manhattan* rationalized, "I gotta model myself after someone." What we know pales in comparison with who we are.

Part of the identity work of heretics includes discovering their unique constellation of gifts, the unique combination that makes them a one-of-a-kind person, and appreciating the points of differentiation from the rest of the human family. Nick Craig, president of the Authentic Leadership Institute, and Scott Snook, the MBA Class of 1958 Senior Lecturer of Business Administration at the Harvard Business School, indicate that an executive's most important role is to be a steward of the organization's purpose. However, they report that less than 20 percent of leaders have a strong sense of their individual purpose, and even fewer can distill their purpose into a concrete statement. They believe that "the process of articulating your purpose and finding the courage to live it—what we call purpose to impact—is the single most important developmental task you can undertake as a leader."

Heretics create the condition of freedom where their followers may identify and celebrate their uniqueness and make a world of difference.

Freedom To Be Radically Practical

"In the psychology of possibility," Ellen J. Langer, in *Counter Clockwise*, remarks, "we search for the answer to how to improve, not merely to adjust."

Heretics don't aspire to be in the adjustment business. They initiate and deliver practical change that puts their unique constellation of gifts to work to accomplish a specific purpose by radical means, in the spirit of radical that derives from the Latin *radix*, which means 'rooted.' They identify an impossible need, a problem, an opportunity, a challenge, or a threat, and address it with a radically practical approach. Heretics agree with singer-songwriter Bob Dylan when he remarked: "A hero is someone who understands the responsibility that comes with his freedom." The efforts of heretics support the lives of others. As President John F. Kennedy expressed, "We stand for freedom. That is our conviction for ourselves— that is our commitment to others." Nelson Mandela reflected, "For to be free is not merely to cast off one's chains, but to live in a way that respects and enhances the freedom of others."

An article's title, "This CEO Is Out for Blood: Elizabeth Holmes and Her Secretive Company Theranos Aims to Revolutionize Health Care," caught my attention. Holmes founded her revolutionary blood diagnosis company, Theranos, when she was nineteen, and now it's worth more than $9 billion, and poised to change health care. The name *Theranos* is an amalgam of the words 'therapy' and 'diagnosis,' and the Palo Alto-based corporation has over 500 employees. Theranos' tests can be performed on just a few drops of blood, or about $1/100^{th}$ to $1/1000^{th}$ of the amount that would ordinarily be required, an extraordinary potential boon to frequently tested hospital patients or cancer victims, the elderly, infants, children, the obese, those on anticoagulants, or simply anyone with an aversion to blood draws. Over seventy tests can be done on a sample obtained by pricking a finger. Holmes believes her company is about doing good for patients and the health system.

Bill Gates, a radically practical entrepreneur himself, who wrote the foreword for *Edison and the Rise of Innovation*, describes Edison as America's greatest inventor. Gates points out: "One of America's greatest gifts to the world is our capacity for innovation. From light bulbs and telephones to vaccines and microprocessors, our inventions and ideas have improved the lives—and even saved the lives—of countless people around the globe."

Edison's inventions were radically practical, perhaps revolutionary. Gates describes Edison as "a very practical person. He learned early on that it wasn't enough to simply come up with great ideas in a vacuum; he had to invent things people wanted. That meant understanding the market, designing the products that met his customer's needs, convincing his investors to support his ideas, and then promoting them. Edison didn't invent the light bulb; he invented the light bulb that worked, and the one that sold."

Heretics cultivate a climate of engagement where there is freedom to be uniquely oneself, radically practical, and outrageously audacious, a dynamite combination in any field.

Freedom To Be Outrageously Audacious

"The key to thinking free is first to allow your mind to contemplate really outrageous ideas," recommends Steven Sample, "and only subsequently apply constraints of practicality, practicability, legality, cost, time, and ethics."

Heretics model a contrarian standpoint and create a climate of engagement that gives their followers freedom to think and feel outrageously audacious, and also gives them permission and encouragement to act in a similarly outrageously audacious fashion.

"Make no little plans," wrote Daniel Burnham, the Chicago architect whose vision recreated the city after the great fire of 1871. "They have no magic to stir men's blood and probably themselves will not be realized. Make big plans. Aim high in hope and work, remembering that a noble, logical diagram, one recorded, will never die but long after we are gone will be a living thing, asserting itself with ever-growing insistency. Remember that our sons and grandsons are going to do things that would stagger us. Let your watchword be order and your beacon beauty." Burnham encourages others to think big, bigger, biggest!

I'm taking Burnham's advice to heart and am planning a virtual global book tour for this book. With my other seven books, my book tour consisted of visiting major bookstores in several major cities in North America. But now, I have the freedom to be outrageously audacious. With reasonably inexpensive technology available to connect me to people around the globe, and a vital message for leaders everywhere, I'm going to plug in *Lead Like a Heretic* to a substantial targeted audience not just in bookstores but to computers everywhere. Stay tuned.

Elon Musk, a South-African-born Canadian-American business magnate, founder of SpaceX, and co-founder, CEO, and product architect of Tesla Motors, predicted, "The world is going to change so dramatically in the 21st century, one thing is to identify something, try to aim for a big problem rather than a small problem, just look for industries that are functioning poorly and that have been stagnant for some period of time." The movie *Selma*, where Martin Luther King Jr., Lyndon Baines Johnson, and the civil rights marches changed America, reveals how an outrageously audacious idea can be achieved. The tag line for the movie, "One Dream Can Change the World," sums up this idea. And I believe it can. I wrote *The Compassionate Conspiracy: A Field Guide to Changing the World* with the express purpose of inviting Millennials to join a movement with an outrageously audacious dream of One World One Family.

Would your organization pass the audacity test? "The greatest danger for most of us is not that our aim is too high and we miss it," cautioned Michelangelo, "but that it is too low and we reach it." Sir Audacity himself, Richard Branson, advocates: "Dream big by setting yourself seemingly impossible challenges. You then have to catch up with them."

David Armstrong, author of *Managing by Storying Around: A New Method of Leadership*, advises: "If people aren't laughing at your ideas, you aren't being creative enough." It's hard to hear their laughter, but consider it a sign that you're onto something. When I shared my dream with Nairobi, Kenya, city officials that Kibera Slum of 1.2 million residents could become an economically viable city, they laughed so hard I felt like a stand-up comedian. Their laughter disappointed me especially since my proposal positively addressed the critical issues of poverty, unemployment, and sanitation in Kibera. One of the city officials chuckled and chided: "Keep dreaming, Doctor!" He certainly underestimated my commitment to work alongside the "Slummers" with more resolve than ever to make our dream a reality. I remember people laughing at President John F. Kennedy's outrageously audacious vision of going to the moon, and then watching the very same people cheering Neil Armstrong's Immortal Footprint.

Heretics believe wholeheartedly that together there is nothing we cannot do. Compare this positive orientation with the person I saw recently who wore a T-shirt with the message "Born to be Mild."

Cultivating a climate of engagement where persons have the freedom to be outrageously audacious can be good for business and improve your bottom line. Gary Hamel, a corporate leadership consultant, confirms this perspective: "Audacity, imagination, and zeal are the ultimate wellsprings of competitive differentiation."

4.2 INTEGRITY

"I look for three things in hiring people," reports Warren Buffett. "The first is personal integrity, the second is intelligence, and the third is high energy level. But if you don't have the first, the other two will kill you."

Heretics cultivate a climate of engagement where integrity permeates their movements from top to bottom. The word integrity derives from *integer* that means one or wholeness, soundness, or unimpaired. Although many organizations act with the utmost integrity, the behavior of a large number of entities suggests that we do have an integrity crisis. To borrow a line from the musical *Music Man*, "There's trouble in River City." The media influences our perceptions of integrity by reporting mostly on organizational breaches of trust especially at the top. The headlines shout out that integrity constitutes a rare commodity. David Brooks, *New York Times* columnist and author of *The Road to Character*, notes, "The post-2008 economy has taught all of us that greed, selfishness and short-sighted leadership aren't sustainable. Today's global marketplace requires better judgment from our leaders."

Abraham Lincoln put integrity in perspective: "It is true that you may fool all the people some of the time; you can even fool some people all of the time; but you can't fool all of the people all of the time." Occasionally, one of my students will plagiarize, even blatantly, like the one who submitted a term paper and even attached a copy of the paper from which he had plagiarized. Exploring how the student decided to plagiarize can be helpful in appreciating the student's particular circumstances. In this case, I discovered that the student worked at two jobs in order to support his family and pay his tuition. Instead of punishment, I offered him praise for his good ideas and gave him an extension so he could complete his assignment.

Francis Bacon, an English philosopher, summarized the nature of integrity: "It's not what we eat but what we digest that makes us strong; not what we gain but what we save that makes us rich; not what we read but what we remember that makes us learned; and not what we profess but what we practice that gives us integrity."

Let's explore how heretics practice integrity in three inter-related dimensions: responsibility to oneself, accountability to others, and respectability to build and sustain a reputation.

Responsibility

"Leadership is not rank, privileges, titles, or money," stated Peter Drucker. "It is responsibility."

Drucker knows from first-hand experience. Hailed by *BusinessWeek* as "the man who invented management," Drucker directly influenced a huge number of leaders from a wide range of organizations across all sectors of society.

Integrity is an inside job that requires responsibility to oneself with adherence to a strict ethical code to tell the truth and walk the talk. Consistent alignment with the truth constitutes the foundation of integrity for the individual leader. Nelson Mandela encouraged leaders: "The first thing is to be honest with yourself. You can never have an impact on society if you have not changed yourself. Great peacemakers are all people of integrity, of honesty, but humility."

"You owe it to yourself, to your family, and to your organization," I sensitively recommended to a corporate president I was coaching, "to deal with your addiction to alcohol." His uncharacteristic response, "You're fired!" told me volumes about the denial of his deteriorating condition. I did take a chance and in the short term paid a price. However, he did get help and today we remain good friends.

Good Business International (also known as GoodB), whose tag line is "Better Business for a Better World," encourages a five-star approach to good business: human, ethical, profits and purpose, green, and common good. GoodB describes the state of business today: "We have entered the extraordinary era of 'personal responsibility' in business. No modern business of good conscience can practice the indifference of the past. The world's suffering has landed at our doorstep and we can no longer turn away." GoodB does not position itself as judge and jury over the business community, but seeks collaborators in the process of the good business revolution.

The heretic accepts that he or she presents himself or herself as a model of integrity however imperfect. Nobody's perfect and everybody I know has a skeleton in their closet. The Biblical image presented in the book of Proverbs (20:5 in *The Message*) rings true: "Knowing what is right is like deep water in the heart; a wise person draws from the well within." Heretics practice that kind of inner responsibility to oneself, and accountability to others, to which we turn our attention.

Accountability

Here's how a heretic spells accountability: DWYSYWD: Do What You Say You Will Do.

Brené Brown, in her book *Daring Greatly: How the Courage to Be Vulnerable Transforms the Way We Live, Love, Parent, and Lead*, offers a succinct definition of a leader: "Anyone who holds her- or himself accountable for finding potential in people and processes." When heretics commit to an impossible dream, they consider themselves accountable to themselves but also to others for everything they think, feel, speak, and do. Mutual accountability provides a solid foundation for trust to be initiated and sustained.

"As we must account for every idle word," advised Benjamin Franklin, "so must we account for every idle silence." Unfortunately, many leaders act inconsistently. Thomas R. Horton, author of *The CEO Paradox: The Privilege and Accountability of Leadership*, reflects: "Until those at the top perceive their accountability as a sacred trust, and accept only the privileges they fully deserve, the troubling CEO paradox will persist."

Servant-leaders recognize that it's both a privilege to serve and a responsibility to guide others with transparency. They practice accountability by keeping a "promise log" that helps them register and deliver on their promises. Leaders report that the simple act of entering the promises they make, especially in speeches, reminds them to do what they said they would do. Leaders know that fulfilling promises for their associates constitutes a small investment that results in big dividends for the short- and long-term life of the enterprise.

Gostick and Elton, in their book *All In*, echo Horton's assessment: "A lack of accountability is one of the most corrosive elements of ineffective work cultures and leads to people failing to take responsibility, missed deadlines, errors in judgment, misunderstandings, overpromising, disagreements, and so on ... When accountability is instituted in positive ways, it helps people feel the satisfaction of achieving a goal and performing up to expectations. It also allows them to understand when they're falling short and where improvements are needed."

Our actions usually speak louder than our words. Annette Simmons, in *The Story Factor: Inspiration, Influence, and Persuasion through the Art of Storytelling*, urges leaders to practice what they preach: "'We value integrity,' means nothing. But tell a story about a former employee who hid his mistake and cost the company thousands, or a story about a salesperson who owned up to a mistake and earned so much trust her company doubled his order, and you begin to teach an employee what integrity means." When heretics act accountably, they take ownership of and responsibility for their dream, and feel a certain modest pride. They also demonstrate increased energy, a sense of fulfilment, and a willingness to make tough choices and take a stand.

A journalist asked *Downton Abbey* star Michelle Dockery, "If you ruled the world, what's the first thing you would change?" Her answer reflects the concern of many about contemporary leaders and their perception of their accountability: "I would put someone else in charge."

Respectability

"It takes 20 years to build a reputation and five minutes to ruin it," reflects Warren Buffett. "If you think about that, you'll do things differently." Keshavan Nair, Professor of Surgery, echoes Buffett's belief: "The reality is that we lose respect for our leaders if we do not approve of their conduct—public or private. Leaders who do not command our respect reduce the legitimacy of their leadership and lose our trust."

Heretics cultivate a climate of engagement in which they live with integrity to themselves, accountability to others, and develop respectability with others inside and outside their movements. That's how they build and sustain their reputation. Most of us can spot respectability in the public square. There are a few local figures we know who personify integrity. I've been blessed with wonderful role models of respectability throughout my life beginning with my parents who showed me on a daily basis how to live with compassion and grace. The list of people outside my family I admire includes: Dr. Ed and Valetta Brown, Deaconess Edith Lucas, Rev. Earl Leard, Joy Lawrence, Chuck Royce, and Joyce Decker, to name a few.

In my community of Grand Rapids, Michigan, I would acknowledge the life of Ralph Hauenstein, a 103-year-old military hero, business leader, and philanthropist (March 20, 1912–January 10, 2016). He sat at the table with former Presidents Gerald R. Ford, a boyhood friend, and Dwight D. Eisenhower, and with generals such as George Patton and Omar Bradley, as well as Secretary of State George Marshall, author of the Marshall Plan. Hauenstein headed Allied intelligence operations during WWII, edited the *Grand Rapids Herald* newspaper, and started several successful companies. At ninety-nine, he joined the Grand Rapids Rotary Club. When I asked him why he was joining, Ralph replied, "I always wanted to join but never got around to it."

"In the twentieth century," said Hauenstein, "I saw with my own eyes the worst that leaders are capable of. In the twenty-first century, I was able to encourage the best leadership possible, so that the world will be better for my children's children." In his honor, Grand Valley State University established the Hauenstein Center for Presidential Studies, an institution dedicated to teaching students to be ethical and effective leaders. His legacy lives on.

4.3 TRUST

"The first job," observed Doug Conant, former CEO of the Campbell Soup Company, "for any leader is to inspire trust."

Heretics cultivate a climate of engagement where freedom, integrity, and trust form a solid foundation for leadership today and tomorrow. "Trust is everything," claimed Bill George, former chief of medical technology pioneer Medtronic, "because success depends upon customers' trust in the products they buy, employees' trust in their leaders, investors' trust in those who invest for them and the public's trust in capitalism. If you do not have integrity, no one will trust you, nor should they."

Stephen Covey begins his classic book, *The Speed of Trust: The One Thing that Changes Everything*, with a similar claim: "There is one thing that is common to every individual, relationship, team, family, organization, nation, economy, and civilization throughout the world—one thing which, if removed, will destroy the most powerful government, the most successful business, the most thriving economy, the most influential leadership, the greatest friendship, the strongest character, the deepest love. On the other hand, if developed and leveraged, that one thing has the potential to create unparalleled success and prosperity in every dimension of life. Yet, it is the least understood, most neglected, and most underestimated possibility of our time. That one thing is trust."

Covey went on to identify five waves of trust: Self Trust (credibility, from the Latin *credere*, which means "to believe"), relationship trust (consistent behavior), organizational trust (alignment), market trust (reputation), and societal trust (contribution). Heretics ride each of these waves by earning the trust of others who in turn fully engage in the organization's life and work. These waves do not stand alone but intersect with each other depending on the context and circumstances that either affirm or reduce trust. Leaders need to be keenly aware that the trust factor must be appreciated with every facet of their role, and that waves of trust influence each other.

In their previously mentioned book *All In*, Gostick and Elton note the critical nature of the leader's behavior: "Character-based trust moves an organization forward. It is created by a leader's consistent behavior, adherence to principles, openness, honesty, and dependability." Most of my executive coaching practice involves identifying how trust eroded and offering strategies to build lasting trust relationships. Precisely identifying the present reality of trust in an organization and how it evolved can be as elusive as trying to put socks on an octopus. Probably the most important dimension of building trust comprises a willingness to focus on the future and to make a fresh commitment to the process. Dealing effectively with the past can be helpful but dwelling on it can be disastrous.

United States Business Hall-of-Famer Max De Pree reminds us of the precarious nature of trust: "Trust can only be won slowly. It can be lost in a twinkling of an eye." Let's explore three kinds of trust heretics develop: mutual, unconditional, and compassionate.

Mutual Trust

"Trust is the lubrication," claim Warren Bennis and Burt Nanus in their book *Leaders: Strategies for Taking Charge*, "that makes it possible for organizations to work."

Mutual trust stands at the pinnacle of human motivation and encourages people to perform at their best. As my friend, motivational speaker Zig Ziglar, used to say, "Every sale has five basic obstacles: no need, no money, no hurry, no desire, no trust." For example, IBM has established a culture of values built around trust. An interviewer asked Randy MacDonald, who is responsible for IBM's human resources worldwide, how the company trains global leaders. MacDonald responded, "Being an IBMer is not about a line of business. It's not about a function. It's not about a team. It's not about you. It's about the enterprise. Those values are built around the client, around innovation for both the company and society, around trust and personal responsibility and the way we treat each other."

Psychologist Robert Hogan, who profiles executives for Fortune 500 companies, maintains that followers want four things: integrity, confidence, decision-making, and clarity. According to Hogan, "The key to the relationship is trust, and if they don't trust you, you're done." Andrew Sobel, author of *All for One: 10 Strategies for Building Trusted Client Partnerships*, encourages leaders to use questions to build trust: "One of the key elements of trust is believing the other person is focused on your agenda and your needs, not just their own interests. Trust, after all, can be defined as 'the belief that you will meet my expectations of you.'" I endorse Sobel's insight. In my MBA classes, I've discovered that paying attention to building trust through focused attention on students, particularly with asking questions, results in creative interaction. The use of questions honors students as capable and forms a connection for a mutually authentic relationship. One of the first things I do with a new class is briefly find out who they are and enquire what they want to get out of the class. From their answers, I can tailor our dialogue with illustrations that fulfil their expectations. I focus primarily on their success. And when I promise to answer their questions and keep my promise, everybody wins.

Building trust can be slippery at best. Amy Cuddy, a psychologist at the Harvard Business School, who has been studying first impressions for more than a decade, indicates that she and her colleagues found that we make snap judgements about other people that answer two primary questions: Can I trust this person? And can I respect this person's capabilities? Cuddy's research shows that trust is the most important factor.

A Latin proverb offers heretics wise advice: "It is equally an error to trust all men or no man."

Unconditional Trust

Jack Welch, former CEO of GE, remarked that only two words matter for leaders today: truth and trust.

Unconditional trust engages others in a relationship so powerful that it affects every aspect of organizational life. There are no hidden agendas and no strings or conditions attached like "I'll scratch your back if you scratch mine." For many, that kind of experience of trust in the workplace amounts to fantasy. The National Leadership Index published by Harvard's Kennedy School concludes with this stark reality: "We don't trust our leaders."

Glenn Llopis, a contributor to *Forbes* magazine, reminds us of a prominent leader who personified unconditional trust: "As the world mourns the loss of Nelson Mandela and commemorates his greatness as a leader, we would do well to remember that one of the many hallmarks of his leadership was trust. The greatest leaders in the world gravitated toward Mr. Mandela because he was genuinely trustworthy and his purpose to support peace, prosperity and unity not only in South Africa—but throughout the world. Mandela was able to lead people in ways that many find impossible to do. As he famously said, 'It always seems impossible until it's done.'"

In his article "Seven Reasons Employees Don't Trust Their Leaders," Llopis also points out seven early warning signs that employees are having trouble trusting their leaders: lack courage, hidden agenda, self-centered, reputation issues, inconsistent behavior, don't get their hands dirty, and lack a generous purpose.

"Trust your instruments" constitutes the most important maxim for fighter pilots. In my paratrooper training, we learned to unconditionally trust each other to pack our parachutes. Similarly, heretics need to develop that kind of trust among members of the movement. A friend of mine, Doreen Bolhuis, shared with me the role of unconditional trust in her avocation as a trapeze artist. She described how she places unconditional trust in her "catcher." In my role as a pastor, my congregants expect me to act as the "catcher," especially when tragedy strikes for a family or the community. I'm amazed at the power of unconditional trust to help us deal with unfortunate situations and rise like the phoenix.

Heretics nurture unconditional trust through small trustworthy acts. For example, Emma Winter, a gracious senior, supports Kibera Kids Kitchen, our feeding program in Kibera Slum in Nairobi, Kenya, with a check every month. Emma calls her contribution, "A drop in the desert," and I'm honored by her ocean of trust. Albert Einstein, who developed the general theory of relativity, one of the two pillars of modern physics, commented, "Whoever is careless with truth in small matters cannot be trusted with important matters."

In *Teach Like Your Hair's on Fire*, Ray Esquith describes the context he's created for learning in a fifth grade public school classroom called Room 56 in a Los Angeles neighborhood plagued by poverty and violence: "It's a world where character matters, hard work is respected, humility is valued, and support for one another is unconditional." Like Esquith's fifth graders, movements progress primarily due to a solid foundation of trust in each other to achieve their impossible dreams.

Let me close this section by quoting Chinese philosopher, Lao-Tzu, who shared this wisdom about unconditional trust:

The best rulers are barely known to men.
The next best are cherished and extolled.
The next are feared, and the least are scorned.
Distrust cannot summon trust.

Compassionate Trust

"Compassion," believes His Holiness the Dalai Lama, "is the radicalism of our time."

Daniel Goleman, who wrote *A Force for Good: The Dalai Lama's Vision for Our World*, points out, "The Dalai Lama's version of compassion is more muscular than the Sunday-school stereotypes of a benign but soft and flabby kindness." According to the Dalai Lama, compassion has a progressive contagious quality: "If you are a compassionate person, then you build a compassionate family and then a compassionate community and then a compassionate world ... I feel fortunate. The first seeds of my compassion came from my mother." Goleman and I have this good fortune in common. My mother, Mary Anne (Sawyer) Johnson, deeply and firmly planted the seeds of compassion in me, and I'm appreciative of the wisdom of her heart every day. In fact, she provided the impetus for me to write *The Compassionate Conspiracy: A Field Guide to Changing the World*, in which I particularly encourage Millennials to become 'radical global servant-leaders' where the primary principle and driving force is compassion.

Heretics commit themselves to show compassion, from the Latin *compassio*, which means, "to suffer," toward others to alleviate their suffering. Dr. Kristin Neff, a professor and researcher at the University of Texas at Austin, coordinates the Self-Compassion Research Lab that studies how we develop and practice self-compassion. According to Neff, in her book

Self-Compassion: Stop Beating Yourself Up and Leave Insecurity Behind, self-compassion has three elements: self-kindness, common humanity, and mindfulness. Jesus rooted his understanding of compassion in these three elements when he urged his followers: "Love your neighbor as yourself." Heretics ignite a passion for compassion. Acts of compassion serve the greater good contagiously.

Heretics cultivate a climate of engagement that includes freedom, integrity, and trust.

CHAPTER 5

Incite A Movement

"If you are what you should be," advised Saint Catherine of Siena, a tertiary of the Dominican Order, scholastic philosopher, and theologian, "you will set the whole world on fire."

Heretics, by definition, incite movements. That's their calling. Max De Pree, in his book *Leading without Power: Finding Hope in Serving Community*, describes a movement as "a collective state of mind, a public and common understanding that the future can be created, not simply experienced or endured." And when heretics ignite the potential of a movement, the impossible dream becomes possible.

Heretics, committed to their impossible dream, engage their followers with two principles: invite them to incite a movement, and involve them to evolve the movement. They incite movements with the key question they initially asked themselves in discerning an impossible dream, but now ask potential members of the movement to co-create the impossible dream. They invite potential members of the movement to embrace the seeds of their vision and commit to co-create it as vital participants in the visioning process.

Christoph Lueneburger, who heads up the New York-based private equity practice at Egon Zehnder, argues that the most successful companies are those that are the most purpose-driven, and that the pursuit of sustainability is the most reliable blueprint for building a culture of purpose. According to Lueneburger, the challenge for corporate leaders is to find the right team, who will not see the pursuit of sustainability as a set of problems to be solved, but rather as the necessary foundation for long-term value creation.

A Chinese proverb articulates the power of purpose succinctly: "Tell me, I'll forget. Show me, I'll remember. Involve me, I'll understand." In one of my MBA classes, I conducted an experiment where I invited the students to make up the 'mandatory' final exam. At first, they were surprised and confused. One student observed, "If we make up the test, then we'll know the answers." I applauded her insight, and the class ended up preparing a test that was more difficult than any I would have created. The students felt actively engaged in their learning to master the course content, trusted in their capacity to develop a credible exam, and valued the opportunity to practically apply their learning to their professional responsibilities.

Inflame a movement with the sparks of your impossible dream. Mike Figliuolo, author of *One Piece of Paper*, believes that everyone needs a little revolution: "You need that one seminal event of one influential voice to get the unsure masses to join the mob. As the leader, you have a responsibility to either be that spark or find someone else who can be one. Recruit a star. Lead a protest. Promote an event that shows people you're serious about revolution. That spark can detonate the powder keg of discontent which unleashes your revolution."

On a visit to the Houston Space Center, I noticed a sign at Mission Control that has implications for inciting a movement: "No Lift-off without Heat." Heretics are in the ignition business: igniting hearts, minds, and souls.

5.1 SET HEARTS ON FIRE

"If you want to build a ship, don't drum up the men to gather wood, divide the work, and give orders," recommended Antoine de Saint-Exupéry, a French poet, journalist, and pioneering aviator. "Instead, teach them to yearn for the vast and endless sea."

The dare-to-dream heretic must now dare to declare the dream, to ignite the hearts of potential followers individually and collectively. In fact, in most wise and ancient cultures, people customarily talked to their heart. The heretic, Jesus, so committed to his calling, sought to write his words on his followers' hearts. Thanks to Mark C. Crowley, the author of *Lead from the Heart: Transformational Leadership for the 21st Century*, drawing on recent scientific discoveries, and contrary to one of the most widely accepted and long-enduring paradigms in business, we now know that the path to engaging workers is through their hearts.

The HeartMath Institute, whose purpose is expanding heart connections, provides tools that connect people with the heart of who they truly are for living healthier, fulfilling lives and building a brighter future. Since 1991, the HeartMath Institute has researched and developed reliable, scientifically based tools to help people bridge the connection between their hearts and minds, and deepen their connection with the hearts of others.

According to Dr. Rollin McCraty, HeartMath's Director of Research, they've discovered the heart, as 'an organ of perception and intelligence,' is a huge part of the equation. We now know that the heart and the brain are in a constant two-way communication and that the heart sends more information to the brain than vice versa. The signals the heart sends affect the brain centers involved in our decision-making and in our ability to perceive.

If your desire is to be a leader who attracts and retains the best people all-the-while producing truly uncommon and sustainable performance, here are two things you must know about the power and influence of the human heart: the heart is the primary driver of optimal human performance and emotions drive performance. Although the prevailing belief in leadership studies is that emotions undermine good decision-making and other cognitive tasks, and have no place in the workplace, the new research clearly indicates that the repression of them greatly inhibits human functioning.

Daniel Goleman, Richard Boyatzis, and Annie McKee, in *Primal Leadership*, confirm the central role of emotions in leadership: "The emotional task of the leader is primal—that is, first—in two senses: It is both the original and the most important act of leadership ... Great leaders move us. They ignite our passion and inspire the best in us. When we try to explain why they are so effective, we speak of strategy, vision, or powerful ideas. But the reality is much more primal: great leadership works through the emotions. Understanding the powerful role of emotions in the workplace sets the best leaders apart from the rest—not just in tangibles such as better business results and retention of talent, but also in the all-important intangibles, such as higher morale, motivation, and commitment."

Heretics probe the depths of their imaginations to invent an incredibly wonderful future of impossibility for their followers and for the global family. They set hearts ablaze with a spark of glory and create excitement. They make the invisible visible, radiate passion, and declare a sense of urgency.

Make The Invisible Visible

The major task of heretics in our contemporary visual culture consists of painting a picture that tells a story to ignite individual and collective passion for their impossible dream.

German writer and statesman Johann Wolfgang von Goethe counseled, "A great artist must be shaken by the naked truths that will not be comforted. This divine discontent, this disequilibrium, this state of inner tension is the source of artistic energy." Often the picture that heretics paint disrupts the status quo as it should.

In the article "TED Talks Are Wildly Addictive for 5 Scientific Reasons," Carmine Gallo, communication coach and author of *The Presentation Secrets of Steve Jobs* and *Talk like TED: The 9 Public-Speaking Secrets of the World's Top Minds*, contends, "It's well established in the neuroscience literature that pictures trump text when it comes to searing an idea into a person's memory. It's called 'picture superiority.'" Simply put, if you hear information, you are likely to remember about 10 percent of that information three days later. Add a picture, however, and your recall rate will soar to 65 percent."

In a study conducted by researchers Brendan Nyhan from Dartmouth University and Jason Reifler from Georgia State, they discovered that our brains privilege visual information over any other kind. More processing power is devoted to it. Studies have shown that we understand images more quickly than words and remember them longer. When what we see conflicts with what we hear, our brains choose vision over sound. And neurological experiments show that the brain has to work much harder to process words than pictures, creating more opportunities for the information to be corrupted, manipulated, modified, or misunderstood.

As a result, the researchers point out, we're more likely to see visuals as 'true' and words as, literally, 'debatable.' When evidence is presented in words, our brains tend to view them as part of an 'argument.' So when the evidence contradicts our beliefs, the brain begins creating counterarguments. Present that same evidence visually, however, and we process it differently. We see it as 'real' in a way that mere words are not.

Heretics create and instill their impossible dreams memorably through the medium of story. I once invited a CEO I was coaching to paint a picture/story of his company. He surprised me by taking a piece of paper, and instead of drawing on the page as I had anticipated, scrunched it up tightly in a ball. That simple artistic exercise helped him tell the story of the turmoil in his company. Stories inform, illuminate, inspire, and start movements. John Neffinger and Matthew Kohut, in their book *Compelling People: The Hidden Qualities that Make Us Influential*, indicate the intrinsic power of stories: "There are two rhetorical forms that naturally project strength and warmth together: stories and humor."

Maya Angelou shares the path stories take: "The idea is to write it so that people hear it and it slides through the brain and goes straight to the heart." Whenever I paint the picture/story about Kibera Kids Kitchen, our mission work feeding hungry kids in the slums of Nairobi, it goes straight to the hearts of grownups and kids. My granddaughter Elsa called me and asked if I would be available to come to her school, Morley School #60 in West Hartford, Connecticut, to speak to her first-grade class about my mission work in Africa. Her class was studying African geography, food, and customs that semester. I dressed as a Massai herdsman and invited them to jump in the air like they do. Then I shared how some of the kids we fed were really, really hungry. In fact, I told them that some children go hungry sometimes for two or three days. Their eyes got very big in disbelief. On the way from the school to Elsa's home, her neighbor and best friend, Ella, met me on the sidewalk and asked me to wait while she ran into her house. She came back with a baggie of pennies. "This is for the kids in Africa," she said. I was touched with Ella's understanding of my story about hunger and of her compassionate generosity. "And a little child shall lead them."

Heretics plot their impossible dream picture/story. Daniel Pink, in his book *To Sell is Human: The Surprising Truth about Moving Others*, offers the method successfully and profitably used by Pixar Animation. I call it the "Picture Perfect Pixar Method," and have used it extensively in teaching leadership at the university and in coaching senior leaders to plot their organization's future picture/stories. The Pixar Method uses six sequential sentences. Warren Buffet uses a similar method where he asks repeatedly: "And then what happens?"

Here's an example from the plot of the movie, *Finding Nemo*:

Once upon a time, there was a widowed fish named Marlin who was extremely protective of his only son, Nemo.

Every day, Marlin warned Nemo of the ocean's dangers and implored him not to swim far away.

One day, in an act of defiance, Nemo ignores his father's warnings and swims into the open water.

Because of that, he is captured by a diver and ends up in the fish tank of a dentist in Sydney.

Because of that, Marlin sets off on a journey to recover Nemo, enlisting the help of other sea creatures along the way.

Until finally, Marlin and Nemo find each other, reunite, and learn that love depends on trust.

Here's your opportunity to plot your movement's or organization's picture/story.

Once upon a time, _____.

Every day, _____.

One day, _____.

Because of that, _____.

Because of that, _____.

Until finally, _____.

Radiate Passion

"Trust yourself," advised Golda Meir, the fourth Prime Minister of Israel. "Create the kind of self that you will be happy to live with all of your life. Make the most of yourself by fanning the tiny, inner sparks of possibility into flames of achievement."

Heretics create and instill their impossible dreams by radiating passion that derives from the Latin *passio*, which means "to suffer." In their hearts, they are aware, care, and act to relieve the suffering of others by being and selling their picture/story. And fortunately, like a virus, passion is wonderfully contagious. Heretics trust themselves to be the passion, to personally identify fully with, and become the embodiment of their impossible dream picture/story. They and their message are one.

DR. PHIL JOHNSON

Dr. Gerald May, in *Will & Spirit: A Contemplative Psychology*, describes this integration of person and message: "This is the unitive experience, the self-losing experience that is the fundamental, paradigmatic experience of consciousness, mystery, and being. It constitutes true intuition and radical spontaneity. It is the keystone of contemplative spirituality."

I witnessed this integration when Desmond Mpilo Tutu, the South African social rights activist and retired Anglican bishop who rose to worldwide fame during the 1980s as an opponent of apartheid, spoke to a packed audience at the Van Andel Arena in Grand Rapids, Michigan. Tutu and his message were one! I felt like he was talking directly to me and inviting me personally to join the passionate quest for equality and freedom for all people. Others revealed after that they had experienced similar feelings. Tutu radiated a contagious passion. I witnessed this integration as well when John Verineau, associate conductor for the Grand Rapids Symphony, played a clarinet solo of the Christmas carol "Silent Night." He and the carol presented as one.

Heretics, be and sell your picture/story. Yes, sell your story. Daniel Pink reminds us that everybody sells. In his above-mentioned book *To Sell is Human*, Pink offers a fresh look at the art and science of selling. Whether we're employees pitching colleagues on a new idea, entrepreneurs enticing funders to invest, or parents and teachers cajoling children to study, we spend our days trying to move others. "Like it or not," contends Pink, "we're all in sales now."

And you may be surprised who makes the best salesperson. Pink points out, "The conventional view that extroverts make the finest salespeople is so accepted that we've overlooked one teensy flaw: there's almost no evidence it's actually true." Ambiverts, a term coined by social scientists in the 1920s, are people who are neither extremely introverted or extremely extroverted. They strike a good balance because they "can talk smoothly but also listen keenly, who know when to turn on the charm but also when to turn it off, who combine the extrovert's assertiveness with the introvert's quiet confidence." Heretics take note: the best leaders embody a combination of extrovert qualities (fierce sense of love and drive, a passion) and introvert qualities (shy, quiet, unassuming).

Heretics, get out your trumpets and tell your picture/story through your unique lens to make the invisible visible, radiate passion to make it memorable, and declare it with a sense of urgency.

Declare A Sense Of Urgency

"We are on this planet together," reflected the 14th Dalai Lama. "We are all brothers and sisters with the same physical and mental faculties, the same problems, and the same needs. We must all contribute to the fulfillment of the potential and the improvement of the quality of life as much as we are able. Mankind is crying out for help. Ours is a desperate time. Those who have something to offer should come forward. Now is the time." An African proverb echoes the Dalai Lama's declaration of a sense of urgency: "For tomorrow belongs to the people who prepare for it today."

Heretics believe in their hearts that they have "something to offer" in their impossible dreams, and they step forward and lead their movements. A certain amount of stress, *eustress*, good healthy stress, keeps the adrenaline flowing and provides for a sense of urgency. The job of change agent is not just presenting high-minded ideas. It summons a sense of urgency inside and outside the movement, and turns that urgency into action. If there's no need, there's no hurry. So the three questions heretics must ask are: What must be done now to achieve the impossible dream? How long will the window of opportunity be available? Will there be another opportunity?

At a dinner party, I asked a dear friend of mine what he would do if he had twenty-four hours to live. Here's his revealing answer: "I think I need a day to think about that." Heretics don't often have that option of long pauses and appreciate they must live and breathe with a sense of urgency. The term "Blue Moon" describes the second full moon that appears in a month. Typically, each month yields only one full moon, so we have the expression "Once in a Blue Moon." And if you're not stargazing at the precise time, you'll miss it.

Heretics frame their presentations to declare a sense of urgency. Stephanie Scotti, a strategic communication adviser, identifies three kinds of presentations: Expert, Interpreter, and Catalyst. The Expert informs in detail the who, what, and why of a situation. The Interpreter clarifies a core message, organizes the content into logical chunks of information, and crafts a story that has an identifiable purpose and structure. The Catalyst recognizes that his or her job goes beyond getting the audience to understand; the mission is to inspire change and move people to action. Catalysts craft a story that is easy for listeners to relate to and act on. Heretics, although they use elements of the Expert and Interpreter strategies, predominantly adopt the role of the Catalyst.

Heretics declare a sense of urgency and resonate with the novel *If Not Now, When?* by the Italian author Primo Levi, first published in 1982 under the title *Se non ora, quando?* The title is taken from a well-known rabbinical saying attributed to Hillel the Elder: "If I am not for myself, who will be for me? And when I am for myself, what am 'I'? And if not now, when?"

Heretics set minds on fire as well as hearts. Nelson Mandela observed: "A good head and a good heart are always a formidable combination." Thomas R. Horton, in his book *The CEO Paradox*, says, "Once you capture the hearts of your people, their minds will follow."

5.2 SET MINDS ON FIRE

"The mind is not a vessel to be filled," commented Greek historian Plutarch, "but a fire to be ignited."

Heretics set minds on fire by integrating the energy and vitality of the head and the heart. Ned Herrmann and Ann Herrmann-Nehdi, in their book *The Whole Brain Business Book*, describe contemporary leaders: "Today's effective leaders are 'thought' leaders, highly skilled thinkers ... What you can't hire is your own ability to think critically, creatively, and strategically, to think visually, intuitively, and globally—to be able to project your leadership out into the future."

The popularity of "TED (Technology, Entertainment, and Design) Talks" affirms its slogan brand position: "Ideas worth spreading." And heretics not only listen to but present TED Talks to ignite and spread their impossible dreams in peoples' minds that consist of about 100 billion neurons. If all these neurons were to be lined up, it would form a 600-mile-long trail. It's interesting to note that the word "ted" is an old English verb that means "to spread."

Heretics aim to rock a "TED Talk" and follow the eighteen-minute rule, where no TED speaker is allowed to speak for more than eighteen minutes. When you give people too much information it results in what scientists call "cognitive backlog"—the more information you ask someone to retain, the more likely they are to forget everything. It's tremendously helpful to have experienced persons who can open, captivate, and inspire our minds on many levels.

Heretics need to be "negotiation savvy" to get their movements off the ground and to keep them growing. It's not a mind game but a process of nurturing clear, responsible, and creative thinking. Harvard Business School Professor Michael Wheeler, the author of *The Art of Negotiation: How to Improvise Agreement in a Chaotic World*, reminds us that one has to learn how to make a deal in three seconds flat. When you've made a connection, three important rules for any negotiation apply: You won't get anywhere until you have your counterpart's attention, never ask questions that are easy for others to say 'no' to, and to engage somebody else, you've got to be engaged yourself.

Albert Schweitzer, a French-German theologian, organist, philosopher, and physician, observed: "As soon as man does not take his existence for granted, but beholds it as something unfathomably mysterious, thought begins." Heretics agree with Schweitzer and set minds on fire.

Throw Out The Box

"If everyone had to think outside the box," observed Malcolm Gladwell, author of *What the Dog Saw*, "maybe it was the box that needed fixing."

We've all heard the common expression regarding creativity: "Think outside the box." Heretics approach "the box" differently and throw out the box because it restricts their imagination and creative capacity. I once asked a CEO I was coaching whether he thought he considered himself an "outside-the-box thinker." His response helped me understand his thought process: "Let's come back to that question at our next monthly meeting." A month later, he answered my question: "I think I just need a bigger box." From his vantage point, he gave a truthful answer. But from my perspective, he limited the scope of his obvious creative capacity by literally trapping himself in his own categories, no matter how much bigger the box could get.

The great cellist Yo-Yo Ma, a citizen artist and a forensic musicologist, decodes the work of musical creators across time and space. In his art, he resists fixed boundaries, and would like to rename classical music just "music," born in improvisation, and traversing territory as vast and fluid as the world we inhabit. For him, music happens between the notes. Ma considers performance as hospitality, not about proving something but sharing the dream.

Heretics understand that in order to accomplish their impossible dream, they need to get out of their minds. Daniel Kahneman explains, in his book *Thinking Fast and Slow*, how we think of ourselves as being in control of our minds, but in reality we have two systems that govern how our mind works: one that we control, and another we do not control. System 1 represents the conscious self that makes choices and decides what to do. System 2 represents the instinctual mental processes that allow us to make quick decisions with little mental energy. John Maynard Keynes, an English economist whose ideas fundamentally changed the theory and practice of modern macroeconomics and the economic policies of governments, adds this insight: "The difficulty lies, not in the new ideas, but in escaping from the old ones, which ramify, for those brought up as most of us have been, into every corner of our minds."

Warren Bennis first used the term "first-class noticer" in the leadership context. Heretics follow Bennis' advice and actively cultivate the art of being "first-class noticers." Ellen Langer, a social psychologist and a professor in the Psychology Department at Harvard University, has done considerable research into the science of mindlessness and mindfulness. In her book, *Counter Clockwise*, she reports that "actively noticing new things is literally and figuratively enlivening. Not only is it not tiring, it's exhilarating. It is the way we feel when we are fully engaged."

On a recent trip to Ecuador, I followed our guide along a jungle path next to the Amazon River. As we came around a curve in the path, I saw what I initially thought was a robust vine that went from the ground all the way up to the top of the very large tree. For a moment, I thought that the heat was affecting my eyesight, because "the vine" appeared to be moving, and it was! When I got closer, I discovered millions of ants travelling up the tree on the right and down the tree on the left.

Heretics set minds on fire. They throw out the box, sharpen their skills as "first-class noticers," and personally guide a Familiarization (FAM) Tour of their impossible dream.

Guide A Virtual FAM Tour

Heretics enthusiastically invite their potential followers to come with them on a virtual Familiarization (FAM) Tour of their impossible dream. Travel companies, for a reduced attractive rate, invite tourists on a tour to give them a sample of what the destination site offers, so they will get others to come with them on a tour. Imagine Rick Steves and your potential followers, with guidebook in hand, visiting your impossible dream site.

Heretics personally take interested parties "there," to the imaginary place where the impossible dream lives, and to imagine themselves being part of making the impossible dream come true. Heretics adopt the role of tour guide to explain, experience, and explore their impossible dream. Heretics explain to the impossible dream "tourists," the why of the dream, provide an opportunity to affirm their tentative interest and investment in the movement, and address areas of clarification, questions, and concerns. In my mind, I have a picture of a bright young college student in her early twenties I met at the San Diego Science Center, whose name badge indicated her specific exemplary role: "The Explainer."

On my FAM Tour to Israel, Jordan, and Egypt, I particularly appreciated Mendy, our knowledgeable tour guide who explained Jewish history, traditions, and holidays, and informed us about various attractions including the Wailing Wall, the Via Dolorosa, and the Aqueduct. Mendy engaged us. He not only showed us the sights, but he transported us as back-in-time travelers so that we viscerally experienced history as if we actually lived there over 2,000 years ago. He informed and enlivened my understanding of the Biblical record I studied in seminary and touched my soul in the streets of Jerusalem where Jesus walked. Heretics guide tours that are unforgettable.

On their FAM Tour, heretics explain and enable visitors to experience the impossible dream. The Dutch post-Impressionist painter, Vincent Van Gogh, advised, "You have first to experience what you want to express." Heretics take Van Gogh's guidance and immerse potential followers in the dream so they can feel like they've actually been to the future heretics have imagined. One could visit the site by video or Skype or use virtual reality with an Oculus VR headset, but it's not the same sensually. When persons come and see, hear, touch, and taste for themselves, they take away long-lasting memories.

Mendy awakened our senses walking in ice-cold water up to our knees, in complete darkness, in "Hezekiah's Tunnel," enjoying a "David Wrap" of medicinal mud, swimming, or actually floating in the salty water of the Dead Sea, and eating a tasty St. Peter's fish dinner. Mendy took us to sites where we could experience the vibrancy of the people and their culture.

We walked 'with Paul' on the famous road to Emmaus, celebrated the *eucharist* on the site of the Feeding of the Five Thousand, and sailed on the Sea of Galilee. I had the once-in-a-lifetime opportunity to preach in Jesus' hometown, Bethlehem. By visiting up close and personal, one can catch the fullness and vibrancy of a vision and imprint the unforgettable feeling of being a participant in the impossible dream.

When I take visitors to our mission in Nairobi, Kenya, hugging a hungry child can produce miracles of generosity. A picture may be worth a thousand words, but hugging a hungry two-year-old-child can make an incredible difference in the world for all of us. One can know the statistics about poverty, but experiencing it face-to-face, especially with a child, not only gives meaning to the data, but bursts open avenues of human connection and compassion that transform both "huggers." Barriers fall. Arms go around. The human family rejoices.

One of the most satisfying aspects of the FAM Tours I've taken involves free time to explore on my own the things I found interesting or intriguing. Adventuresome potential members of the movement will welcome the opportunity to explore the impossible dream from their own particular perspective, and this may spark other concerns, questions, or insights they have for the fulfillment of the dream you can address.

On our Israel FAM Tour, I explored the Old Jerusalem Market where I bartered for olive wood sculptures and enjoyed the varied smells and sounds, took time to follow the steps of Jesus on the Via Dolorosa, buy a watercolor painting of the Sea of Galilee in a little shop in Tiberias, and photograph the Nike swish in a sarcophagus.

I can't think of a better way to connect with potential followers than taking them on a virtual FAM Tour of your impossible dream, to inspire them to seriously consider committing to the dream. Create a remarkable experience that they can tell others. Create vivid touchstones for future reference. Create memories that stick.

Outline A Strategy

A goal without a plan is just a wish. That's what Pablo Picasso believed: "Our goals can only be reached through the vehicle of a plan, in which we must fervently believe, and upon which we must vigorously act. There is no other route to success." Some people who are attracted to a movement need very little in the way of strategy. Others, however, may need to have you present a thoughtful more detailed strategy to reach the destination presented to them in order to gain their full commitment.

In organizational strategy, we paint a picture of the future and then work backward to determine how to organize to reach it. "Great people are attracted to great visions," asserts Sal Khan, founder of Khan Academy. "It's important to have a sense of what might be possible, but not to be dogmatic about the way something must be done." Heretics make it happen with a simple, specific, and synergistic strategy.

Some call it the KISS strategy: Keep it Simple, Stupid. Timothy Devinney, a professor of strategy at University of Technology, Sydney, Australia, reports on a study of twenty major corporations in five industries in Australia that demonstrates company strategy often falls on deaf ears. Only 29.3 percent of employees could correctly match their company to its espoused strategy, and a whopping 70 percent of employees could not identify the publicly presented corporate strategy of their employer.

Make the strategy specific by painting the broad strokes of the picture of promise and match them with the appropriate action to get there. Heretics engage in backward planning to fulfill their impossible dreams. If the dream is to have dinner at the Space Needle revolving restaurant in Seattle at table 42 at 6:00 p.m. on Monday July 8, 2017, then the strategy would outline the specific actions to get from here to there on time, and presumably hungry.

Outline a strategy that's simple, specific, and synergistic, where various parts of a strategy are working together to produce an enhanced result. Heretics anticipate that when parts work together, they accomplish more than they could alone. I recognized synergy in action on a tour of the Waterford Crystal Factory in Waterford, Ireland, where I met a glass-blower craftsman engraving a larger than life goblet for the Ryder Cup. "This is the 'just-in-case' goblet. If something happens to the one we've shipped, we've got a back-up." That's a very simple, specific, and smart synergistic strategy.

Heretics incite movements. They set hearts on fire, minds on fire, and souls on fire, to which we now turn our attention.

5.3 SET SOULS ON FIRE

"The most powerful weapon on earth," claimed Marshal Ferdinand Jean Marie Foch, the Commander-in-Chief of the Allied Armies during the final year of the First World War, "is the human soul on fire."

Heretics appreciate the critical dimension of souls on fire in a movement. Let me clarify that I'm using "soul" in the broad sense that is not necessarily religious, although it could be, but certainly is spiritual. Jim Loehr and Tony Schwartz, in their book *The Power of Full Engagement: Managing Energy, Not Time, Is the Key to High Performance and Personal Renewal*, claim that the most fundamental source of energy is physical, and the most significant is spiritual. Unfortunately, many leaders today do not subscribe to the significance of spiritual energy.

"Visionary leaders are the builders of a new dawn, working with imagination, insight and boldness," argues the Center for Visionary Leadership. "They present a challenge that calls forth the best in people and brings them together around a shared sense of purpose." Impossible dreams integrate the rich quality of heart, mind, and soul. But heretics must be careful to honor the freedom to choose. Heretics set souls on fire by invitation only. One cannot establish a vision by edict or coercion but by actively and persuasively igniting the fire of commitment in potential followers to embrace a compelling vision for the future. With souls aligned, heretics can lead their followers to do the impossible. Wise leaders avoid the "curse of yes" where followers offer their reluctant commitment.

In my coaching practice, I often hear leaders of large organizations comment that their very size makes it difficult to nurture their organization's soul. While it's true that smaller organizations generally find it easier to generate soulfulness, I urge these thoughtful leaders to secure the overall development of and commitment to the entity's soul, and then to offer the freedom to smaller sections of the organization like divisions or special function groups, to use the overall theme of soul as a foundation to foster their own appreciation of their corporate soul.

"Dance is the hidden language of the soul," observed Martha Graham, an American modern dancer and choreographer. So let's dance as we consider how heretics set souls on fire with the trilogy of faith, hope, and love.

Faith

"To accomplish great things," noted Anatole France, a French poet, journalist, and novelist, "we must not only act, but also dream, not only plan, but also believe."

Heretics have faith, often a religious faith, but not necessarily tied directly to a particular faith or religion. Guided from the irrepressible standpoint of the sacred, their faith on fire heats up the environments and people and places they touch. The Rev. Maurice McLuhan, brother of Marshall McLuhan, once told me that my role as a pastor was to "hot up the environment." Faith and doubt are partners in the life adventure with many different points of view. "Where there is no longer any opportunity for doubt," contended Swiss physician Paul Tournier, "there is no longer any opportunity for faith either."

Theologian and writer Frederick Buechner summed up the heretic's main task to find purpose with these words: "Find the place where your greatest love meets the world's greatest need." Ken Robinson, in his book *The Element: How Finding Your Passion Changes Everything*, echoes Buechner's perspective and refers to calling as "the element." The element is the point at which natural talent meets personal passion. When people arrive at the element, they feel most themselves and most inspired, and they achieve at their highest levels.

Robinson chronicled Gillian Lynne's discovery of her element or purpose. Her school thought she had a learning disorder so arranged an appointment with a psychologist. She sat on her hands for twenty minutes, after which the psychologist and her mother left the room. But, before leaving the room, the psychologist turned on the radio with music. The psychologist, looking through the window in the door, saw that Lynne moved to the music. "Your daughter isn't sick," he declared. "She's a dancer!" Gillian Lynne described the discovery of her element, "I can't tell you how wonderful it was. I walked into this room, and it was full of people like me. People who couldn't sit still. People who had to move to think." Lynne later became a dancer, and choreographer of *CATS* and *The Phantom of the Opera*.

Annette Simmons, author of *Whoever Tells the Best Story Wins*, offers a refreshing understanding of the role of faith in people's lives: "People don't want more information. They are up to their eyeballs in information. They want faith—faith in you, your goals, your success, in the story you tell. It is faith that moves mountains, not facts. Facts do not give birth to faith. Faith needs a story to sustain it—a meaningful story that inspires belief in you and renews hope that your ideas do indeed offer what you promise. Genuine influence goes deeper than getting people to do what you want them to do. It means people pick up where you left off because they believe."

Douglas MacArthur expressed the role of faith in life: "You are as young as your faith, as old as your doubt; as young as your self-confidence, as old as your fear; as young as your hope, as old as your despair." Heretics set souls on fire with not only faith but also hope, to which we now turn our attention.

Hope

United Nations Secretary-General Ban Ki-moon, speaking to the world leaders at the General Assembly meeting in October 2014, urged them to take the lead on solving global challenges and crises: "Leadership is precisely about finding the seeds of hope and nurturing them into something bigger." Heretics seize the opportunity to find and plant seeds of hope to nurture spiritual energy and to look toward the future with hope.

Heretics, already with their souls on fire with hope, recruit "fire carriers." Bobette Buster, author of *Do Story: How to Tell Your Story So the World Listens*, notes how stories are the fire we carry to each other. In Cormac McCarthy's novel, *No Country for Old Men*, Sheriff Bell recalls that his cowboy father would carry the embers from the fire of one camp to the next in an animal horn. It was a tradition passed to the cowboys by the Native American Indians. In the novel, this important act had another meaning: to have hope and continue the quest, but also to maintain humanity. The "fire carrier" held a special position in the tribe and for their society.

Heretics have been and will continue to be the "fire carriers" who ignite hope in their followers. For almost five decades, I've had the privilege of being a "fire carrier" as an ordained minister conducting ceremonies of hope: baptisms, marriages, and funerals. At a recent funeral for a dear saint in our congregation, we celebrated the legacy of Joyce Decker's life of faithful love and generosity. Everybody knew she was an avid fan of the Detroit Red Wings and the Detroit Tigers. So at the conclusion of her service, I placed on her casket three baseball hats: one for the Wings, one for the Tigers, and one for the Detroit Lions in the hope that when Joyce got to heaven she would put in a good word for the football team. As the congregation recessed, we joyce-fully sang "Take Me Out to the Ball Game."

Mother Teresa exemplifies a "fire carrier" by bringing hope to the poorest of the poor. She established Missionaries of Charity, an order that has grown to over 4,000 members in 697 foundations in 131 countries.

On September 4, 2016, on the eve of the nineteenth anniversary of her death, the Pope granted Mother Teresa sainthood. After visiting her ministry in the slums of Calcutta, someone once remarked to Mother Teresa, "I wouldn't do what you do for a million dollars." Looking back at the observer, the seasoned missionary replied, "Neither would I."

Joseph Addison, English playwright and poet, offers a life perspective: "Three grand essentials to happiness in this life are something to do, something to love, and something to hope for."

Love

"The compass heading that orients people most directly, even when you get blown off course, is loving and being loved," maintain Heifetz and Linsky, in their book *Leadership on the Line.*

Heretics combine faith, hope, and love to give meaning to people's lives. "When people work for love," observed Max De Pree, in his book *Leading without Power: Finding Hope in Serving Community,* "leaders help them move toward potential and service." Brené Brown, author of *Daring Greatly: How the Courage to Be Vulnerable Transforms the Way We Live, Love, Parent, and Lead,* agrees with De Pree: "For me, teaching is about love. It is not about transferring information, but rather creating an atmosphere of mystery and imagination and discovery."

I, too, have found that loving my students as co-learners, and understanding the learning process as a labor of love, makes all the difference in the world to the academic atmosphere and to the pursuit of learning for life. One of the ways I try to validate my students is to always greet them by name and to enquire how things are going. I don't want to be their learning buddy but I do want them to know I legitimately care about their personal welfare and their academic progress. Their goals are as important as mine. Learning is a collaborative sport.

Love is the basis of servant-leadership and any form of serving others constitutes an act of love. A group of students from Georgia asked Warren

Buffett about his greatest success and his greatest failure. Buffett replied, "When you get to my age, you'll really measure your success in life by how many of the people you want to have love you actually do love you. I know people who have a lot of money, and they get testimonial dinners and they get hospital wings named after them. But the truth is that nobody in the world loves them. If you get to my age in life and nobody thinks well of you, I don't care how big your bank account is, your life is a disaster.

"That's the ultimate test of how you have lived your life. The trouble with love is that you can't buy it. You can buy sex. You can buy testimonial dinners. You can buy pamphlets that say how wonderful you are. But the only way to get love is to be lovable. It's very irritating if you have a lot of money. You'd like to think you could write a check: I'll buy a million dollars' worth of love. But it doesn't work that way. The more you give love away, the more you get."

A fitting conclusion to this comes from St. Paul who summarized in 1 Corinthians 13:13 (*The Message*) the work of the soul and the primary role of love in life and work: "But for right now, until that completeness, we have three things to do to lead us toward that consummation: Trust steadily in God, hope unswervingly, love extravagantly. And the best of the three is love."

CHAPTER 6

Run Up The Flag

"Everywhere Jesus went, there was a riot," mused an Archbishop of Canterbury. "Everywhere I go, they make me cups of tea."

Heretics have imagined, claimed, and expressed an impossible dream. They've cultivated a climate of engagement and incited a movement, setting hearts, minds, and souls on fire. Now it's time to test how people respond to their impossible dream. It's time to "Run up the flag and watch who salutes," a military expression that helps officers determine the commitment of their troops to an idea or proposal or action. It serves as a trial balloon to see if it rises, or a sample size of a new product like a breakfast cereal, to assess if people give it a thumbs up and consider buying it, or a thumbs down. In the same way, marketing, advertising, and communication companies routinely employ focus groups to gauge public opinion about a wide range of issues.

Ryan Hoover, the founder of the San Francisco-based product recommendation site, Product Hunt, built a platform on this principle to recommend products and games, widely considered the place to discover the next big thing in technology. The site curates mostly unknown products and startups and lets members vote on, comment, and discuss their favorites. The result is a site with more than $7 million in funding that gives entrepreneurs another avenue to get discovered and find venture backing.

The primary challenge for heretics, as indicated by leadership specialists Heifetz and Linsky, in their book *Leadership on the Line*, involves appreciating the political reality of running up the flag: "There are six essential aspects of thinking politically in the exercise of leadership: one for dealing with people who are with you on the issue; one for managing those who are in opposition; and four for working with those who are uncommitted but wary—the people you are trying to move."

Heretics present their impossible dreams and run up the flag to see the response of potential followers. In this chapter, let's consider how heretics understand purposefully questioning the unquestionable. And then, we'll watch and identify how two groups respond: the ones who salute and the ones who don't salute.

6.1 QUESTION THE UNQUESTIONABLE

Heretics follow the wise counsel of Ratan Tata, Chairman of the Tata Group: "Question the unquestionable." They show the courage to question the most ingrained 'sacred cows' of conventional wisdom.

Robert J. Kriegel and David Brandt, in their insightful book *Sacred Cows Make the Best Burgers: Developing Change-Ready People and Organizations*, demonstrate why the latest business panaceas of re-engineering, virtual teams, outsourcing, reinventing, restructuring, and downsizing, almost always prove unsuccessful. The authors define, from a business perspective, a "sacred cow" as an outmoded belief, assumption, practice, policy, system, or strategy, generally visible, that inhibits change and prevents responsiveness to new opportunities.

I served a terrific congregation that took the risk of questioning the unquestionable. The worship committee boldly took on the "sacred cow" of the exclusive use of classical music, and recommended a separate service using rock music. Almost all hell broke loose, and many were so upset that they left the church. But teens and young families returned and brought with them a fresh spirit of commitment. One grandmother vowed to me that she would never be caught dead at "that contemporary service" until she realized that her whole family came to the rock service. One Sunday, as I came into the sanctuary, I realized she'd had a change of heart—well, sort of. Beside her family, there she sat with a smile, and her earmuffs on!

Leading an entity to question the unquestionable can be dangerous. The word 'leader' comes from the Indo-European root word *leit*, the name for the person who carried the flag in front of an army going into battle and usually died in the first enemy attack. "The hope of leadership lies in the capacity to deliver disturbing news and raise difficult questions in a way people can absorb," assert Heifetz and Linsky, "prodding them to take up the message rather than ignore it or kill the messenger." They also throw light on the dynamics of leadership intervention: "Four types of interventions constitute the tactics of leadership: making observations, asking questions, offering interpretations, and taking actions."

Let me offer a word of caution. Heretics, as servant-leaders, need to question the unquestionable sensibly and sensitively. Friedrich Wilhelm Nietzsche, a German philosopher, wisely advised: "Whoever fights monsters should see to it that in the process he does not become a monster." So how does one identify a heretic?

Heretics apply the following three methods to question the unquestionable: probe, disrupt, and confront.

Probe

Heretics question the unquestionable by probing, enquiring into an issue or a circumstance, to get the whole picture, to find out the who, why, when, where, and how. Recent examples of probing include the 9/11 Commission, the 2012 Benghazi attack, the NFL's Deflate Gate scandal, and the Flint, Michigan, lead-contaminated water crisis.

Probing openly exposes old thinking. Albert Einstein defined insanity as "doing the same thing over and over again and expecting different results … We cannot solve our problems with the same thinking we used when we created them." A commonly held view contends that if you do what you've always done, you'll get what you always got. Well, that may be true in rare cases, but hardly ever true in an age of constant change. Gostick and Elton, in their book *All In*, report, "Our research shows incontrovertible evidence that employees respond best when they are recognized for things they are good at and for those actions where they had to stretch." Many progressive business schools, although they still use the case study model, have added a future focus model to imagine what the future might look like.

Probing with astute questions can be profitable. Several years ago, when the Betty Crocker Company first began selling their cake mixes, they offered a product that only needed water. All you had to do was add water to the mix that came in the box, and you would get a perfect, delicious cake every time. It bombed. No one bought it and the company couldn't understand why, so they commissioned a study that brought back a surprising answer. It seemed that people weren't buying the cake mix because it was too easy. They didn't want to be totally excluded from the work of preparing a cake; they wanted to feel that they were contributing something to it. So, Betty Crocker changed the formula and required the customer to add an egg in addition to water. Immediately, the new cake mix was a huge success.

A manufacturing company hired me as a consultant to discover why deliveries of their products were delayed. In the course of my investigation, I visited the shipping dock and identified three large chicken wire cages full of boxes of product. I asked the head of the shipping dock to explain how he used the cages. He mumbled his response and I realized I needed to gently probe to get a satisfactory answer. I found that the cages represented his retaliation for what he considered unfair treatment concerning his pension. We met with the Human Resources department and resolved the situation. The contents of the cages were delivered that day.

Probing often brings out the worst in organizations because habits that provide stability are hard to give up. They also challenge closely held values and beliefs, and activate resistance. Heretics probe with an intention to uncover and discover, and as a consequence, disrupt the status quo.

Disrupt

Questioning the unquestionable almost always disrupts the status quo because it introduces a different way of thinking. Apple's 1997 campaign slogan captures the company's commitment to a spirit of disruption: "Think Different."

Heretics think and act disruptively. In *The Innovator's DNA: Mastering the Five Skills of Disruptive Innovators*, the authors, Jeff Dyer, Hal Gregersen, and Clayton M. Christensen, point out that all innovation is by definition disruptive and that the challenge is to cultivate a healthy disruptive context where disruptive thinking is encouraged and rewarded. "Only when we're brave enough to explore the darkness, will we discover the infinite power of our light," reflected Snape, a character in *Harry Potter*, written by J. K. Rowling.

A disruptive innovation, contends Mark Johnson, senior partner with Innosight, a strategic innovation consulting company that he founded with Clayton Christensen, is one that "transforms a complicated, expensive product into one that is easier to use or is more affordable than the one most readily available ... In other words, a disruptive product opens up a market that wasn't being served, by offering a simpler, more accessible or more convenient option. Ultimately, you don't have to slay Goliath. Instead of aiming to displace industry leaders, aim to improve people's lives." Johnson also encourages dispelling these four myths of disruption: driving disruption isn't necessarily about developing something entirely new; innovation isn't only about technology; technologies don't simply replace other technologies; and customers don't care about inventions or innovations.

Travis Kalanick, the CEO of Uber, plans on continuing his disruption of the taxi transportation business. With a $51 billion valuation, the company dispatches low-cost taxis and limousines operated by more than 1 million independent active drivers in fifty-nine countries. Max Chafkin, in his Fast Company article, "What Makes Uber Run," describes Kalanick as "the architect of all this disruption," whose transportation service has become a global brand, an economic force, and a cultural lightning rod.

Aristotle's notion of *phronesis* is a mixture of the Greek words and notions for knowledge and wisdom. Our students today think of the acquiring of knowledge as retrieval. Older generations still think about the acquiring of knowledge as retention.

Confront

Leadership expert Howard Gardner, in his book *Leading Minds: An Anatomy of Leadership*, reports, "Among the early markers of the leader's personality, the most telling indication is a willingness to confront individuals in authority." Perhaps heretics have a natural disposition toward practical confrontation.

Heretics take the risk to confront an issue head-on and usually create a "discomfort zone" for the organizations being confronted. The word "confront" derives from the Latin *confrontare*, which literally means, "turn your face toward something," or "face something frontally." When leaders confront others with a loss of pride, status, influence, power, legitimacy, standing, or reputation, leadership becomes dangerous. Heretics need therefore to be acutely aware that confronting what they consider to be injustice in any form may bring out robust resistance.

Only change that people can believe will save the day. That's why it's critical to confront with the intention and resolve to do no harm. Meanness doesn't work well in the short- or long-term. As John Gardner, former U.S. cabinet secretary and founder of Common Cause and Independent Sector, put it: "All too often, on the long road up, young leaders become 'servants of what is' rather than 'shapers of what might be.'"

Examples of confrontation abound, including the movie *Spotlight*, which shines a laser-light on the true story of how the Boston Globe uncovered the massive scandal of child molestation and cover-up within the local Catholic Archdiocese, and then confronted and shook the entire Catholic Church to its core. The Boston Globe, whose driving force is due diligence in the service of a moral imperative, chronicled the exposé of the Catholic Church's sexual-abuse scandal. The title of the movie refers to the Globe's Spotlight team, four journalists, coincidentally all lapsed or casual Catholics with roots in the city, and who know the difficulties they face in exposing one of Boston's cornerstone institutions as corrupt, are dedicated to deep-dive investigative pieces. One reviewer wrote: "The film probes society's need for truth in all contexts: political, societal or personal. We watch as these characters wholly commit themselves to a cause larger than themselves, a compulsion that's not the sole property of journalists, but of good, strong, upstanding people."

Heretics take the risk to confront and shine the spotlight on the status quo, take a stand, and start movements to make the status quo better or to create a completely new status quo. They resolutely question the unquestionable, run up the flag, and watch who salutes to determine whether potential followers desire to be engaged, energized, and empowered.

6.2 AND WATCH WHO SALUTES

Sometimes we're surprised by the responses to an invitation to join a movement. We have hunches about what the response might be, but only raising the flag and watching who salutes will give you an accurate assessment.

The "Run up the flag and watch who salutes" exercise signals the moment of truth. Did the targeted audience resonate with the pitch? Did they catch fire with the impossible dream? Did they move from "me" to "we"? Heretics need to be adept at reading the obvious signs as well as the subtle signs that can give significant clues to analyze and take the next appropriate step.

If people resonate with the impossible dream presented, the movement is off to a good start. It may be helpful to enquire what triggered their salute and perhaps their eventual commitment to the movement. Even though they show a keen interest, enquire whether they have questions or concerns that could be addressed.

A vice-president of sales at a company where I was consulting told me that he'd run out of ideas to turn around their sagging sales. I asked how expectations for salespeople were set and he answered he set the expectations. I probed further and learned that his sales team was not part of the process. "I set the quotas and then it's up to them," he said. I recommended that he engage his salespeople in that process and he resisted strongly. However, he offered to give it a try and to his surprise, sales not only improved but his associates expressed their satisfaction at being involved.

Marci Harris, CEO of Popvox, offers this perspective: "Commitment to the vision trumps funding, technology, gold-plated degrees, and press. It remains our primary qualification. Everything else can be taught." I find it helpful to divide persons who salute into three categories: engaged, energized, and empowered. Their ultimate salute is an integration of these three attributes, but keep in mind that these attributes can vary from person to person. Pay close attention to those who salute, who respond positively to the impossible dream, and learn why they respond as they do.

Engaged

"When a leader triggers resonance," report Goleman, Boyatzis, and McKee, in their book *Primal Leadership*, "you read it in people's eyes: They're engaged and they light up." When a potential supporter engages, it's like the sun rising and shining on the impossible dream.

The lack of a clear concise definition of engagement makes deciphering engagement difficult. However, even though there is no universally accepted definition of workplace engagement, or an objective standardized process for identifying it or measuring it, there has been considerable progress made especially by Gallup. Gallup's Q12, an annual Employee Engagement Survey, is a twelve-item employee engagement assessment tool that determines an individual's level of engagement with his or her workplace. Gallup argues that when properly measured, engagement extends beyond an assessment of how happy your employees are on the job. It also reveals whether that happiness manifests itself in superior performance.

Gallup's report is based on the results of a survey, administered to more than 25 million employees in 189 countries, in which respondents answer "yes" or "no" to a dozen statements. Through rigorous research, Gallup has identified twelve core elements that link powerfully to key business outcomes. These questions, Gallup says, constitute "the best predictors of employee and workgroup performance."

The Twelve Questions, the Q12, are:

1. Do you know what is expected of you at work?
2. Do you have the materials and equipment to do your work right?
3. At work, do you have the opportunity to do what you do best every day?
4. In the last seven days, have you received recognition or praise for doing good work?
5. Does your supervisor, or someone at work, seem to care about you as a person?
6. Is there someone at work who encourages your development?
7. At work, do your opinions seem to count?
8. Does the mission/purpose of your company make you feel your job is important?
9. Are your associates (fellow employees) committed to doing quality work?
10. Do you have a best friend at work?
11. In the last six months, has someone at work talked to you about your progress?
12. In the last year, have you had opportunities to learn and grow?

Guy Kawasaki, the former chief evangelist of Apple, and author of *Enchantment: The Art of Changing Hearts, Minds and Actions*, takes a different approach by considering engagement as enchantment. "I define enchantment as the process of delighting people with a product, service, organization, or idea. The outcome of enchantment is voluntary and long-lasting support that is mutually beneficial." Kawasaki adds that enchantment "transforms situations and relationships. It converts hostility into civility and civility into affinity. It changes skeptics into believers and the undecided into the loyal."

I experienced an integration of these two concepts of flow and enchantment in my undergraduate abnormal psychology class at Wilfrid Laurier University, where my professor, Dr. Mary Kay Lane, made learning, to use Kawasaki's frame of reference, remarkably enchanting. Lane animated the course material so dramatically and effectively that we would remember it long after the class ended. The fact that I'm writing about her decades later proves my point. She modeled engagement and engaged us in the process. No one missed her classes. We listened. We laughed. We learned. We remembered.

Heretics welcome those who engage with the impossible dream, and then determine whether they are energized.

Energized

Ralph Lauren, an American fashion designer, philanthropist, and business executive, observed, "A leader has the vision and conviction that a dream can be achieved. He inspires the power and energy to get it done." Like Lauren, heretics energize people. They give them the strength and vitality required for sustained physical or mental activity. They energize them by inspiring them to devote themselves to the impossible dream. People who have a foundation of engagement seek and thrive on being energized for the task of achieving the impossible dream.

I have found the very best resource on engagement, and one whose principals have positively influenced my coaching and consulting practice, in *The Power of Full Engagement: Managing Energy, Not Time, Is the Key to High Performance and Personal Renewal* by Jim Loehr and Tony Schwartz. The book's subtitle provides a significant differentiation between the management of time and energy. The authors present four sources of energy: physical capacity they define by quantity of energy, emotional by quality of energy, mental by focus of energy, and spiritual by force of energy. When one is fully engaged, one is therefore physically energized, emotionally connected, mentally focused, and spiritually aligned. Full engagement also provides mental, emotional, physical, and spiritual resilience.

Engaged, energized persons express their willingness to commit, commence, and complete the movement's mission. Commitment to the impossible dream focuses energy from the inside out. Towers Watson's research on how the most profitable companies work on the inside, identified twenty-five companies with a total of 303,000 employees that enjoyed high-performance business results, and posted them on what it called The Global High-Performance list. The core finding was that in the highest-performing cultures, "leaders not only create high levels of engagement—manifest in strong employee attachment to the company and a willingness to give extra effort—but they also create environments that support productivity and performance, in which employees feel enabled. And finally, they help employees feel a greater sense of well-being and drive at work; in other words, people feel energized."

Heretics motivate others to commence achieving the impossible dream, to get the show on the road and hit the ground running. Often, persons who hear the heretic's pitch express an engaged, energized, and enthusiastic perspective and ask, "When do we start?" Notice an important shift from the "me" to "we"—that's a key indication of the focus of their energy. They may appear like energizer bunnies and their energy may have to be channeled. In any case, they bring a genuine receptivity to the impossible dream and infuse the movement with their contagious energy. Energized heretics model the tone of the movement but don't need to feel like miracle-workers.

One important dimension of energized engagement is the early determination of potential members of a movement to complete the mission. Do you recognize in their response an excitement and readiness to do whatever it takes to reach the visionary destination, to finish strong? Samuel Johnson, the great English lexicographer, commented, "Genius is that energy which collects, combines, amplifies, and animates."

Empowered

Potential members of a movement may have saluted because they not only felt engaged and energized but also empowered to pursue together the impossible dream.

Jesus, from my perspective, the ultimate heretic, provides a model of empowerment. He charged his disciples to fulfill their high calling in what is referred to as "The Great Commission," recorded in the Gospel of Matthew 28:18-20 (*The Message*).

18-20 Jesus, undeterred, went right ahead and gave his charge: "God authorized and commanded me to commission you: Go out and train everyone you meet, far and near, in this way of life, marking them by baptism in the threefold name: Father, Son, and Holy Spirit. Then instruct them in the practice of all I have commanded you. I'll be with you as you do this, day after day after day, right up to the end of the age."

Jesus valued and trusted his followers. He practiced what he preached by valuing everyone who chose to come with him on a journey of faith. His actions spoke louder than his words. In fact, Jesus put his life on the line for them. Jesus' disciples knew that he valued, trusted, and supported them to fulfill their calling with his promise of eternal presence: "I'll be with you as you do this, day after day after day, right up to the end of the age." Jesus was ahead of his time in attracting and choosing a diverse group of followers.

By effectively empowering his followers, Jesus began a movement that continues to this day. I encountered the idea of Jesus as a heretic creating a movement at a seminar held at The Earlham School of Religion, a graduate division of Earlham College, located in Richmond, Indiana, the oldest graduate seminary associated with the Religious Society of Friends. The seminar's presenter, Dr. Clarence Jordan, captured my attention then and more passionately today, with a single phrase, "The God Movement," that he repeated during the three memorable days. For Jordan, "The God Movement" described the engaged, energized, and empowered action of the followers of Jesus.

As a seminary student, I had the privilege and honor to room with Dr. Jordan and witnessed first-hand his fervent resolve to offer dignity to everyone including Blacks in the southern United States. Jordan followed the tradition of Jesus by being a heretic himself. A farmer and New Testament Greek scholar, he founded Koinonia Farm, a small but influential religious community in southwest Georgia. He also wrote the *Cotton Patch* paraphrase of the New Testament, and was instrumental in formulating Habitat for Humanity. Jordan's translations of scripture portions led to the creation of a musical, *Cotton Patch Gospel*, telling the life of Jesus Christ, using his southern style and set in Georgia. As a pastor, I accept my primary role to empower congregants. I'm in the empowerment business that enables them to go out and engage, energize, and empower others. Together, we act as evangelists for "The God Movement."

A leader may be defined as one who has a following. If even only one saluted, you have the beginnings of a movement. If no one responded by saluting, if no one was on fire or even slightly smoldering, you might have to go back to the drawing board and reassess your impossible dream, and/or your presentation and its timing.

6.3 AND WATCH WHO DOESN'T SALUTE

"To fly, we have to have resistance," observed Maya Ying Lin, an American designer and artist who is known for her work in sculpture and landscape art, and who first came to fame at the age of twenty-one as the designer of the Vietnam Veterans Memorial in Washington.

For heretics presenting their impossible dreams, resistance comes with the territory. It's a given. Michael "Mike" Hammer, a fictional hard-boiled detective created by the American author Mickey Spillane in his 1947 book *I, the Jury*, points out that people's resistance to change is "the most perplexing, annoying, distressing, and confusing part" of reengineering. "People resist change in all kinds of ways," reveal Kriegel and Brandt, in their book *Sacred Cows Make the Best Burgers*. "They resist actively, passively, consciously and unconsciously, by sabotage and subterfuge. They resist it rationally, emotionally, and sometimes spiritually."

What enables heretics to initiate major change without being harmed or 'killed,' as has regrettably happened in the past, depends on how you treat persons who don't salute. Give them the same attention and respect you pay to the ones who salute, and let your behavior send a clear message that you're leading with fairness and an open mind. Why don't people embrace change? In a nutshell, for most, change feels unpredictable, uncomfortable, and unsafe.

Rosabeth Moss Kanter, a professor of business at the Harvard Business School, where she holds the Ernest L. Arbuckle Professorship, and in addition, who directs and chairs the Harvard University Advanced Leadership Initiative, compiled an excellent list of ten reasons why people resist change. I find her checklist helpful as a tool when assessing organizational resistance, and particularly helpful for leaders of change, by understanding the predictable, universal sources of resistance in each situation and then strategizing around them. Kanter's list of the ten most common universal sources of resistance includes the following: loss of control, excess uncertainty, everything seems different, loss of face, concerns about competence, more work, ripple effects, past resentments, sometimes the threat is real, and surprise.

Heretics deal effectively with resistance respectfully, openly, and calmly. The first, respectfully, means heretics listen to those who don't salute non-judgmentally with an appreciation for their perspective. "Your management of an attack," advised Heifetz and Linsky, in their book *Leadership on the Line*, "more than the substance of the accusation, determines your fate." The authors add that as far as it is possible, keep the opposition close because "People who oppose what you are trying to accomplish are usually those with the most to lose by your success." Treat them with understanding, legitimize their feelings, grieve with them, and memorialize their potential loss.

Openly recognizing that the actions proposed may result in some casualties signals the heretic's commitment to the organization, as well as a willingness to consider all the responses as legitimate and worthy of review. Expect and welcome resistance to change by soliciting feedback from those who resist the proposed change in order to improve the process of gaining their eventual acceptance for change.

Usually, a senior member of the community may give clues about what's happening in the organization under the radar. Oscar Wilde believed that "Skepticism is the beginning of faith." If Wilde is right, and I think he is, be open to consider that some of your best support may appear to be hidden. Years ago, in my congregation where I was pastor, a newspaper columnist, who had caused me a lot of grief, became one of my biggest supporters.

Heretics deal effectively with resistance with a confident non-anxious presence. Heretics gain nothing by attacking resisters, so indicate their opinions matter and their opinions have a right to be heard. Assure them, as African-American social reformer, abolitionist, orator, writer, and statesman, Frederick Douglass, noted: "If there is no struggle, there is no progress." And don't take personally the unwillingness of others to embrace the recommended changes.

John Gardner, an American novelist, observed, "Pity the leader who is caught between unloving critics and uncritical lovers." Heretics describe persons who didn't resonate with the changes proposed as fence-sitters, disengaged, and CAVE people.

Fence-Sitters

Margaret Thatcher observed, "Standing in the middle of the road is very dangerous; you get knocked down by the traffic from both sides."

An example of fence-sitting may be found in the Illinois legislature where members have on their desks in front of them three color-coded buttons to push, green (yes), yellow (fence-sitter), and red (no), indicating their response to proposals. The fence-sitters most often choose yellow.

Fence-sitters feel vulnerable and anxious. They feel vulnerable for a variety of reasons including concerns about the impact of the impossible dream on them personally, and lingering questions about the direction of the organization especially if they distrust the present leadership to lead them into the future, and have their backs and their best interests in mind. Their institutional memory may block any effort to change their mindset.

Often, fence-sitters are resistant to change of any kind, and when the change is significant, it may trigger increased vulnerability. "We never did it that way before," they declare. Heifetz and Linsky confirm this possibility. "In fact, there's a proportionate relationship between risk and adaptive change: The deeper the change and the greater the amount of new learning required, the more resistance there will be and, thus, the greater danger to those who lead."

Fence-sitters feel vulnerable and anxious, caught between a rock and a hard place and not aligned with the new direction anticipated by the impossible dream. They can't envision themselves as an integral part of the proposed movement. Some thoughtful fence-sitters need your assurance you'll do what you're promising to do, and if you do, they may become, in time, passionate champions of the impossible dream. What heretics don't want, as Kriegel and Brandt note in their book *Sacred Cows Make the Best Burgers*, are potential followers responding with "vicious compliance or the kiss of yes." Part of the anxiety fence-sitters experience may involve the fear of loss of power, influence, and stability.

Heifetz, Linsky, and Alexander Grashow, authors of *The Practice of*

Adaptive Leadership: Tools and Tactics for Changing Your Organization and the World, offer what for me personally and professionally continues to be a most liberating concept: "What people resist is not change per se, but loss. When change involves real or potential loss, people hold on to what they have and resist the change." French poet, journalist, and novelist, Anatole France, reflects, "All changes, even the most longed for, have their melancholy; for what we leave behind us is a part of ourselves; we must die to one life before we can enter another."

Disengaged

Lewis Carroll, in *Alice's Adventures in Wonderland*, expressed the mind- and heart-set of the disengaged:

"'Would you tell me, please, which way I ought to go from here?' said Alice.

"'That depends a good deal on where you want to get to,' said the Cat.

"'I don't much care where,' said Alice.

"'Then it doesn't matter which way you go,' said the Cat."

In this book's introduction, I referred to the disengagement of people in the workplace. While many would consider this a huge problem, heretics view this issue as an incredible opportunity to engage workers to increase innovation, improve productivity, and foster worker satisfaction. Research professor at the University of Houston Graduate College of Social Work, Brené Brown, in her book *Daring Greatly*, describes the disengaged succinctly: "When we're disengaged, we don't show up, we don't contribute, and we stop caring." One can describe the 'disengaged' in the word "whatever," which can be gauged on a sliding scale of disengagement from mild to intense where people purposely sabotage their organization. The primary challenge for heretics regarding the disengaged involves engaging the disengaged to disengage, so they can be open to fully engaging.

Heretics may encounter a disengaged response that most often results from two factors: a poor fit and poor leadership. A poor fit emerges from a poor attitude and poor skills alignment. In fact, if a heretic receives no resistance, the chances are the dream stretches their audience's imagination minimally. It's just not big enough. Rob Markey, in his article, "The Four Secrets of Employee Engagement," in the Harvard Business Review Blog, confirms that employee engagement remains a challenge for companies worldwide. Recently, Bain & Company, in conjunction with Netsurvey, analyzed responses from 200,000 employees across forty companies in sixty countries, and found three troubling trends: Engagement scores decline with employee tenure, meaning that employees with the deepest knowledge of the company typically are the least engaged; engagement scores decline as you go down the organization chart, so highly engaged senior executives are likely to underestimate the discontent on the front lines; and engagement levels are lowest among sales and service employees, who have the most interactions with customers.

People disengage because of poor leadership. Brené Brown highlights what she calls the disengagement divide: "We disengage to protect ourselves from vulnerability, shame, and feeling lost and without purpose. We also disengage when we feel that the people who are leading us—our boss, our teachers, our principal, our clergy, our parents, our politicians—aren't living up to their end of the social contract."

In the article, "The Different Impact of Good and Bad Leadership," the Barna Group explores the leadership maxim: "People don't quit jobs, they quit bad bosses." In a study among Americans in the workplace, done in partnership with Leadercast, Barna Group found that two in five work for someone they consider a "bad" leader. When asked to attribute positive and negative characteristics to their supervisors, these 40 percent of workers assign at least four of the six attributes to their boss. Another two in five workers (40 percent) say their leader displays one to three of those negative attributes, classifying that leader as 'average.' In contrast, only one in five workers (19 percent) assigns only positive attributes qualifying them as "good" bosses.

So what do people say makes for a bad leader? Workers most often identified three complaints when it comes to poor leadership: at least three in ten Americans say their supervisor lacks clear vision and direction (32 percent), that the poor leadership at work is the most stressful part of the job (33 percent), and that their boss makes them feel controlled, manipulated, or defensive (31 percent). Additionally, one-quarter of workers (25 percent) feel their career progress is limited because of their boss's poor leadership. About one in six (17 percent) say they would prefer a new boss over a raise. And a majority (62 percent) say they wouldn't follow their boss if their paycheck didn't depend on it.

Heretics register the response of persons who don't salute not only as a common courtesy, but also as a way to understand how and why the fence-sitters, the disengaged, and the CAVE dwellers view the impossible dream. This last group, in my experience, comprises the most difficult to reach, appreciate, and inspire.

CAVE Dwellers

They all laughed at Fulton and his steamboat
Hershey and his chocolate bar
Ford and his Lizzie kept the laughers busy
That's how people are.
– George Gershwin, "They All Laughed"

Citizens Against Virtually Everything (CAVE) describes citizen activists who regularly oppose any changes within a community. The phenomenon is linked to the so-called Not In My Back Yard (NIMBY) phenomenon in which residents oppose a development as being inappropriate for their local area. While the NIMBY phenomenon is typically related to development issues, CAVE people, as the name implies, oppose virtually everything.

Heretics will inevitably encounter CAVE Dwellers. Steven Browning Sample, the tenth president of the University of Southern California, and author of *The Contrarian's Guide to Leadership*, identifies the challenge for heretics: "Congenital naysayers are among the greatest stumbling blocks to thinking free." The upside to CAVE Dwellers is their negative consistency. Their body language often gives a clue to their stance regarding the future. On the speaking circuit and in the boardroom, I meet these folks whose arms are folded securely on their pumped-up chests with a distinct direct message: "Just try to engage me!" They prefer the presumed safety of opposition.

One can generally characterize CAVE Dwellers by their ignorance and/or indifference. They often don't know and don't want to know. With their close-minded eyes, they ask: "What? You talking to me?" They are like ballet critics who leave no turn un-stoned. Mark Twain remarked, "Anyone with a new idea is a crank until the idea succeeds."

CAVE Dwellers may respond to an impossible dream with indifference for a whole spectrum of reasons. They contend that an impossible dream cannot be done and consider any idea outside the norm to be outrageous, audacious, and ridiculous. In response to this viewpoint, heretics need to follow the wisdom of German philosopher Arthur Schopenhauer who aids our understanding of change when he noted: "All truth passes through three stages. First, it is ridiculed. Second, it is violently opposed. Third, it is accepted as self-evident." Go forward confidently in the spirit of this Chinese proverb, "One who says it cannot be done must not prevent one who is doing it."

Heretics don't summarily dismiss CAVE Dwellers. They can positively surprise you with their change of heart, mind, and soul, and commit their unswerving commitment. On a flight from my mission in Nairobi to Amsterdam, I sat next to a gentleman who enquired what I was doing in Kenya. I answered that I fed hungry kids in the slums. He responded in a somewhat typical CAVE Dweller fashion: "I hate you goddamn globe-trotting do-gooders." I calmly reached into my briefcase, pulled out a picture of a child in our program, and gave it to him along with my business card. About two weeks after I returned, I received in the mail a letter from the gentleman based in Europe, and a generous check. I wrote him an email and thanked him for his generosity, and suggested that he consider, like many of our contributors, to support our project monthly. And thankfully, he continues to do so.

Heretics can anticipate resistance in many forms including fence-sitters, the disengaged, and CAVE Dwellers. The persons who don't salute deserve your attention as much as the people who saluted. The way heretics treat those who don't salute will speak volumes to them and to those who did salute.

PART THREE

Lead Like A Heretic: Energize

CHAPTER 7

Maintain Momentum

The French proverb, *Pierre qui roule n'amasse pas mousse*, which means, "A rolling stone gathers no moss," provides a clue to the importance of maintaining momentum in a movement's success. The discipline of physics defines momentum as the property or tendency of a moving object to continue moving. Heretics understand that momentum means increasing the forward motion of the movement, and just like a boulder rolling down a hill gains momentum, advancing a movement follows the same principle.

Perhaps one of the easiest aspects of fostering momentum is the first push to get the movement going. Heretics usually express great excitement like a horse race announcer: "This field is now in motion!" But the real work of sustaining momentum starts even before the gates fly open. The continuing challenge is how to keep the momentum going and the movement growing with everybody moving forward in the same direction with the same purpose at the same time.

Movement momentum involves encouraging the ones who saluted, as well as those who did not, to come together for the welfare of the entity. Heretics appreciate the ones who did not initially salute, because they may, in the end, become some of the strongest supporters. Build a foundation of commitment on which to grow the movement and energize followers to rise up, take the banner, and boldly press on.

Every heretic faces the momentum challenge including candidates running for political office, for whom momentum can be a deciding factor in them staying in or dropping out of the race. We saw this reality play out in the United States 2016 Presidential race. In fact, there were a number of forces at work to increase or decrease momentum of candidates, especially those leading the field. Undecided voters had an increasing impact as well.

Momentum can be considered a science and an art in politics, business (Stock market), sports (March Madness Brackets), and entertainment (*Dancing with the Stars*). Many factors contribute to the speeding up or the slowing down of momentum including unrealistic goals, poor strategy, unexpected setbacks, and fatigue. Heretics employ three key strategies to maintain their movement's momentum: instill purpose, nurture values, and foster community.

7.1 INSTILL PURPOSE

"The best companies," believes Guy Kawasaki, "enchant us with purpose, affection, empathy, coolness, and grit."

The word "evangelist" derives from the Greek *euangellion*, *eu* (good), and *angellion* (messenger), which literally means "messenger of good news." One can find use of the term evangelist in both religious and secular contexts. Heretics see themselves as the bearers of good news of a prosperous future for their movements. They offer their followers a source of meaning that attracts the brightest and the best of passionate creative associates.

Jeff Weiner, CEO of LinkedIn, echoes Luyeneburger's perspective: "Leadership, to me, is the ability to inspire others to achieve shared objectives. The important word there is inspire. The key difference between managers and leaders is that managers tell people what to do, while leaders inspire them to do it. Inspiration comes from three things: clarity of one's vision, courage of their conviction and the ability to effectively communicate both of those things." Leadership consultant Ron Heifetz, author of *Leadership without Easy Answers,* points out the long-term benefits of establishing a strong sense of purpose: "Preserving a sense of purpose helps one take setbacks and failures in stride."

In my coaching practice, I initially explore with senior leaders their personal and corporate purpose because it provides the foundation not only for purposeful coaching but also for exceptional leadership. Most of the time, they present themselves as obviously possessing a deep internal purpose, but have never been challenged to articulate it clearly and without hesitation. Part of my privilege in coaching involves teasing out the essence of a leader in order to enable him or her to authentically instill purpose in their followers. Leaders have expressed to me how liberating the process of distilling a passionate sense of purpose can be.

Heretics maintain momentum by instilling the movement's vision, mission, and drive.

The Vision

"Where there is no vision, the people perish."
– Proverbs 29:18 (King James Version)

A key to maintaining momentum is instilling purpose with a compelling vision held in common by members of the movement who *see* a new preferred future. Vision, as central to the movement, provides "the why," a unifying catalyst that drives the organization toward its chosen destination. Vision makes it worth the pain to strive for and achieve the impossible dream.

Heretics engage everybody everywhere in the movement to know the movement's vision by heart, and then live out that vision from their hearts. Some leaders don't get the importance of a loyal commitment to a vision. I once interviewed a CEO of a Fortune 500 company and asked him to tell me the vision of his organization. To my surprise, he struggled to put the picture he had in his mind into a comprehensive sentence. A little embarrassed, he started looking under his desk blotter to find the piece of paper with the results of a weekend retreat that had formulated the vision. Leaders who do get the "vision thing" engrave their vision on their hearts and minds and souls.

Heretics live and breathe their impossible dream and instill their vision not just as a picture of the future, but a here-and-now palpable heartbeat for the organization. It's all about the future. Mary Parker Follett, an American social worker and pioneer in the fields of organizational theory and organizational behavior, describes the primary function of a collaborative leader: "The most successful leader of all is one who sees another picture not yet actualized. He sees the things which belong in his present picture but which are not yet there … Above all, he should make his co-workers see that it is not his purpose which is to be achieved, but a common purpose, born of the desires and activities of the group."

My friend and fellow Rotarian, the late Dr. Bill Sprague, a retired physician of obstetrics, dedicated himself to his dream of eradicating polio—a common purpose he shared with 1.2 million members in 35,000 Rotary International clubs. In 1985, Rotary established the PolioPlus Program, which works globally and especially in Africa, to eradicate this debilitating disease. Dr. Bill vaccinated over a billion children for polio. Rotarians, whose motto is "Service above Self," have contributed more than $1.6 billion and countless volunteer hours to immunize more than 2.5 billion children in 122 countries.

In the article, "Leading in the 21st century: An interview with Ford's Alan Mulally," writer Rik Kirkland asked the president and CEO of the Ford Motor Company to describe his leadership style. Mulally responded: "At the most fundamental level, it is an honor to serve … Starting from that foundation, it is important to have a compelling vision and a comprehensive plan. Positive leadership—conveying the idea that there is always a way forward—is so important, because that is what you are here for—to figure out how to move the organization forward."

Dave Ulrich and Wendy Ulrich, in their book *The Why of Work: How Great Leaders Build Abundant Organizations That Win*, indicate the influence of a heretic's vision: "Leaders are meaning makers: they set direction for others to aspire to; they help others participate in doing good work and good works; they communicate ideas and invest in practices that shape how people think, act, and feel."

Heretics instill purpose with commitment to their vision and to their mission, to which we now turn our attention.

The Mission

"If you can't fly then run, if you can't run then walk, if you can't walk then crawl," encouraged civil rights activist Martin Luther King, Jr., "but whatever you do you have to keep moving forward."

Coupled with instilling a vision as a key to sustaining momentum, heretics instill a permeating sense of mission. They differentiate their vision, the *why* of their movement, from their mission, the *how* of their movement. Vision derives from the Latin *visio*, which means "to see," and mission from *missio*, which means "to send out." Readers may be familiar with the latter that refers to the focus of the Roman Catholic Mass that reaffirms the calling and commitment of the people to the mission and then their being 'sent out on a mission' to be God's missionaries in the world.

Heretics pay special attention to developing a clear inspiring memorable mission that can resonate with the hearts and minds and souls of their members. For example, I've met a number of persons who have served in the United States Peace Corps (USPC) and every one had an extremely strong sense of their mission. The USPC provides service opportunities for motivated change-makers to immerse themselves in a community abroad, working side by side with local leaders to tackle the most pressing challenges of our generation. Its mission is to promote world peace and friendship by fulfilling three goals: to help the people of interested countries in meeting their need for trained volunteers, to help promote a better understanding of Americans on the part of the peoples served, and to help promote a better understanding of other peoples on the part of Americans.

The United States Marine Corps, another example, serves as a versatile combat element, and is adapted to a wide variety of combat operations. It has a unique mission statement, and, alone among the branches of the U.S. armed forces, "shall, at any time, be liable to do duty in the forts and garrisons of the United States, on the seacoast, or any other duty on shore, as the President, at his discretion, shall direct." In this special capacity, charged with carrying out duties given to them directly by the President of the United States, the Marine Corps serves as an all-purpose, fast-response task force, capable of quick action in areas requiring emergency intervention.

Stan Doerr, Executive Director of Blood:Water, describes its mission as a grassroots organization that empowers communities to work together against the HIV/AIDS and water crises in Africa. It considers itself an equipping agency that partners with African grassroots organizations to address the HIV/AIDS and water crises. It does this by identifying Africa's hidden heroes and coming alongside their vision for change. Through technical, financial, and organizational support, Blood:Water expands the reach and effectiveness of African civil society organizations and the communities they serve.

I noted earlier that heretics cultivate a climate of engagement so that members of their movements have the freedom to grow to their own personal potential and the collective potential of the movement. They create an atmosphere of encouragement as a learning organization for visionary missionaries where workers can realize their professional advancement goals and develop necessary expertise.

Heretics understand that good ideas and education have to be put into practice. Yehudi Menuhin, an American-born violinist and conductor, who is widely considered one of the greatest violinists of the twentieth century, observed, "The difference between a beginner and the master—is that the master practices a whole lot more."

The Drive

Henry Ford, founder of the Ford Motor Company, reflected coincidentally on the concept of drive: "Enthusiasm is the yeast that makes your hopes shine to the stars. Enthusiasm is the sparkle in your eyes, the swing in your gait. The grip of your hand, the irresistible surge of will and energy to execute your ideas."

Drive constitutes an internal positive energy. Daniel H. Pink, a heretic in his own right, in his classic book *Drive: The Surprising Truth about What Motivates Us*, turns the motivational world on its head. The secret to high performance and satisfaction in today's world, he claims, is the deeply human need to direct our own lives, to learn and create new things, and to do better by ourselves and our world.

Drawing on four decades of scientific research on human motivation, Pink exposes the mismatch between what science knows and what business does, and how that affects every aspect of our lives. He demonstrates that while the old-fashioned carrot-and-stick approach worked successfully in the twentieth century, it's precisely the wrong way to motivate people for today's challenges. In *Drive*, he calls for a renaissance of self-direction, of taking responsibility for one's life, and reveals the three elements of true motivation: autonomy, the desire to direct our own lives; mastery, the urge to get better and better at something that matters; and purpose, the yearning to do what we do in the service of something larger than ourselves.

Persons who have lived in the service of something larger than themselves inspire heretics. And heretics major in instilling drive in members of their movements. James M. Kouzes and Barry Z. Posner, authors of *Encouraging the Heart: A Leader's Guide to Rewarding and Recognizing Others*, claim: "Passionately believing in people and expecting the best of them is another prerequisite to encouraging the heart ... Encouraging the heart, then, is about the dichotomous nature of leadership. It's about toughness and tenderness. Guts and grace. Firmness and fairness. Fortitude and gratitude. Passion and compassion. Leaders must have the courage themselves, and they must impart it to others."

Heifetz and Linsky, in their book *Leadership on the Line*, connect the concept of drive with leading with an open heart: "Leading with an open heart helps you stay alive in your soul. It enables you to feel faithful to whatever is true, including doubt, without fleeing, acting out, or reaching for a quick fix. Moreover, the power of a sacred heart helps you to mobilize others to do the same—to face challenges that demand courage, and to endure the pain of change without deceiving themselves or running away ... The virtue of a sacred heart lies in the courage to maintain your innocence and wonder, your doubt and curiosity, and your compassion and love even through your darkest, most difficult moments."

On June 26, 2015, we witnessed a moving example of leading with an open heart when President Barack Obama delivered a eulogy for the Rev. Clementa C. Pinckney, who was among nine killed in a shooting by a twenty-one-year-old racist terrorist during Bible study at Charleston, South Carolina's Emanuel African Methodist Episcopal Church. "As a nation, out of this terrible tragedy, God has visited grace upon us for he has allowed us to see where we've been blind," Obama said. "He's given us the chance, where we've been lost, to find our best selves." The President's thoughtful meditation on race in America at the funeral will be remembered mostly for his heartfelt singing of "Amazing Grace" that brought mourners to their feet to join him in song. It may be acknowledged as one of the most powerful moments of his presidency.

"Courage," Winston Churchill defined, "is going from failure to failure without losing enthusiasm." Heretics maintain momentum by instilling purpose and nurturing ideals.

7.2 NURTURE IDEALS

"Nobody grows old merely by living a number of years," claims poet Samuel Ullman. "We grow old by deserting our ideals. Years may wrinkle the skin, but to give up enthusiasm wrinkles the soul."

Heretics, as I am presenting them, lead from a foundation of being servants, dreamers, and challengers in the best interest of others. They, like physicians taking their medical oath, honor the spirit of *Primum non nocere*, a Latin phrase that means "first, do no harm."

Every organization operates with an ideology, a system of ideas and ideals that guides the thinking and behavior of its members. And heretics identify the ideals they want to nurture in their movements, and from these ideals, formulate guidelines for values and behavior for the movement as it moves toward achieving its impossible dream.

In my senior executive coaching, I ask leaders a series of questions to identify their ideals. What habits do you and your organization encourage? What's expected and affirmed? What is punished, frowned upon, a cause for immediate dismissal, or completely unacceptable? What would you have to do around here to get in big trouble? Their answers, what they said and what they didn't say, offer significant clues about the ideals of the organization. One of the challenges is to read between the lines. Very few indicated that they feel encouraged to think like a heretic. The most fascinating responses addressed what they have to do to get in big trouble. For example, a young executive confided that making love to the President's spouse on the President's desk did not help his career. Now, that's not exactly an ideal image!

Heretics understand that movements put their ideals into action. That's what heretic Samantha White did. In an article, "How the Bard Saved a City: Sam White launches an against-all-odds campaign to transform Detroit with Shakespeare," by Drew Philp in Southwest the Magazine, we learn how White launched the unlikeliest of startups and transformed her downtown. "Shakespeare in Detroit" reveals that in desperate times some respond by dreaming dreams that are bigger and wilder than ever before.

Of course, for native Detroiter White, an experienced actor, all the city's a stage. She also used her decade of experience as a journalist to create awareness in the community, and reflected, "You have to have a healthy, thriving creative community to have a successful city. As artists, we have a responsibility to bring people together." Shakespeare's King Lear, the monarch who went mad, compelled her to contemplate what sanity really means. "Perhaps a little bit of insanity is needed to go after your dreams," she said, "because there is nothing simple or comfortable about it."

Heretics sustain momentum by instilling purpose and nurturing ideals of openness, respect, and empathy. Let's begin our exploration of nurturing ideals by considering the ideal of openness.

Openness

Heretics understand openness as an overarching concept or philosophy that is characterized by an emphasis on transparency and free, unrestricted access to knowledge and information, as well as collaborative or cooperative management and decision-making rather than a central authority. Openness can be said to be the opposite of secretive.

Two terms usually describe a person's or an organization's state of mind: closed or open. The closed mind describes the attitude of a person impervious to ideas, arguments, facts, and logic, who clings stubbornly to some mixture of unwarranted assumptions, tribal prejudices, and emotions. Meanwhile, the open mind may be described as an objective, unbiased approach to ideas and willingness to examine ideas and issues critically.

Heretics nurture in their movements the ideal of openness, of an open transparent mind, to consider new ideas and constructive criticism. They encourage their followers to share their ideas no matter how wild and wacky they may seem. They encourage and welcome workers' concerns, insights, and creative ideas about strategy, new products or services, or the future of the movement. Nothing is off limits. That's probably why

Google supports their associates to devote 20 percent of their time to do their creative thinking, musing, and doodling.

With openness, heretics strive to honor, unlock, and endorse creativity. Heretics encourage not only dedicated research and development of persons and departments, but invite everyone in the operation to fill the pipeline with great ideas to benefit the bottom line. No leader has all the great ideas. Openness can be productive and profitable. For example, at one of my church board meetings, a member suggested that we not have the annual fundraising dinner that had been traditionally held for over seventy-five years. Instead, she recommended that we convene a "No Dinner Dinner," where church members, because their calendars were so full already, would welcome the opportunity to pay not to attend, and instead could spend quality time with their families. The idea passed and we had the most profitable dinner in the church's history. Indeed, that congregation annually celebrates the "No Dinner Dinner."

Unfortunately, many organizations do not create the conditions conducive to sharing without judgment. Alan Weiss, author of *Million Dollar Consulting*, persuasively articulates an open-minded approach to diverse points of view: "Consensus is something you can live with, not something you would die for. We need to accommodate legitimate, diverse points of view. Too often we move from the issue to the person. Once we question the legitimacy of the other person, we end honest debate and emotion precludes logic. We need to disagree without despising, debate without demeaning, understand without undermining. We'll never gain influence if we demonize those who disagree with us."

My wise grandfather Johnson counselled me never to call someone a "horse's ass." He believed that if you used that kind of derogatory language, it probably would be difficult to cultivate a friendship, establish a business connection, or exist peacefully in the same stable in the future. He did, however, offer a caveat: if someone repeatedly acted like a "horse's ass," then they deserved my honesty of giving them the notable title.

Heretics are open to new ideas and welcome constructive criticism from their followers. They recognize improvement as a two-way street and nurture an environment of trust that provides a foundation for openness to work together collaboratively and positively. Honest criticism becomes an organizational asset based on mutual trust that enables everyone to actively seek a preferred solution. Heretics purposefully nurture ideals of openness and respect.

Respect

In the movie *The Imitation Game*, English mathematician and logician, Alan Turing, helps crack the Enigma Code during World War II. "I'm just a mathematician," he declared. The film repeatedly winds back to 1928, when, as a public schoolboy, Turing is bullied for his strangeness, but befriended by one other boy, Christopher Morcom, who tells him, "Sometimes it is the people who no one imagines anything of who do the things that no one can imagine."

Heretics possess a healthy respect for themselves and others, and model respectful behavior for their followers. They create an attitudinal framework for life, love, and work that celebrates others' similarities as well as their differences individually and collectively. "Trust begins with a personal commitment to respect others, to take everyone seriously," observes Max De Pree, in his book *Leading without Power*. "Respect demands that we first recognize each other's gifts and strengths and interests; then we must integrate them into the work of the organization." Poet and activist Audrey Lorde asserts, "It is not our differences that divide us. It is our inability to recognize, accept, and celebrate those differences."

Today many leaders in the United States share with me that they find it difficult to understand, appreciate, and motivate Millennials—youth born between 1982 and 2000, who number 83.1 million and represent more than one quarter of the U.S. population. Wise leaders respect the gifts of all generations including the Millennials, now the largest generation in the workforce. In my research for my book *The Compassionate*

Conspiracy: A Field Guide to Changing the World, whose target audience is Millennials, I discovered that all Millennials are not alike. They're a multi-faceted generation that may surprise you. Most of them are industrious, collaborative, community oriented, financially prudent, entrepreneurial, and eager to build a better planet. Leaders with a compelling vision take note: Millennials seek a cause bigger than themselves.

A. G. Lafley, former CEO of Proctor & Gamble, praises diversity in the workplace: "All the data we've seen, and all of my personal experience, convinces me that a diverse organization will out-think, out-innovate, and out-perform a homogeneous organization every single time. Winning will come from taking full advantage of our diversity."

Bennis and Nanus, in their book *Leaders: Strategies for Taking Charge*, articulate the practical importance of nurturing respect: "Therefore, the challenge to leaders will be to act as compassionate coaches, dedicated to reducing stress by ensuring that the whole team has everything it needs—from human and financial resources to emotional support and encouragement—to work together effectively and at peak performance most of the time.

"Recognizing, developing and celebrating the distinctive skills of each individual will become critically important to organizational survival. In the new global, multicultural workplace where employees have different languages, values and loyalties, this may well challenge leaders to new heights of interpersonal sensitivity, understanding and commitment to the best that human diversity has to offer."

"Treat people as if they were what they ought to be," recommended Johann Wolfgang von Goethe, a German writer and statesman, "and you help them become what they are capable of being." Heretics nurture within their movements the ideals of openness, respect, and empathy.

Empathy

Arthur P. Ciaramicoli and Katherine Ketcham, authors of *The Power of*

Empathy, describe the contagious power of empathy: "Empathy shines its light on our deepest needs, never allowing us to forget that our very survival depends on our ability to accurately understand and sensitively respond to each other."

Self-aware leaders who are attuned to their inner signals offer their colleagues authentic empathy, an opportunity for members of the movement to have face-to-face pivotal connections. Gay Hendricks and Kate Ludeman, in their book *The Corporate Mystic*, note how empathy works: "Creative leaders find ways of stepping into the shoes of other people and asking, 'How would I feel and what would I want if I were this person?'"

Atticus Finch, the fictional lawyer in *To Kill a Mockingbird* observed, "You never really understand a person until you consider things from his point of view … until you climb into his skin and walk around in it." That's precisely why, every week, in preparation for my Sunday worship message, I go to our church's sanctuary and sit in the chairs where I know members sit—there's something to be said for tradition—and ask, what does this person need from me this week? Sometimes, it's a little eerie when someone tells me after the service that it felt like I was talking directly to them.

A study by The Center for Creative Leadership (CCL) in Colorado Springs adds to the growing body of evidence that emotional intelligence (EQ) can be more important than IQ in predicting success in organizations. Daniel Goleman, in his groundbreaking book on the subject, refers to emotional intelligence (EQ) as "a master aptitude, a capacity that profoundly affects all other abilities, either facilitating or interfering with them." Elsewhere, Goleman says that of the five dimensions of EQ, empathy is the "fundamental skill of management." Heretics endorse the practice of empathy in their movements by being attuned to themselves and to others.

Empathy and kindness go hand in hand. Perhaps kindness is empathy's secret weapon of mass construction. I met empathy and kindness personified when Dr. Christopher-Stine, an Associate Professor of Medicine and Neurology and the Director of the Johns Hopkins Myositis Center, a multidisciplinary clinic formally established in 2007 and one of the largest, most comprehensive centers of its kind worldwide, examined me. In a phrase, she practices "amazing grace."

Heretics maintain momentum by nurturing the ideals of openness, respect, and empathy that together foster community.

7.3 FOSTER COMMUNITY

John Donne's poem "For whom the bell tolls" helps us appreciate how to foster community:

No man is an island
Entire of itself,
Every man is a piece of the continent
A part of the main.
If a clod be washed away by the sea,
Europe is the less.
As well as if a promontory were.
As well as if a manor of thy friend's
Or of thine own were:
Any man's death diminishes me,
Because I am involved in mankind,
And therefore never send to know for whom the bell tolls;
It tolls for thee.

Heretics maintain movement momentum, the theme of this chapter, by instilling purpose, nurturing ideals, and fostering community that lives with harmony, optimism, and perspective. The word 'community' appears today in all sorts of contexts: African-American, Latino, LGBT, evangelical, liberal, medical, legal, educational, pro-life, anti-abortion, immigrant, and rural, to name a few. Community derives from the Latin *communis*, which means, "common, public, general, or shared by all or many."

In an article, "The Desire for Community: Illusion, Confusion and Paradox," in the Community Development Journal, Jeremy Brent comments, "Community is constantly invoked as an 'answer' to problems of power, voice and social peace, yet never arrives." He poses important questions about the nature of community in contemporary society: "So, is community an illusion within the globalized world? Does it fetishize the face-to-face? Is it a challenge to power, or a conservative idea of ecological adaptation?" Brent then answers his questions. "While the imprecision and ambiguity of community leads to a desire for clarity, simple definitions do not work. A more complex analysis is needed to unravel the insubstantial but powerful characteristics of community. Community is a desire, continually replenishing itself as people seek voice and connectedness, in all their imperfections."

Brent hit the nail on the head here. There never was, is, or will be a perfect community. Healthy communities, however, embrace imperfection as a reality of their life together, constantly evolve to meet the needs of their members, and entertain no illusion of winning a perfect community seal of approval. As a pastor of small and large congregations, I encountered "church-hoppers" who were looking for the perfect church. I must confess I never felt or expressed regret when they continued their search. These unhappy hoppers remind me of a woman in my congregation who decided after the death of her husband to remarry. "I'm looking for the perfect husband," she told me confidently. Occasionally, I would ask her how the search was going, and over a period of eighteen months she went from looking for "the perfect husband," to "Mr. Alright," to "Mr. Warm and Breathing." When I finally met the result of her extensive search, I didn't have the heart to tell him the whole story.

The longing and hunger for community runs deeply, pervasively, and substantially in both individual and organizational life. Worldwide, people young and old seek communal well-being. Heretics encourage the development of a deep sense of community with an enduring commitment to the vision and to the people who share it.

Movements draw people together with a common interest, purpose, and passion. People coalesce with a feeling of fellowship as a result of sharing common attitudes, perspectives, and goals. They celebrate a particular *esprit de corps* in belonging to the same tribe with their commonality and diversity, and embrace each other as well their local and global community. P. M. Forni, cofounder of the Johns Hopkins Civility Project, and author of *Choosing Civility: The Twenty-Five Rules of Considerate Conduct*, offers sound advice regarding civility in community: "To live a long, healthy, and serene life, we need the help of a network of caring people—we need social support."

Let's begin our discussion of how heretics foster community by exploring harmony.

Harmony

Mahatma Gandhi offered a practical definition of harmony: "Happiness is when what you think, what you say, and what you do are in harmony."

Heretics foster community by promoting harmony so that their movements may go forward toward realizing their impossible dreams. Often, movements fizzle and die because there is little or no harmony among the members. Harmony is like an invisible glue that bonds members to each other and to their common cause, the why of their existence, to move forward together as one body. Goleman, Boyatzis, and McKee reveal, "The glue that holds people together in a team, and that commits people to an organization, is the emotions they feel."

The field of music brings valuable insights to the development of harmony within a movement. Professional cellist and psychiatrist Ronald Heifetz, author of *Leadership without Easy Answers*, offers this insight: "As a musician, I bring several metaphors from music to the study of leadership. Music teaches that dissonance is an integral part of harmony. Without conflict and tension, music lacks dynamism and movement. The composer and improvisational musician alike must contain the dissonance within a frame that holds the audience's attention until resolution is found … Creating music takes place in relation to structures and audiences.

Structural limits provide scaffolding for creativity."

I experience this musical dimension of harmony when I listen to jazz that engages me in a form of constructive conflict with honest interaction and resolution. Heretics provide their movements with an environment that invites members to become an enlarged jazz combo dedicated to realizing their impossible dream together. In addition, the jazz metaphor informs my mediation/arbitration practice.

Heifetz highlights our human approach to conflict: "For good reason, most people have a natural aversion to conflict in their families, communities, and organizations … Indeed, many organizations are downright allergic to conflict, seeing it primarily as a source of danger, which it certainly can be. Conflicts can generate casualties. But deep conflicts, at their root, consist of differences in fervently held beliefs, and differences in perspective are the engine of human progress."

Desmond Mpilo Tutu offered his sage advice on conflict resolution: "Forgiveness is never cheap, never easy. Ultimately, real reconciliation can happen only on the basis of truth. In reality, there can be no future without forgiveness, for revenge merely begets further violence, causing an inexorable spiral of reprisal, provoking counter-reprisals ad infinitum." Of course, knowing Tutu's wry sense of humor, he'd enjoy Oscar Wilde's perspective: "Some cause happiness wherever they go; others, whenever they go."

"In an interdependent, turbulent world," Kerry Patterson, Joseph Grenny, David Maxfield, Ron McMillan, and Al Switzler, authors of *Influencer: The Power to Change Anything*, remind us, "our biggest opponents—the mortal enemy of all families, companies, and communities—may well be our inability to work in concert." Heretics have their work cut out for them in fostering community with harmony.

Optimism

Chinese-American artist, philosopher, and teacher Deng Ming-Dao tells this intriguing story: "There was an old man who began an orchard upon his retirement. Why plant trees? They told him he would never live to see a mature crop. He planted anyway and he has seen them blossom and has eaten their fruit. We all need that type of optimism."

Heretics project optimism like a form of play. They agree with Stuart Brown, in his book *Play: How It Shapes the Brain, Opens the Imagination and Invigorates the Soul*, when he described play as "intensely pleasurable. It energizes us and enlivens us. It eases our burdens. It renews our natural sense of optimism and opens us up to new possibilities."

Martin Seligman, a renowned psychologist and author of *Learned Optimism: How to Change Your Mind and Your Life*, has studied optimists and pessimists for over twenty-five years. Pessimists believe that bad events are their fault, will last a long time, and undermine everything. They feel helpless and may sink into depression. Optimists, on the other hand, believe that defeat is a temporary setback or a challenge and it doesn't knock them down. "Pessimism is escapable," asserts Seligman, "by learning a new set of cognitive skills that will enable you to take charge, resist depression, and make yourself feel better and accomplish more."

Heretics predominantly wear what Maltese physician and psychologist, Edward de Bono, who originated the term 'lateral thinking,' called in his book *Six Thinking Hats*, 'yellow hats.' Persons wearing the yellow hat project positive warmth, a sunny disposition, and positive optimism. Yellow signals constructive thinking and making things happen with a focus on the benefit. Apparently, Winston Churchill wore a yellow hat when he declared, "I am an optimist. It does not seem too much use being anything else." So did Norman Vincent Peale, who wrote *The Power of Positive Thinking*. And if yellow hats had been available, the cast of the Monty Python movie *Life of Brian*, would have worn them during the singing of "Always look on the bright side of life ..."

Optimism possesses a contagious quality that can be a substantial benefit for heretics. Heretics foster community by encouraging harmony, optimism, and perspective.

Perspective

Many years ago, a British shoe manufacturer sent two salesmen to Africa to investigate and report back on market potential. The first reported back, "There is no potential here—nobody wears shoes." The second reported back, "There is massive potential here—nobody wears shoes."

Comedian George Carlin framed perspective this way: "Some people see the glass half full. Others see it half empty. I see a glass that's twice as big as it needs to be." Heretics, in their efforts to maintain momentum by fostering community, must keep their perspective through the good times and the tough times. And be assured, there will be both. The word 'perspective' derives from the Latin *perspicere*, which means "to inspect or to look closely at." It also means "to look through," the meaning that most helps heretics understand the role of perspective in fostering community. The heretic needs to recognize his or her own perspective, as well as the perspectives of others in order for the movement to survive and thrive, to look through to make it through. Ron Heifetz recommends, "To withstand such pressure demands a broad perspective and extra measures of patience, maturity, strength and grace." The recession of 2008-9 caught many leaders by surprise. And the real tragedy is that some of them went into a recession mode of operation and stayed there even after the recovery.

Heretics recognize the wisdom of Dr. Mihaly Csikszentmihalyi, who claimed: "Of all the virtues we can learn, no trait is more useful, more essential for survival, and more likely to improve the quality of life than the ability to transform adversity into an enjoyable challenge." William Arthur Ward, one of America's most quoted writers of inspirational maxims, observed, "The pessimist complains about the wind; the optimist expects it to change; the realist adjusts the sails." That's what Father Michael Lapsley did after he lost both hands when a letter bomb exploded. He adjusted the sails and went on to establish the Institute for Healing Memories.

In the spring of 1949, Harvard Business School graduated its most successful class of all time, issuing MBAs to future corporate titans such as Xerox's Peter McColough, Johnson & Johnson's James Burke, and Bloomingdale's Marvin Traub. The class of 1949 succeeded in part because of its wartime experiences, says biographer Laurence Shames, which gave them passion, conviction, and perspective. "They had a sense of life and death," he explains, "and they had a perspective of how important business was and wasn't."

Heretics, in order to energize their movements, maintain momentum by instilling purpose, nurturing ideals, and fostering community. They also create a common culture.

CHAPTER 8

Create A Common Culture

Mark Twain mused about culture: "You go to heaven for the climate and to hell for the company." However, the Biblical book of Proverbs 13:20 (*The Message*) issues a warning: "Become wise by walking with the wise; hang out with fools and watch your life fall to pieces." We are known by the company we keep and what we have in common with them.

Creating a common culture can be a key to superlative energized leadership. The dynamic of a common culture as a living breathing entity that's constantly changing constitutes the movement's "inside structure" that enables progress toward the fulfillment of the impossible dream. Marcus Aurelius, Roman Emperor from 161 to 180, and the last of the Five Good Emperors, advised, "We must be arched and buttressed from within, else the temple will crumble to dust."

Dr. Stanley D. Truskie, author of *Leadership in High-Performance Organizational Cultures*, points out that before executives can transform their organization's culture, they first need to transform themselves. He recommends that leaders increase their self-awareness by using the L4 Strategy model offered by the Myers-Briggs Assessment Inventory (MBTI). Correlated with effective organizational performance, the four cultural patterns they assess include cooperation, inspiration, achievement, and consistency.

"Culture isn't part of the game," says Lou Gerstner, in his book *Who Says Elephants Can't Dance*, "it is the game." He should know. Gerstner, former chairman and CEO of IBM, led this blue-chip giant back from the brink of bankruptcy and mainframe obscurity to the forefront of the technology business. Transformational leadership of this kind involves the reshaping of an organization's culture, perhaps one of the most critical responsibilities of senior executive leadership.

In my experience as a leadership coach and consultant, a common culture is unfortunately uncommon. However, a few heretical leaders I have encountered in both the profit and not-for-profit sectors have forged strong and vibrant common cultures that continue to produce remarkable results for their customers and for themselves. These remarkable leaders approach culture with an obsession for creating, developing, sustaining, and celebrating their commonness. They accept themselves as trustees of their common culture including the purposeful integration of the gifts of all their followers. They practice what I call constellation leadership that aligns the various "planets" or distinctive parts in a culture to spin in a common orbit and keeps them bound to one another. They nurture what is common and live it every day in every way. Everybody is on the same page.

Let's visit their world of a common culture comprised of a common core, a common connection, and a common cause.

8.1 A COMMON CORE

"To be a leader who has great impact," recommended Tim Irwin, author of *Impact: Great Leadership Changes Everything*, "we must build and protect a strong core."

Heretics adopt a principle of inside-out leadership where the movement's identity, its DNA, recognizes a common core, the heartbeat of the individual members of the movement, as well as the collective heartbeat of the entire movement.

In a Harvard Business Review article, "Developing Mindful Leaders," Polly LaBarre, Editorial Director of the Management Innovation eXchange, explored how leaders can cultivate a successful inner life. She began by asking, "What if, instead of stuffing people with curricula, models, and competencies, we focused on deepening their sense of purpose, expanding their capability to navigate difficulty and complexity, and enriching their emotional resilience? What if, instead of trying to fix people, we assumed that they were already full of potential creating an environment that promoted their long-term well-being? In other words, what if cultivating a successful inner life was front and center on the leadership agenda?"

Pierce and Weiss distilled a list of principles that became the "Personal Excellence Program" (PEP), a short course in unleashing human capability, resilience, compassion, and well-being. These principles include: developing people is a process not an event, people don't grow from the neck up, put mindfulness at the center (but don't call it that), it's hard to grow alone, and everybody deserves to grow.

Heretics model the attributes of the common core. They lead the way by example and invite members of the movement to behave with a similar motivation and consistent action. With an instilled sense of vision, mission, and drive, heretics encourage members of the movement to act from the common core with one voice to direct the movement from the inside out.

When I coach a CEO, after I've earned his or her trust and promised strict confidentiality, I ask a very probing personal question: How would you describe the core of your being? At first, there is understandable reluctance to explore and articulate their essence, mostly because of the possible ramifications for their image in the context of their organization as well as in the public sphere. I find that leaders by and large tend to confuse their own personhood and their leadership role, although these concepts are not mutually exclusive. Their answers to this critical dimension of identity provide substantial clues for me to enable them to unleash their full potential.

Thomas Jefferson, the American Founding Father who acted as the principal author of the Declaration of Independence, wrote these words of advice for heretics: "In matters of style, swim with the current; in matters of principle, stand like a rock."

Heretics create a common culture with the core components of character, beliefs, and values.

Character

"Leadership is a potent combination of strategy and character," observed United States Army General H. Norman Schwarzkopf. "But if you must be without one, be without the strategy."

Peter Gadol, in *The Long Rain*, paints an unsettling portrait of contemporary leadership: "Here we are at the end of the century, drifting through a hero-less age. We have no leaders we can trust, no visions to invest in, no faith to ride. All we have are our own protean moralities, our countless private codes, which we shape and reshape according to our own selfish needs. We don't dare to think too far ahead. We can't see too far ahead. Here we are, trapped by whatever season we find ourselves enduring, waiting out the weather, staring at a drought sun, stupefied, helpless—or scrambling like fools to make it home before the rain really comes down and the dry river floods and the hills crash into the valley. Where do we find the courage to do what is right?"

Heretics to the rescue! The word 'character' derives from the Greek *karakter*, which means 'engraved' or 'stamped.' By extension, heretics fulfill the role of engravers who shape and stamp the core of their movements. I had the pleasure of meeting David Brooks after a presentation about his book *The Road to Character*, in which he paints a rather dismal picture of the state of character in contemporary leadership. In an article in the *New York Times*, Brooks noted, "Highly educated young people are tutored, taught, and monitored in all aspects of their lives, except the most important, which is character-building. But without character and courage, nothing else lasts."

John Neffinger and Matthew Kohut, authors of *Compelling People: The Hidden Qualities that Make Us Influential*, report on the work of psychologists Martin Seligman and Christopher Peterson, who studied how different cultural traditions around the world define character, and found that there are six moral virtues at the core of all of them. I appreciate the research and have found their categories very helpful in discerning the character of leaders in the workplace. Half are forms of strength, and half are forms of warmth:

Courage: the force of will to act in the face of danger.

Temperance: the principled exercise of self-control.

Wisdom: intellectual competence in its highest form.

Justice: a commitment to fairness for humanity.

Humanity: a deep and abiding concern for people's well-being.

Transcendence: looking beyond day-to-day concerns to achieve a sense that we are all connected.

Joel Peterson, Chairman of JetBlue Airways, highlighted the critical nature of character in life and work when he commented, "Success in life is rooted in aligning our actions with our values, until our choices flow naturally, and without calculation, from our character."

Beliefs

"Leadership is much more an art," said Max De Pree, "a belief, a condition of the heart than a set of things to do."

The heretic's beliefs constitute the mental acceptance that something is true or false, valid or invalid. As communication professor W. Barnett Pearce indicates, one's beliefs form the core of her or his being, and expand to influence a person's values, the ideals by which one judges what is important and moral, and a person's attitudes, the predisposition to evaluate, positively or negatively, persons, objects, or symbols.

Simon Sinek, author of *Start with Why*, describes the role of the leader regarding beliefs: "As a company grows, the CEO's job is to personify the 'why.' To ooze of it. To talk about it. To preach it. To be a symbol of what the company believes." Gostick and Elton report on the work of psychological researcher Andrew Newberg who has done pioneering work in brain science and belief. Newberg reveals, "Beliefs are intimately woven with human biology, and our biology compels us and allows us to have beliefs. The involuntary mental drive is the cognitive imperative; it is the almost irresistible, biologically driven need to make sense of things."

In the Jewish tradition, Shema Yisrael, "Hear, [O] Israel" are the first two words of a section of the Torah (Deuteronomy 6:4-9), and is the title, sometimes shortened to simply Shema, of a prayer that serves as a centerpiece of the morning and evening Jewish prayer services: "Hear, O Israel: The Lord our God, the Lord is one. Love the Lord your God with all your heart and with all your soul and with all your strength. These commandments that I give you today are to be on your hearts. Impress them on your children. Talk about them when you sit at home and when you walk along the road, when you lie down and when you get up. Tie them as symbols on your hands and bind them on your foreheads. Write them on the doorframes of your houses and on your gates."

Heretics turn beliefs into action for their members and for their "neighbors" in the human family. Here heretics act on a secular or religious belief foundation consistent with their profile of being servant leaders. For example, the Navy SEAL Creed simply states the personal purpose of its beliefs in action: "I humbly serve as a guardian to my fellow Americans always ready to defend those who are unable to defend themselves."

Elie Wiesel, Nobel laureate and memory keeper of the Holocaust, who died at eighty-seven on July 2, 2016, gave us a stellar example of turning beliefs into action. A heretic, he used his moral authority to force attention on atrocities around the world. Presidents summoned him to the White House to discuss human rights abuses in Bosnia, Iraq, and elsewhere, and the chairman of the Norwegian Nobel Committee called him a "messenger to mankind."

"Elie Wiesel was one of the great moral voices of our time, and in many ways, the conscience of the world," President Obama said in a statement, describing Mr. Wiesel as "a dear friend." The president continued, "After we walked together among the barbed wire and guard towers of Buchenwald where he was held as a teenager and where his father perished, Elie spoke words I've never forgotten: 'Memory has become a sacred duty of all people of goodwill.'"

Heretics turn their beliefs into action. They agree with theologian and author Frederick Bueckner, who commented, "Either life is holy with meaning, or life doesn't mean a damn thing."

Values

"Who you are, what your values are, what you stand for," contends Anne Mulcahy, Chair and CEO of Xerox, "are your anchor, your north star. You won't find them in a book. You'll find them in your soul."

Heretics recognize that their core values are the ideals by which they judge what is important or moral. Terrence E. Deal and Allan A. Kennedy, in their book *The New Corporate Cultures: Revitalizing the Workplace after Downsizing, Mergers, and Reengineering*, state, "A movement's beliefs and values constitute the bedrock of culture."

In her article, "Getting Back to the Heart of Leadership," Lisa Petrilli, CEO of C-Level Strategies, Inc., points out the connection between vision and values: "The leader, whether it be of a country, a religion, the company you work for, or the company you're creating, is responsible for setting and clearly communicating a vision of where the organization is headed under their leadership, and the values to which members will be held accountable. Thus the heart of your leadership beats with the passion of your vision and the conviction of your values."

Core values are prominently posted on walls at most corporate offices for all to see, but will be assessed as meaningless unless those values are inculcated into the hearts and minds and behavior of the people in the organization and reinforced through celebrations. I've noticed in my leadership consulting practice that great organizations take every opportunity to celebrate their values and thereby reinforce them and their vision. Contemporary society faces a significant challenge of leadership immorality that requires nothing less than a moral renaissance.

Douglas MacArthur, an American five-star general and Field Marshal of the Philippine Army, encouraged leaders to always take the high ground: "Moral courage, the courage of one's convictions, the courage to see things through. The world is in a constant conspiracy against the brave. It is the age-old struggle—the roar of the crowd on one side and the voice of your conscience on the other."

Heretics build and develop within their movements a common core and a common connection.

8.2 A COMMON CONNECTION

"Connection is why we're here," declares Brené Brown. "We are hardwired to connect with others. It's what gives purpose and meaning to our lives, and without it there is suffering."

Heretics embrace the concept and practice of a common connection. Jan Bruce, a health and wellness media entrepreneur and contributor to *Forbes*, in an article titled, "Mequilibrium," offers insight into connection: "Meaningful work comes from one of the building blocks of resilience: connection. When you believe what you do has a positive purpose in the world, you are connected to your values, to your ideals. You are likely connected to a group of people whose lives you somehow want to make better. You are a part of a long line of others who worked in this field or in this manner, and you're connected to all those who will build on your contribution."

The connection between work and how it serves the human family plays an important role in every generation, but especially among Millennials, who believe it's cool to care. They deliberately seek out employment that has a set of cultural values that permeates every aspect of the organization's life and work and complements their own. The organization must declare and demonstrate a "why" for its existence or they'll simply leave for another opportunity. "Throughout our research on Millennials over the years," remarked Roxanne Stone, Editor-in-Chief at the Barna Group, "we've seen them demonstrate a consistent desire to make an impact in the world." Millennials don't just want to pay their bills but want to work with a team devoted to a cause bigger than themselves.

A Stanford research project asked nearly 400 Americans whether they thought their lives were either happy or meaningful, or both. The dissonance, in part, was how the two groups approach social interactions. Happiness is associated with being a 'taker.' Meaningfulness, in contrast, comes from being a 'giver,' suspending what one wants and desires for a fair amount of self-sacrifice. In other words, to amplify meaning at work, we must temper our 'taking' tendencies and dial up our acts of giving. Meaning is premised on an entirely different way of interacting, that is, giving to others in service of the greater good.

Heretics solidify a common connection among members of their movements. They create the environment and the social context to connect with one another. Adam Grant confirms this strategy: "Meaning is made in moments, and what matters most is the people we create those moments with."

For example, at Pixar Animation Studios, an American computer animation film studio based in Emeryville, California, and a subsidiary of The Walt Disney Company, all employees are called filmmakers whether they work as a night watchman, receptionist, or animator. And if you work at Pixar, and have a child born during the making of a movie, they get credit too in the "Production Babies" list. People have been known to induce labor for such an honor.

Psychologist Mihaly Csikszentmihalyi maintains that "creativity does not happen in people's heads" but in the interaction between a person's imagination and a social context. That's why heretics connect people to each other and to a common future in an adventure to realize an impossible dream. Seth Godin, marketing guru, and author of *Tribes: We Need You to Lead Us*, describes what he calls our "post-industrial connection economy," in which we're invited and stretched in whatever we do to be artists and create in ways that matter to other people.

A robust common connection results in working together as collaborative partners. Patricia Martin, in her book *Renaissance Generation: The Rise of the Cultural Consumer—And What It Means to Your Business*, indicates that collaboration is the new model of connection. A white paper authored by Cap Gemini, a worldwide consulting practice, put it this way: "Collaborative working is perhaps the single most important factor in achieving competitive advantage and long-term success for organizations."

Heretics create a common connection within their movements by supporting three strategies: all for one-another, the team as hero, and corporate spirit.

All For One-Another

"There are no passengers on Spaceship Earth," noted Marshall McLuhan. "We are all crew."

Heretics create a common connection that mirrors the slogan of the famous Three Musketeers: "One for all and all for one." With respect, I've adapted their slogan for heretics who follow the primary principle of interdependence. The "all for one-another" theme resonates with the African spirit of *ubuntu* where a person is a person only through other persons. Desmond Mpilo Tutu writes extensively about this concept in his book *God Is Not a Christian and Other Provocations*. "Ubuntu," Tutu informs us, "is the essence of being human. It speaks of how my humanity is caught up and bound up inextricably with yours. It says, not as Descartes did, 'I think, therefore I am' but rather, 'I am because I belong.' I need other human beings in order to be human."

William Barclay, a Scottish author and Professor of Divinity and Biblical Criticism at the University of Glasgow, advised, "Always give without remembering and always receive without forgetting." That's exactly what LaSalle Street Church in Chicago did when it received $1.6 million from a real estate deal, and with the leadership its Pastor, Laura Truax, it divided 10 percent of the windfall, $160,000, a typical 10 percent tithe, among the 320 regular attendees. Each attendee received a $500 check to do something positive for anything or anyone, including themselves. Pastor Truax commented, "I hoped that they would recognize the power they had to bless others and change somebody's life." Although she admits that the measure was an unorthodox gesture, she confirmed that LaSalle is "a gutsy little church" with a history of making waves around socially progressive causes it embraces. Sounds a bit like something the heretic Jesus would cheer.

A Chinese proverb says an invisible red thread connects those destined to meet, despite the time, despite the place, despite the circumstances. The thread can be tightened or tangled, but never be broken. Heretics form that kind of lasting connection, living and breathing all for one-another. How wonderfully magical it is to encounter people with this "invisible red thread" despite time, place, or circumstance.

I have experienced this connection with my dear friend Vince Radzik. In the early nineties, I received a telephone call from Vince, a Vice President at the Ford Motor Credit Company headquartered in Dearborn, Michigan. He indicated that the President of the company had heard me make a speech in Toronto and had asked him to engage me for a speech at an upcoming conference. Part of my research involved me going to meet with Vince in Dearborn. I did meet with him and in the course of our conversation he indicated we would be having lunch with the President. The lunch turned into a leadership-coaching contract with the President. I also travelled with Vince to various locations of the company and got to appreciate him and meet his wife, Fran, and their children. I performed the wedding of one of Vince and Fran's daughters. Time passed and we kept in touch. Another daughter of theirs, Patti, who attended a church in Birmingham, Michigan, connected me with Melody, an associate pastor of her church who shortly thereafter became my wife. And in November 2016, I attended Vince and Fran's sixtieth wedding anniversary where they greeted me like a member of their family. The "invisible red thread" will never be broken.

Let's move on to consider another dynamic of a common connection: the team as hero.

The Team As Hero

"Individual commitment to a group effort," noted Vince Lombardi, "that is what makes a team work, a company work, a society work, a civilization work." Winston Churchill offered a similar perspective: "If we are together, nothing is impossible. If we are divided, all will fail."

Heretics commit themselves to the team's vision, mission, and drive, and to the team members with an attitude trumpeted by Harry S. Truman, who framed this concept of the team as hero with these words: "It is amazing what you can accomplish if you do not care who gets the credit." When I was in high school, I played football with a team that modelled Truman's spirit of the team getting the credit. I must admit that it helped that we never lost a game. Our coach encouraged each player to contribute to the team to the best of his ability.

In his classic book on leadership, *Leading Minds: An Anatomy of Leadership*, Howard Gardner, a developmental psychologist and the John H. and Elisabeth A. Hobbs Professor of Cognition and Education at the Harvard Graduate School of Education at Harvard University, identified four factors crucial to the practice of effective leadership: a tie to the community, a certain rhythm of life, an evident relation between stories and embodiments, and a centrality of choice. Heretics enjoy the integration of Gardner's four factors with their commitment to the team as hero. So do hospital Emergency Room teams who flexibly perform their respective tasks in life and death circumstances. They calmly and singularly focus their activities on the welfare of the patient.

An African proverb summarizes and celebrates the common connection of the team as hero: "When spider webs unite they can entangle a lion." Heretics also create a common connection by attending to a movement's corporate soul.

Corporate Soul

"A sure sign of a soul-based workplace is excitement, enthusiasm, real passion; not manufactured passion, but real involvement. And there's very little fear," writes David Whyte, an English poet and author of *Crossing the Unknown Sea: Work as a Pilgrimage of Identity.*

While the concept of a corporate soul may be considered religious, as is the case with ServiceMaster, as I'll refer to later, it may also be legitimately understood within a spiritual or secular framework. However, one should always use caution when mixing religion with anything. As William Penn Adair "Will" Rogers, an American cowboy, vaudeville performer, and social commentator reminds us, "Mixing politics and religion is like mixing manure and ice cream. It doesn't do much to the manure, but it surely does ruin the ice cream." When I'm on the speaking circuit, I'm very careful about my role and don't present as a theologian but from the perspective of a life and leadership coach.

In the lobby of the headquarters of ServiceMaster in Downers Grove, Illinois, one can see a curving marble wall that stretches ninety feet and stands eighteen feet tall. Carved prominently in the stone of that wall, in letters nearly a foot high, are four statements that constitute the objectives of the company: "To honor God in all we do, to help people develop, to pursue excellence and to grow profitably." C. William Pollard, the former CEO of ServiceMaster, reported, "Few people find fault with our commitment to a set of principles. Quite frankly, it is the 'God language' that raises eyebrows."

Mark Pagel, an evolutionary biologist, explores in his book, *Wired for Culture: Origins of the Human Social Mind*, how culture and biology have intertwined to create modern human beings with shared ways of thinking and learning that result in a sense of kinship among those who are part of our culture, and created a feeling of otherness toward those who are not. Pagel observed, "What our history has demonstrated is that we humans will get along with anyone who wishes to play the cooperative game with us. Our received culture is more like software than hardware."

Simon Sinek, author of *Leaders Eat Last: Why Some Teams Pull Together and Others Don't*, expresses a similar sentiment: "It is not the work we remember with fondness, but the camaraderie, how the group came together to get things done." Heretics engender and celebrate the collective soul in their movements—a spirit, a palpable pulse, and an undefinable bonding that connects one to another and to the world. Together, they create a common culture with a common core, connection, and cause.

8.3 A COMMON CAUSE

Heretics agree with Jamie Dimon, the CEO of JP Morgan Chase, who claimed, "Leaders demand loyalty, not to themselves but to the cause for which they stand."

Heretics discover their own personal passion that provides a foundation for enabling others to discover their collective passion for helping others. They rise to the major challenge of igniting and aligning the various passions of followers to row together in the same direction at the same time for the same common cause. C. William Pollard recognized, "People want to work for a cause, not just for a living."

We're wired to seek and connect with a common cause. As human beings, we yearn for a vital cause to support for the benefit of ourselves and others. Perhaps it is nature's way of helping us bond together for the sake of the human family to survive and thrive. Millennials certainly are attuned to a common cause and are positively responsive to cause marketing. Upon this foundation I wrote *The Compassionate Conspiracy*, to help Millennials discover what needs to be done in the world, to dream of how they could fulfill that need, and then have the dedication to deliver on their promises. Heretics who come together around a common cause can produce incredible results.

Wharton marketing professor Americus Reed, in his article, "The New Philanthropists: More Sophisticated, More Demanding—and Younger," identifies a significant shift in the business community: "Business is almost trying to rebrand itself. I'm seeing, institutionally and in terms of overall values individually with the students, that the whole Wall Street crisis caused business schools to reevaluate their own priorities and tell a different story. It's okay to make money—but also, give back. You don't go to Wharton, get a job on Wall Street, then go to work for a hedge fund and retire at 40. That whole MO (modus operandi) is out the window." Whatever the driver, some say the concept of giving has become a part of the core of identity. Reed notes, "Students are saying, 'I want to be a captain of industry, but I don't want to be out there just chasing materialistic objects. I need something deeper. I need self-actualization in addition to the materialistic metrics of success in business.'"

Starbucks' "Make Your Own Mark Program" allows employees time off, and in some cases, grants monies to take on socially meaningful pursuits that benefit the community. A Starbucks' spokesperson explained, "We are looking to grow and nurture young baristas. Whether they stay with Starbucks or not, if we encourage them to make things happen through their own initiative, we make the world a better place. We send that talent out there into the world. In the short term, the work of the community is getting done. Long term, we make change in the world."

Dedication

Victor Frankl, Austrian neurologist and psychologist, in his book *Man's Search for Meaning*, articulates the meaning of dedication: "For success, like happiness, cannot be pursued; it must ensue, and it only does so as an unintended consequence of one's personal dedication to a cause greater than oneself."

Gostick and Elton begin their book *All In* with a chapter titled, "Get in the Wheelbarrow." They tell a story about the Great Blondin crossing Niagara Falls pushing a wheelbarrow. About 25,000 onlookers turned out on June 30, 1859, to witness the flamboyant, mustached Frenchman step out onto a three-inch cord that stretched across the roaring falls.

Before he started, Blondin asked the crowd, "Do you believe I can cross the falls with this wheelbarrow?"

"Yes!" they yelled as one.

"Wonderful," he said. "Then who will get in?"

Many in the crowd laughed but then fell silent as they realized he wasn't joking. Then Blondin's agent, Harry Colcord, took off his silk top hat and waved it high above his head and volunteered. A few months later, Blondin carried Colcord across the falls on his shoulders.

Relatively few of the leaders and managers I've encountered in my consulting business know how to engage and energize their followers to get 'all in.' Gostick and Elton comment on energizing others through dedication: "This book is clearly not about daredevils or tightrope walkers, but about a related drama that is taking place in organizations every day, all around the world. While most managers by now understand that their most reliable competitive advantage comes though their people, few of them actually know how to get their people 'all in'—convincing employees to truly buy into their ideas and the strategy they've put forward, to give that extra push that leads to outstanding results." Heretics accept the task of inspiring their followers to get 'all in.'

I personally know two women in their twenties who chose a higher purpose and invited others to get 'all in,' to support an annual event, "Nana's Run," to raise funds to find a cure for amyotrophic lateral sclerosis (ALS), a progressive neurodegenerative disease that affects nerve cells in the brain and the spinal cord. The progressive degeneration of the motor neurons in ALS eventually leads to death. ALS was first found in 1869 by French neurologist Jean-Martin Charcot, but it wasn't until 1939 that Lou Gehrig brought national and international attention to the disease. These two women experienced first-hand the excruciating pain and suffering of the disease that claimed the life of their beloved grandmother, and now unselfishly dedicate themselves to their dream of a cure.

Heretics dedicate themselves and their followers to a common cause with laser-like focus. They recognize, as Martin Luther King Jr. did, that "Human progress is neither automatic nor inevitable … Every step toward the goal of justice requires sacrifice, suffering, and struggle; the tireless exertions and passionate concern of dedicated individuals."

Focus

Dear Polio,

We have bad news for you. Very, very, very bad news.
Today we stand extremely close to eliminating you.
We still have more work to do, but we'll get there.
Someday, we'll live in a world where you no longer exist.
So prepare to exit stage left.

Adios. Ciao, Au revoir. Sayonara. Toodles. Goodbye.

Sincerely,

Rotary

This open letter to "Polio," which appeared on the cover of the September 2015 edition of *The Rotarian*, reveals the sharp focus of Rotary International and its partners to eradicate the disease. On April 12, 2015, the world celebrated the sixtieth anniversary of Jonas Salk's discovery of a vaccine for polio, the contagious crippling virus.

"The very job of leaders," points out Morten T. Hansen, in his book *Collaboration*, "is to unite people to pursue a common goal." Gary Hamel adds, "A noble purpose inspires sacrifice, stimulates innovation, and encourages perseverance." Heretics focus their collective gifts and energy on their common cause with razor-like accuracy.

At corporate meetings, Amazon founder Jeff Bezos likes to make sure one chair is kept empty to represent the customer, "the most important person in the room." That focus on the customer gives Amazon the confidence to innovate freely without fretting about the short-term results. "We don't focus on the optics of the next quarter; we focus on what is going to be good for customers," he explains. "This aspect of our culture is rare."

In *Up and Out of Poverty: The Social Marketing Solution*, my friend and legendary marketing expert, Philip Kotler, along with Nancy Lee, write their dedication to the poor, the focus of their mission: "To the four billion poor in our world, and to those working to help them achieve a better life." They consider poverty from a radically different and powerfully new viewpoint—that of the marketer.

Murray Gell-Mann, in "The Quark and the Jaguar," observed, "History shows us clearly that humanity is moved forward not by people who stop every little while to try to gauge the ultimate success or failure of their ventures, but by those who think deeply about what is right and then put all their energy into doing it."

La Yapa

My wife and I recently enjoyed a wonderful tour of Ecuador where our tour guide extraordinaire, Marcello, introduced us to "*La Yapa*," an Ecuadorian expression for giving "something extra." For example, when we stopped for a break, Marcello would buy twelve pieces of sugar cane for his guests and point out that he received thirteen, one extra, one more than expected. This tradition of generosity mirrors the motto of the country: *Ama la vida*, which means "Love life."

I've subsequently observed that persons, families, businesses, and organizations with a *La Yapa* orientation offer themselves unselfishly with no expectation of getting something in return. Fortunately, I grew up in a family that encouraged giving generously of oneself for the other. The idea took root and when I was four years old, I received for Christmas an Indian rubber ball and gave it to my friend Billy who didn't have one.

Apparently, *La Yapa* appears to be contagious, because on another trip, to the Republic of Ireland, we encountered a similar "something extra" with a difference in accent. We arrived in the small quaint town of Portarlington, checked into our hotel, and went searching for a place to have dinner. We searched with no success, until we saw two people sitting at a small table outside an upscale restaurant named The Candied Walnut.

We asked them where they would suggest we find a place to eat and they responded that everything in the town was closed. As we started walking away, Barry Hayden, the owner and head chef of the restaurant that had just opened five weeks before, called out to us: "Don't you know, we're closed. But you're welcome to come in and take your chances. We sure don't want you to leave hungry." So we accepted his gracious invitation and enjoyed a fabulous dinner consisting of butternut squash soup, Haik (like cod), beef and mushroom potpie in red wine sauce, and a sumptuous calorie-loaded desert.

Healthy corporations improve the lives of their employees, suppliers, customers, as well as their local and global community. It's part of their corporate DNA. For example, the Amway Corporation, a global leader in health and beauty, based in Ada, Michigan, reaches out at home and abroad with its *La Yapa* vision: to help people live better lives and create positive change in people's lives around the world.

Emma Winter, a faithful and gracious woman in her nineties, and whose generosity has supported our mission to feed children in Kibera Slum in Nairobi, included with her monthly check a note that read, "A drop of water in the desert!" It reminded me of the way Saint Teresa once described her mission: "We ourselves feel that what we are doing is just a drop in the ocean. But the ocean would be less because of that missing drop."

John Wesley wrote the Rule of Conduct to guide his people called Methodists, and inspires heretics today to create a common culture.

Do all the good you can,
By all the means you can,
In all the ways you can,
In all the places you can,
At all the times you can,
To all the people you can,
As long as ever you can.

CHAPTER 9

Exploit Potential

"If you're not uncomfortable in your work as a leader," observed Seth Godin, in his book *Tribes: We Need You to Lead Us*, "it's almost certain you're not reaching your potential as a leader." Let's take a look at how heretics exploit potential within their movements.

The word 'potential' derives from the Latin *potens*, which means "power." At birth, we bring into the world a constellation of power to accept graciously and exploit to make a positive impact in society. Max De Pree says, "No question about it: potential is wrapped in great mystery. Like rainbows, which are really circles—we see only the upper halves, the horizon hides the rest—potential never reveals its entirety ... A place of realized potential opens itself to change, to contrary opinion, to the mystery of potential, to involvement, to unsettling ideas."

One of the world's leading researchers in the field of motivation, Carol S. Dweck, conducts research on why people succeed and how to foster success. The Oxford American Dictionary defines mindset as "an established set of attitudes held by someone." However, according to Dweck, a set of attitudes needn't be so set. She proposes that everyone has either a fixed mindset or a growth mindset. A fixed mindset is one in which you view your talents and abilities as fixed. In other words, you are who you are, your intelligence and talents are fixed, and your fate is to go through life avoiding challenge and failure. A growth mindset, on the other hand, is one in which you see yourself as fluid, a work in progress. Your fate is one of growth and opportunity. I wish our son, Tim, had met her. Mid-way through high school, he had an interesting insight: "Dad, I think I might have too much potential."

Heretics exploit potential. Although people often use the word 'exploit' to convey a negative connotation, to make use of selfishly or unethically, I choose to use it in the derivative sense from the Latin *explicare*, which means "to unfold, fully utilize, or to employ to the greatest possible advantage." Potential, even when used in minimal ways, exerts a significant influence. From small beginnings, movements can influence others and produce remarkable results.

"Jesus had the uncanny ability to look at everyone with grace-filled eyes," Philip Yancey, author of *Vanishing Grace: Whatever Happened to the Good News?* observed, "seeing not only the beauty of who they were but also the sacred potential of what they could become." Apparently, persons responsible for leadership development could take a cue from Jesus in the true spirit of education derived from the Latin *educo*, which means "to lead out." Great leaders embrace the presupposition that their principal role involves exploiting the potential, "leading out" what is already naturally inside their followers.

Heretics exploit pockets of potential to realize their impossible dreams. They energize their followers by being present, by inviting members of the movement to get to play, and celebrating who they are and who they may become.

9.1 BE PRESENT

"I've learned that people will forget what you said, people will forget what you did," said Maya Angelou, "but people will never forget how you made them feel."

The heretic freely gives her or his passionate purposeful presence, derived from the Greek *praesens*, which means "to be in the presence of, or to stand before."The very act of being present to one another represents the ultimate connection of persons in the human family, as well as the definitive act of leadership. In fact, heretics exhaust their gift of presence by being aware, involved, and responsive.

In wide-ranging conversations held over a year and a half, Peter Senge, Otto Scharmer, Joseph Jaworski, and Betty Sue Flowers explored the nature of transformational change: how it arises, and the fresh possibilities it offers a world dangerously out of balance. Their book, *Presence: Human Purpose and the Field of the Future*, introduces the idea of presence, a concept borrowed from the natural world, that the whole is present in any of its parts, to the worlds of business, education, government, and leadership.

By encouraging deeper levels of learning, the authors contend, we create an awareness of the larger whole, leading to actions that can help to shape its evolution and our future. *Presence* is both revolutionary in its exploration and hopeful in its message. It defines the capabilities that underlie our ability to see, sense, and realize new possibilities in ourselves, in our institutions, and in society itself. I have a deep appreciation for the insight of these authors because my doctoral thesis explored the concept and practice of presence in the context of community.

One cannot overestimate the power of executive presence. In a *Financial Post* article, "'Executive presence' makes a strong leader," Jim Murray, the CEO of Optimal Solutions International, and architect of Becoming CEO, a professional development program for senior executives, discusses the risk leaders take when they don't cultivate this characteristic: "Having a career as a CEO is a risky business. Over the past decade, the rate of dismissals has increased by 300% and turnover exceeds the normal attrition rate for all employees. Forced exits from the C-suite occur for a multitude of reasons ranging from poor cultural fit to misaligned skill sets. At least 40% flame out in their first 18 months. The primary reason, not surprisingly, is under-performance that amounts for a third of all departures. The second reason, perhaps surprisingly, is lack of 'executive presence,' CEOs who neither act nor look like a leader.

"In essence, presence is knowing what to do when others around you don't have a clue. You're not born with it; it's a learned skill. When you possess executive presence, you're more likely to get to the top and stay there longer than most. This secret sauce is knowing how to think on your feet, project poise under extreme pressure, take control of difficult situations, make tough decisions in a timely manner and hold your own with other talented, strong-willed members of the executive team."

When you think of leaders you've encountered with an authentic sense of 'executive presence,' who comes to mind? For me, a few stand out and I consider myself fortunate to have met them face-to-face: the Dalai Lama; Coretta Scott King; Dr. Nido Qubein, President of Highpoint University in North Carolina; Pierre Trudeau, former Prime Minister of Canada, Jennifer Mulhern Granholm, former Governor of the State of Michigan; Ron Tschetter, former Director of the United States Peace Corps; Wayne Gretzky; Rich DeVos, co-founder of Amway; and my mother, Mary Anne Sawyer Johnson.

Heretics recognize the importance of their presence in the development of their movements and seize every opportunity to show up, pay attention, and stay in touch.

Show Up

"Eighty percent of success," said Woody Allen, "is just showing up." Maybe he's right. After a keynote speech to the annual meeting of a Fortune 100 company meeting, its CEO thanked me for showing up. I wasn't sure what he meant, so I asked him and he replied, "Most of our speakers show up with their canned presentations, but you showed up for us."

Heretics take a proactive rather than a reactive stance toward engagement. They show up intentionally with members of their movements, and when they do, they're fully present in body, mind, and spirit. Personal presence may be difficult to define, but you know it when you see it. People with presence look confident and comfortable, speak clearly and persuasively, and think clearly, even under pressure. They act with intention and integrity. What they say and do matches who they really are.

After a trip to Africa, I experienced the influence of showing up at an appointment with an infectious diseases specialist a month earlier than the arranged time. The receptionist told me that I got the wrong date, and I responded that if it was alright, I'd just wait for a cancellation. I explained that when someone did cancel, all she had to do was open the window to the waiting room and point at me. I'd save the practice time and money too. So I waited and met some interesting folks. The next morning at 10:15, the receptionist opened the window, pointed at me, and smiled.

In their role, heretics get to play their authentic selves to serve their organization and advance others, while avoiding the traps of self-promotion along the way. Mastering the art of authenticity may not always get you applause, but it will give you a credible edge as a leader. In a leadership audit of a mid-size company, I asked a long-term employee to comment on the effectiveness of the CEO's monthly visits. His response spoke volumes: "I really appreciate him coming, but when he comes, he's always at his next meeting." The message for heretics: be totally present here and now in body, mind, and soul.

"Engaging authentically with those around you," advises Margie Warrell, an internationally recognized leader in human potential, and passionate about empowering people to think bigger about what is possible for them, "is the first task of genuine leadership … Leadership is far less about what you are doing, than about who you are being. Ultimately, a leader is not judged so much by how well he or she leads, but by how well he or she serves. No carrot or stick of any size will ever trump the effect you have on those around you when you engage with them from a place of genuine service."

Heretics show up with all their humanness, warts and all. Walter

Wangerin Jr., in his book *The Manger is Empty*, tells the story called "Matthew, Seven, Eight, and Nine," about how he tried to stop his son Matthew from stealing comic books. He tried various uses of the law over several years and continued to fail. Finally, Wangerin resorted to something he rarely used: a spanking. He did it deliberately, almost ritualistically, and he was so upset when he finished that he left the room and wept. After pulling himself back together, he went in to Matthew and hugged him. A number of years later, Matthew and his mother were doing some general reminiscing, and Matthew happened to bring up the time when he kept stealing comic books.

"And you know why I finally stopped?" he asked.

"Sure," she said, "because Dad finally spanked you."

"No!" replied Matthew, "No, because Dad cried."

American writer Edith Wharton observes, "There are two ways of spreading light: to be the candle or the mirror that reflects it." Heretics show up and let their light shine.

Pay Attention

"A human moment occurs any time two or more people are together," says Edward M. Hallowell, a psychiatrist and author of *Driven to Distraction*, "paying attention to one another."

Heretics not only show up, they also pay attention. Unlike some leaders who constantly scan a cocktail reception for "more important" conversations, they make their live connections count by focusing on others as a sign of genuine respect. Comfortable in their own skin, they reach out and care for others, and lay a solid foundation for rich dialogue where hearts, minds, and souls can meet and contribute to each other.

Wise leaders take time to connect with people they might need to influence before they need them. They encourage others, take them seriously, convey they care about them, and remain open and available to them here and now. Theodore Roosevelt once observed, "People don't care how much you know until they know how much you care."

"The principal form that the work of love takes is attention," commented psychiatrist Dr. Scott Peck, author of *The Road Less Traveled: A New Psychology of Love, Traditional Values and Spiritual Growth*. "When we love another we give him or her our attention; we attend to that person's growth." Pier Massimo Forni, author of *The Thinking Life: How to Thrive in the Age of Distraction*, believes, "Comprising our faculties of awareness and focus, attention is the very bedrock of thinking. As an enabler of moderation, attention becomes in the words of Epictetus a handmaiden to wisdom. Together with willpower, attention is the top building block of the fully engaged life."

In most human interactions, attention leads to respect, thoughtfulness, and honesty. Heretics who don't pay attention to their followers miss an opportunity to build lasting trusting relationships. Inattention can have disastrous consequences, so they listen actively and connect with others' purpose and passion. They mentally and physically focus all their faculties, and lean in. As a young teenage Boy Scout in uniform, in Kitchener, Ontario, Canada, I can vividly remember standing along the parade route to catch a glimpse of Queen Elizabeth II.

Franklin Roosevelt, who often endured long receiving lines at the White House, allegedly once complained that no one really paid any attention to what was said. One day, during a reception, he decided to try an experiment. To each person who passed down the line and shook his hand, he murmured, "I murdered my grandmother this morning." The guests responded with phrases like, "Marvelous! Keep up the good work. We are proud of you. God bless you, sir." It was not till the end of the line, while greeting the ambassador from Bolivia, that his words were actually heard. Nonplussed, the ambassador leaned over and whispered, "I'm sure she had it coming."

My grandfather Johnson taught me a valuable lesson when he told me, "It's not what you say, it's what they hear that's important." He certainly modeled for me attentive listening with integrity.

Stay In Touch

Winnie the Pooh recommends, "You can't stay in your corner of the forest waiting for others to come to you. You have to go to them sometimes." Heretics practice leadership executive presence; they authentically show up, pay attention, and stay in touch with members of their movements.

"In the most innovative companies, there is a significantly higher volume of thank-yous than in companies of low innovation," observed Rosabeth Moss Kanter, Professor of Business at the Harvard Business School. In fact, research shows that saying "thank you" creates oxytocin, a powerful hormone, which makes people happier and more productive.

Campbell's former CEO, Doug Conant, stayed in touch by sending up to twenty handwritten notes a day to employees celebrating their successes and contributions. "I was trained to find the busted number in a spreadsheet and identify things that are going wrong," he said. "Most cultures don't do a good job of celebrating contributions. So I developed the practice of writing notes to our employees. Over 10 years, it amounted to more than 30,000 notes, and we had only 20,000 employees. Wherever I'd go in the world, in employee cubicles you'd find my handwritten notes posted on their bulletin boards."

Conant's notes were not gratuitous. They celebrated specific contributions. And because the notes were handwritten, they seemed to be treasured more than an email message might be. He shows how important sending authentic messages with a personal touch can be. Conant co-authored a book on the subject, *TouchPoints: Creating Powerful Leadership Connections in the Smallest of Moments*.

My mother taught me the principle of courtesy that Conant practiced. She encouraged me to send a thank-you note to persons who invited me to a birthday party or gave me a gift at Christmas. I followed her counsel and have ever since sent postcards to friends, family, and business associates. At the retirement of a CEO I had coached, he took me to his office, opened a desk drawer, and showed me bound with an elastic band, the cards that

I had sent him from across the globe. Thanks for the advice, Mom.

Heretics send signature communications to stay in touch that affirm and confirm their personal connection and build relationships and trust often lasting a lifetime. They recognize the importance of being here and now when that's possible, but also of being there and then, to stay in touch in virtual reality. Research indicates that superb leaders develop their "remote viewing" skills, critical for those who have associates in several international locations.

In an age of technological advancement, we have a myriad of communication channels from which to choose including e-mail, Facebook, Snapchat, and Instagram. Although they may not have an impact of a handwritten note, electronic communications still fulfill the intention of staying in touch. But here's a word of warning to "save face."

Heretics stay in touch by several means, one of which is leaving a trail of tangibles. I learned about this practice of generosity and memorable communication from my friend, Dr. Nido Qubein, the President of High Point University and Chair of Harvest Bread Company. One Valentine's Day, he sent me a gift of a ten-pound chocolate bar. That I'm telling you about his gift offers proof the practice works. And twenty of my friends who each received a half-pound of delicious chocolate still remember the ceremony where we divided "The Bar."

9.2 LET'S GET TO PLAY

"You're only given a little spark of madness," said the late actor and comedian Robin Williams. "You mustn't lose it."

Heretics recognize play as an essential dimension of everyday work, and create a playful environment that legitimizes and gives permission to play on the job. Secure in themselves to model an attitude of play, they encourage associates and others to play. They understand play as a state of mind rather than an activity and that human beings are wired for play by nature's design.

Organizations bring life to work and work to life through play that honors the child in all of us. Friedrich Nietzsche commented, "The struggle of maturity is to recover the seriousness of a child at play." The research clearly indicates that when work and play coexist as collaborative partners, especially in what we call the "work environment," outstanding performance results.

British historian, Arnold Toynbee, commented, "The supreme accomplishment is to blur the line between work and play." This Zen Buddhist text affirms Toynbee's perspective: "The Master in the art of living makes little distinction between his work and his play, his labor and his leisure, his mind and his body, his education and his recreation, his love and his religion. He hardly knows which is which. He simply pursues his vision of excellence in whatever he does, leaving others to decide whether he is working or playing. To him he is always doing both."

Let me describe the seven common characteristics I've observed in coaching healthy CEOs who epitomize this blurring of work and play.

1. They do what they love and love what they do.
2. They practice presence and patience.
3. They balance effort and rest for peak performance.
4. They foster loving relationships with family and friends.
5. They consider leading a privilege and a responsibility.
6. They treat their associates with respect and compassion.
7. They possess a sense of humor and laugh naturally.

If you only read one book on play, consider *Play: How It Shapes Our Brain, Opens the Imagination and Invigorates the Soul*, by Stuart Brown and Christopher Vaughan. Brown, a psychiatrist and leading expert on the science of play and its essential role in fueling our happiness and intelligence throughout our lives, asserts: "Lifelong play is central to our continued well-being, adaptation and social cohesiveness." By definition, play is purposeless, all consuming, and fun, but as Brown illustrates, play is anything but trivial. We are designed by nature to flourish through play with a biological drive as integral to our health as sleep or nutrition. Play, as he studies it, is an indispensable part of being human, and through play, heretics can learn empathy, trust, irony, and problem solving.

Dr. Brown has spent his career studying animal behavior and conducting more than 6,000 "play histories" of humans from all walks of life—from serial murderers to Nobel Prize winners. Backed by the latest research, *Play* explains why play is essential to our social skills, adaptability, intelligence, creativity, and more. Particularly in tough times, we need to play more than ever, because it's the very means by which we prepare for the unexpected, search out new solutions, and remain optimistic. Play just might be the most important work we can ever do. Play promotes true intellectual curiosity. It has been shown to increase lifetime performance just as adequate recess time leads to increased long-term academic accomplishments.

Heretics create the playful conditions for members to write drunk and edit sober, invent with "improv," and "flexperiment." So, let's play!

Write Drunk And Edit Sober

I live in Grand Rapids, Michigan, voted Beer City USA in national polls and named Best Beer Town and Best Beer Scene by *USA TODAY* readers in 2016. Grand Rapids commends itself as the perfect place for your next "beercation." Our Beer City Ale Trail boasts over forty breweries—that's more incredible craft beer per square mile than just about anywhere else on earth.

Please note that I'm not encouraging the consumption of alcoholic beverages to get drunk, but simply offering an uninhibited metaphor. Heretics know that in order to discover meaning, find solutions, develop strategic thinking and insight, they need to model relaxed intensity. When people relax at play, a whole new world of imagination emerges. I compare it to experiencing vibrant colorful action night dreams, the effect of taking certain medications to prevent malaria when I travel, particularly in Africa. I could hardly wait to go to sleep.

Many of my university students despise writing assignments. To them, I'm the reckless arbiter of curses. So I try to ease their pain slightly by quoting novelist John Irving, when he said, "The reason I can work so hard at my writing is that it's not work for me." They feel no relief. So I quote comedian Steven Wright: "I'm writing a book. I've got the page numbers done, so now I just have to fill in the rest." Even with humor, there's only a faint chuckle. Then I recommend that they write drunk and edit sober. And they cheer wildly—mostly at the former. I encourage them to splash their first draft on the page and express their research with reckless abandon, to let their unconscious stimulate their consciousness. First, the splashing. Then, the editing. Sounds like a Dr. Seuss book for first-year college students. Some do much better with the splashing than the editing. Great editors are worth their weight in gold.

"Despite a lack of natural ability," expressed actor Steve Martin, "I did have the one element necessary to all early creativity: naiveté, that fabulous quality that keeps you from knowing just how unsuited you are for what you are about to do." Playful relaxed intensity encourages humor that requires a turn of phrase, an unlikely consequence, or an image that tickles the funny bone. "Imagine, if you will, that I am an idiot. Then, imagine that I am also a Congressman," commented humorist Mark Twain. "But, alas, I repeat myself."

Here's how Dr. Seuss appreciated life: "I like nonsense. It wakes up the brain cells. Fantasy is a necessary ingredient in living. It's a way of looking at life through the wrong end of a telescope. Which is what I do. And that enables you to laugh at life's realities."

So raise a stein of creativity brew to St. Jude, the Saint of Hopeless Cases, and leave the rest to your editor.

Invent With Improv

"Leadership is an improvisational art," observed Heifetz and Linsky. "You may have an overarching vision, clear, orienting values, and even a strategic plan, but what you do from moment to moment cannot be scripted."

One night, the great jazz trumpeter Wynton Marsalis was playing a gig at the small Village club in New York. He was playing the soulful, mournful ballad "I Don't Stand a Ghost of a Chance with You." At the song's most heart-rending point, a cell phone rang. After a few seconds, Marsalis, without missing a beat, picked up the tune of the cell phone's ring and incorporated it into the song he was playing. He performed variations on it, blending it with what he planned to play, and then drew the whole ballad back to the original theme. Marsalis transformed an interruption into a memorable moment. That's what great musicians do. And that's what good heretics do too.

Josh Linkner, author of *Disciplined Dreaming: A Proven System to Drive Breakthrough Creativity*, and also a talented jazz musician, describes improvisation as "a spontaneous burst of creativity, and to keep the tempo brisk, this book gives a nod to many of the strong and sometimes surprising links between improvisational jazz and business innovation."

"Those who have used music metaphors to describe working together, especially jazz metaphors, are sensing the nature of this quantum world," remarked Margaret J. Wheatley, author of *Leadership and the New Science: Discovering Order in a Chaotic World*. She adds, "This world demands that we be present together, and be willing to improvise. We agree on the melody, tempo, and key, and then we play. We listen carefully, we communicate constantly, and suddenly, there is music, possibilities beyond anything we have imagined."

In an article, "Yes, and: How Improvisation Reverses 'No, but' Thinking and Improves Creativity and Collaboration," Kelly Leonard and Tom Yorton make the connection between improv and business: "We think the skills you need to be successful in business are really the skills that good improvisers have. The ability to create something out of nothing; work well on teams; be nimble and adaptive; deal with failure; be comfortable working in an interactive way where you're co-creating material."

Improv acts as a catalyst for imagination, creativity, and innovation. Watch Second City, the famous Chicago-based improv troupe, or the

TV program, *Whose Line Is It Anyway?* and you'll note the tension that stimulates creativity among the actors. Note that the word 'tension' derives from the Latin *tendere,* which means "to stretch." Improv also produces flexibility, the handmaiden of creativity, often with the element of surprise. "Movement play lights up the brain and fosters learning, innovation, flexibility, adaptability, and resilience," claims Stuart Brown.

Virginia Postrel, author of *The Future and Its Enemies: The Growing Conflict Over Creativity, Enterprise, and Progress,* highlights the need for improv as we invent our future: "It is in curiosity, problem solving, and play that we discover who we are. These are the very qualities and activities that make the future unknown, and unknowable … The future will be as grand, and as particular, as we are. We cannot build a single bridge from here to there, for neither here nor there is a single point. And there is no abyss to cross."

In my leadership coaching practice, I use improvisational theater to unlock the creative potential and foresight of CEOs and their senior executive teams. It takes a variety of forms from simple role play exercises, to when I'm confident that the experience will stretch the leader's inner capacity to deal with a situation that's a little frightening but also incredibly exhilarating, perform on stage at an improvisational theater. One CEO claimed, "I just about peed my pants but learned more in five minutes on stage than in my MBA degree." I've maintained that business schools ought to make a course in the dramatic arts a requisite for graduation.

Here's an apt description of the heretic from French philosopher, playwright, novelist, and political activist, Jean-Paul Sartre: "On a shattered and deserted stage, without script, director, prompter, or audience, the actor is free to improvise his own part."

"Flexperiment"

"I am concerned about losing our ability to experiment, disrupt the status quo, innovate and rebel," said Hossei Moiin, Chief Technology Officer of Nokia Networks. He's not the only one. Heretics appreciate the value of flexperimenting—a combination of flexibility and experimentation, to flex the creative muscles and watch what happens: a breakthrough, failure, and always learning. Life is an experiment and we don't know at the beginning how it's going to work out in the end. For most of us, the simple act of getting in the shower can stimulate flexperimentation of thoughts and ideas.

"When you view leadership as an experiment," Heifetz, Linsky, and Grashow point out, "you free yourself to see any change initiative as an educated guess, something that you have decided to try but that does not require you to put an immovable stake in the ground." In the midst of the Great Recession, United States President Franklin Roosevelt called for "bold, persistent experimentation." Roosevelt framed his approach with these words: "It is common sense to take a method and try it. If it fails, admit it frankly and try another. But above all, try something."

Hunter Doherty "Patch" Adams, best known for his work as a medical doctor and a clown, also claims the role of heretic, a social activist who has devoted over forty years of his life to changing America's healthcare system. He believes that laughter, joy, and creativity are an integral part of the healing process. With the help of friends, he founded the Gesundheit Institute in 1971, a non-profit healthcare organization. It is a project in holistic medical care based on the belief that one cannot separate the health of the individual from the health of the family, the community, the society, and the world. Their mission is to reframe and reclaim the concept of "hospital." In 2006, Adams founded the Gesundheit Global Outreach (GGO) that encompasses humanitarian clowning missions and aid, educational programs, building projects, and community development around the world. The goal of this work is the improvement of the health of individuals and communities in crisis from sickness, war, poverty, and injustice.

Purposeful leadership coaching can take many forms. I flexperiment especially with the location of our regular half-day monthly meetings.

Effective coaching requires uninterrupted time with a leader. That's difficult in the office setting because corporate offices, although comfortable, don't provide the kind of space that easily evokes creative thinking and interaction. Coaching in a corporate aircraft is preferable but it's impossible to go for a long walk. So I mix it up a little by meeting CEOs at locations away from their offices so we can avoid being distracted but be available in case of emergency.

I introduce "field trips" to places that represent a change from the ordinary office setting and give them a leadership challenge. Research led by David Zald of Vanderbilt University shows that novel behavior triggers the release of dopamine, a chemical that helps keep us motivated and increases innovative creativity. Variety is a marvelous teacher at any age and stage. I've experimented with some success, going on a visit to an art gallery, a museum, or a circus. Watching together a movie like *Frozen* that highlights the need to "Let It Go" proves beneficial. My favorite location is what I call a "Mystery Meeting," where we go on a photo-shoot with a professional photographer like Todd & Brad Reed to emphasize the critical importance of focus when envisioning the future.

Heretics exploit potential by enthusiastically inviting their followers: "Let's get to play."

9.3 CELEBRATE!

"There are two things people want more than sex and money," remarked Mary Kay Ash, founder of Mary Kay Cosmetics, Inc., "recognition and praise." In my research, it appears that a large percentage of workers around the world are starved for recognition.

By celebrating the people and their actions in their movements, heretics keep the spirit of their movement alive and fulfill their members' need for affiliation. The word 'celebrate' derives from the Latin *celebrare*, which means "to keep." Heretics celebrate their progress in pursuit of their impossible dreams and bring the various dimensions of a movement together with ritual and ceremony. Healthy organizations use celebrations to praise the achievement of a particular goal or the significant learning from a failure.

The ALS Association (ALSA) has every reason to celebrate the remarkable success of its Ice Bucket Challenge to raise funds for ALS research. According to the national chapter of the ALSA, the challenge brought in a staggering $115 million. Participants also donated an additional $13 million to the Association's regional branches. Over 3 million donors gave contributions that ranged from under $1 to $200,000.

The challenge spread worldwide on Facebook from the United States to the following countries: Australia, New Zealand, Canada, Mexico, Brazil, Germany, Philippines, Puerto Rico, and India. During that time frame, over 28 million people joined the challenge by posting, commenting, or liking a challenge post, and 2.4 million videos. Celebrities, singers and musicians, sports figures, CEOs, and other business leaders participated, According to data curated by media analyst Jeremiah Owyang, the challenge had then been responsible for around 2.33 million YouTube videos. The success of the Ice Bucket Challenge brought with it another perhaps bigger challenge: How does the Association match or go beyond what the Ice Bucket Challenge achieved? Stay tuned.

Terrence E. Deal and Allan A. Kennedy, authors of *The New Corporate Cultures: Revitalizing the Workplace after Downsizing, Mergers, and Reengineering*, point out that celebrations inspire hope: "Celebrations infuse life with passion and purpose. They summon the human spirit. They bond people together and connect us to shared values and myths. Ceremonies and rituals create community, fusing individual souls with the corporate spirit. When everything is going well, ritual occasions allow us to revel in our glory. When times are tough, ceremonies draw us together, kindling hope and faith that better times lie ahead."

The Herman Trend Alert, in an article, "#1 Engagement Driver, Job Rewards," reported Ceridian's Pulse of Talent Survey that revealed employers risk disengagement and high turnover if they fail to address job rewards and other key drivers. According to the study, 'Job Rewards,' receiving monetary or non-monetary compensation for a job well done ranks as the most important engagement driver for the polled employees as a group. In fact, 47 percent ranked job rewards first, above job recognition (42 percent) and job motivation (11 percent).

The Survey also indicates that once employees are satisfied their pay is fair, they want additional rewards, such as compensatory time off, providing state-of-the-art technology, or free meals. However, it is also vitally important that the type of reward be aligned with what the specific employees value. In other words, reward and recognition programs must be tailored to account for generational differences, individual preferences, and technological innovation. 60 percent of respondents' companies are currently offering non-monetary rewards to their employees.

Oprah Winfrey, the American media proprietor, talk show host, and philanthropist, certainly practices what she preaches: "The more you praise and celebrate your life, the more there is in life to celebrate."

Heretics openly and strategically celebrate the devotion, failure, and success of their members and their movements.

Celebrate Devotion

"Silent gratitude isn't much good to anyone," observed novelist G. B. Stern. And yet, the influence of celebrating devotion can be far-reaching. Mark Twain points out, "I can live for two months on a good compliment."

Heretics understand that they must encourage their followers along the way, especially when the going gets tough. And most heretics can attest that from time to time they do face twists and turns on their way to their collective impossible dream. "Winning is not everything," contended Vince Lombardi, legendary coach of the NFL's Green Bay Packers, "but making the effort to win is." Heretics engage their followers to seek and maintain a healthy perspective on the progress of their movements. Philip Yancey, in his book *What Good is God? In Search of a Faith that Matters*, reveals how Bruno Bettelheim, a survivor of the Holocaust, described three different responses he observed among his fellow inmates. Some simply felt debilitated. A second group put up a shield of denial, attempting to resume life as before. The third, the healthiest group, sought instead to reintegrate with life, incorporating into their "different normal" state, lessons they had learned from the camps.

The Olympic Creed captures the essence of celebrating devotion. Pierre de Coubertin got the idea for the phrase adopted as the Olympic Creed from a speech at a service for Olympic champions during the 1908 Olympic Games given by Bishop Ethelbert Talbot: "The most important thing in the Olympic Games is not to win but to take part, just as the most important thing in life is not the triumph but the struggle. The essential thing is not to have conquered but to have fought well."

I witnessed this Creed lived every day in the efforts of David Guthrie, a friend of our family, who lived with us for six months while he trained for the US Olympic Swimming Team trials. He devoted his entire being to secure the privilege and honor of competing with the best athletes in the world. I never understood how a native of Arkansas with a southern drawl could go as fast as he could in the pool. Even though David came close to being selected, I admire his willingness to give everything toward his dream.

Sue Monk Kidd, best known for her novel *The Secret Life of Bees*, tells a story about when her daughter was young and got the dubious part of the Bethlehem star in a Christmas play. After her first rehearsal, she burst through the door with her costume, a five-pointed star lined in shiny gold tinsel designed to drape over her like a sandwich board. "What exactly will you be doing in the play?" her mother asked her. Her daughter answered, "I just stand there and shine."

That's worth celebrating: pure unadulterated devotion and delight.

Celebrate Failure

Tom Watson, Jr., IBM's founder and guide for over forty years, called in an executive, who said, "I guess you want my resignation." Watson replied, "You can't be serious. We've just spent $10 million educating you!"

Celebrate failure? Yes. Welcome it with open arms so that members of the movement have the freedom not only to succeed, but also to fail. Developing a culture of innovation and invention requires that failure must be a necessary and viable option. And yet, I still hear some executives issue to their people what could be considered an untenable edict: "Failure is not an option!"

Michael Eisner, Chair and CEO of the Walt Disney Company (1984–2005), shared how his company understands the nature of failure: "At Disney, we also feel that the only way to succeed creatively is to fail. A company like ours must create an atmosphere in which people feel safe to fail. This means forming an organization where failure is not only tolerated, but fear of criticism for submitting a foolish idea is abolished. If not, people become too cautious. They hunker down, afraid to rock the boat, afraid of being ridiculed. Potentially brilliant ideas are never uttered and therefore never heard."

"One of the reasons people stop learning," observed John Gardner, author of *Excellence and Self-Renewal*, "is that they become less and less willing to risk failure." I find that a large segment of my university students studying leadership and creativity at the graduate level have been exposed to an educational system that has done its best to "stigmatize mistakes," as Ken Robinson and Lou Aronica point out in their book *The Element*. In conversation with my students, they reveal how educators have ridiculed and punished them for an incorrect answer. So they play it safe by not getting involved in class discussions, stay under the radar, and just get through the course. Even though I assure them that in my class it's okay to fail, it's going to be a long time before they trust me or another professor again.

"A child becomes an adult," reflected psychiatrist Thomas Szasz, "when he realizes that he has a right not only to be right but also to be wrong." What you consider to be your worst failure may turn out to be one of your best successes. E. Stanley Jones, a Methodist minister/

missionary for fifty-five years during the early twentieth century in India, formed a close friendship with Mahatma Gandhi, with whom he shared an advocacy for human rights. Shortly after Gandhi's death in 1947, the United Methodist Publishing House released Jones' book, *Christ of the Indian Road*, about his relationship with Gandhi. The book bombed and Jones felt that the publication was his least successful book and its messages completely ignored.

A few years later, a recent graduate of Crozier Theological School and a doctoral candidate at Boston University, checked references about Mahatma Gandhi and found Jones' unsung volume. As he read about Gandhi's commitment to a nonviolent yet non-compliant form of protest, this young pastor and civil rights leader found a basis for forming his own resistance to abuse and oppression, and wrote in the margin: "This is it!" That student, Martin Luther King, Jr., formed and formulated the Montgomery, Alabama, bus boycott and the nonviolent resistance model of the early civil rights movement, partly because he read a "failed" book.

"I've failed over and over again in my life," claimed Michael Jordan, "and that is why I succeed."

Celebrate Success

"Success is a lousy teacher," reflected Bill Gates. "It seduces smart people into thinking they can't lose."

Heretics concur with John Ruskin, the leading English art critic of the Victorian era and a prominent social thinker: "In order that people may be happy in their work, these three things are needed: They must be fit for it. They must not do too much of it. And they must have a sense of success in it." Heretics define their "success" by recognizing their capacity as servant, dreamer, and challenger, their opportunity to strive together for and achieve an impossible dream.

A friend of Baron Pierre de Coubertin, Father Henri Martin Didon, used the discipline of sport as a powerful educational tool. One day, following an interschool athletics meeting, Didon ended his speech quoting three Latin words: *Citius, Altius, Fortius* (meaning "faster, higher, stronger"). Struck by the succinctness of this phrase, Baron Pierre de Coubertin made it the Olympic motto, a motto for people who "dare to try to break records."

The Olympics demonstrate that victory is often by a hundredth of a second, or a single point, or a few centimeters. The victors generate their best performance at exactly the time required, under the greatest pressure, and against the strongest competition. Although only three competitors receive medals at each Olympic event, there's nothing shabby about being the eighth best in the world.

In the article, "A Wall of Honor That's Built by Your Colleagues," Adam Grant interviewed Niraj Shah, co-founder and CEO of Wayfair.com, about the important leadership lessons he has learned. Shah responded, "One thing I've learned over time is that it's important to take a minute and celebrate a win before you move on to the next thing you want to accomplish. One of our values at Wayfair is that we are never done. That speaks to being tenacious—there is good, but you can do it even better. But you have to celebrate wins and let everyone who worked hard on something know that they were successful and that you're proud of the team."

PART FOUR

Lead Like A Heretic: Empower

CHAPTER 10

Lead Without Power

"An empowered organization," commented Stephen Covey, author of *Principle-Centered Leadership*, "is one in which individuals have the knowledge, skill, desire, and opportunity to personally succeed in a way that leads to organizational success." Heretics who lead without power paradoxically empower their organizations. "Leaders accept and act on the paradox of power," contend James Kouzes and Barry Poser, authors of *The Leadership Challenge*. "You become more powerful when you give your own power away."

Max De Pree finds that the most successful organizations of the Information Age operate not as controlled collections of human resources, but as dynamic communities of free people. And in order to mobilize these communities, leaders must know how to lead without power, because free people follow willingly or not at all. De Pree, CEO of Herman Miller from 1980 to 1987, calls such organizations movements, and challenges others to follow their example to transcend the deceptive simplicity of a single bottom line and set standards for leadership and service all organizations should reach for. They lead not with the power of the paycheck or with bureaucratic carrots-and-sticks, he claims, but with the promise of meaningful work and lives fulfilled.

From my research, a universally accepted definition of empowerment does not exist. However, we can indicate with certainty that the foundation of empowerment rests on the idea that giving employees skills, resources, authority, opportunity, motivation, as well as holding them responsible and accountable for outcomes of their actions, will contribute to their competence and satisfaction. Employees receive a certain degree of autonomy and responsibility for decision-making regarding their specific organizational tasks, which allows decisions to be made especially at the lower levels of an organization where employees have a unique view of issues and problems facing the organization.

I have, for three decades, experienced this kind of "empowered employee" first-class service for outerwear, clothing, footwear, and accessories for outdoor recreation at retailer Eddie Bauer. In 1920, the company, which bears the founder's name, made this promise to his customers: "Every item we sell will give you complete satisfaction or you may return it for a full refund." Bauer was one of the first retailers to offer an unconditional guarantee in writing—he was that confident and committed to the quality of his products. And after fifty years in business he said, "My greatest contribution to the consumer was our 100% unconditional lifetime guarantee. That guarantee was part of what I sold." His philosophy still guides the company today. "Every product we sell is designed to be the best and built to last. If anything you buy falls short of those standards, you're invited to return it at any time."

This marks a major power shift so that the powerless become powerful. Alice Malsenior Walker, an American novelist, poet, and activist, commented, "The most common way people give up their power is by thinking they don't have any."

Let's explore how heretics lead without power, how they understand the nature of power as the currency of leadership, set power partnership parameters, and practice the stewardship of power.

10.1 POWER: THE CURRENCY OF LEADERSHIP

Goleman, Boyatzis, and McKee point out, "Increasingly, the best of breed lead not by power alone, but by excelling in the art of relationship, the singular expertise that the changing business climate renders indispensable." Heretics are in the forefront of the art of relationship leadership. They employ a complementary form of relationship currency that symbolizes loyalty and responsibility. Relationships are the key to success.

The writing is on the wall: leadership must change. "To survive in the twenty-first century," claims Warren Bennis, "we are going to need a new generation of leaders." Leadership consultant Gary Hamel observes, "Whatever the rhetoric to the contrary, control is the principal preoccupation of most managers and management systems." The command and control currency of leadership can still be used effectively in specific extraordinary circumstances, but must give way on a regular basis to an empowerment currency of leadership that accurately reflects the needs of today and tomorrow.

Heretics who know and accept themselves, invest their power, their currency of leadership, generously and wisely. So leadership may be defined as a process of social influence that maximizes the efforts of others toward the achievement of a greater good. Authentic leadership is an approach to leadership that emphasizes building the leader's legitimacy through honest relationships with followers that value their input and are built on an ethical foundation. Generally, authentic leaders are positive people with truthful self-concepts who promote openness.

In their book *The Unfinished Leader: Balancing Contradictory Answers to Unsolvable Problems,* authors David Dotlich, Peter Cairo, and Cade Cowan provide a modern handbook for leaders to recognize, face, and inspire others to expose the real issues that underlie paradoxes in modern organizations. Leading through complexity, they point out, requires giving up the illusion of control, consistency, and closure, while embracing the reality of being permanently 'unfinished.' Like other leaders, heretics are works in progress, learning as they go and grow. It takes a combination of time, patience, courage, and wisdom to fully appreciate power as the currency of leadership and how to use and invest it to accomplish their impossible dreams.

Heretics appreciate power as their currency of leadership that can transform their own community as well as the global community. Let's examine how they understand and employ the power puzzle, the power network, and the power play.

The Power Puzzle

'Enigma,' from the Latin *aenigma*, means "a riddle or a puzzle." And by extension, enigmatology, the study of puzzles, informs our exploration of the power puzzle as it relates to heretics.

Howard Gardner, in *Changing Minds: The Art and Science of Changing Our Own and Other People's Minds*, reminds readers, "Any attempt to describe a social process as complex as leadership inevitably makes it seem more orderly than it is. Leadership is not tidy."

Joseph Nye coined the term "soft power," but he says that strategy alone is no longer enough. In *The Future of Power*, Nye explains that in the global information age, superpowers need a "smart power" strategy, the hard power of coercion and payment plus the soft power of persuasion and attraction. He explains the process: "Leadership combines structure and soul—the hard and the soft, the big decision and the small gesture—in order to build or restore confidence."

"One of the great problems of history is that the concepts of love and power have usually been contrasted as opposites," observed Martin Luther King, Jr. "What is needed is a realization that power without love is reckless and abusive, and that love without power is sentimental and anemic."

The French Canadian philosopher and Catholic social innovator, Jean Vanier, has guided my thinking about the leadership puzzle. As a student of Vanier when he taught ethics at St. Michael's College at the University of Toronto, I learned that power is essentially an inside job, a nurturing of the human soul to help others and in the process help ourselves. A teacher of the wisdom of tenderness, Vanier founded the L'Arche (French for 'ark') movement, which focuses on people with mental disabilities, and celebrated its fiftieth anniversary in 2015. L'Arche is in 147 communities in thirty-five countries on five continents. Vanier, who recently received the Templeton Prize, brings the most paradoxical religious teachings to life: there's power in humility, strength in weakness, and light in the darkness of human existence.

According to Jay Deragon, author of *The Relationship Economy* blog, a narrative about the intersection of technology with the human network, many leaders don't get it: "In a connected world of rapid change, the new meaning of smarter is knowing what matters. What mattered for business to win in the 20th century was products, prices and profits. What matters in the 21st century is purpose, people and promises … To be a smarter business in the 20th century you had to be good at measuring, monitoring and managing the tangible assets so they produced the desired results. To be smart in the 21st century you have to be good at learning to improve upon the intangibles by identifying, measuring and managing them according to the expected results of the stakeholders."

Abraham Lincoln put the power puzzle in perspective: "Nearly all men can stand adversity; but if you want to test a man's character give him power."

Let's move on to see how heretics create and use the power network.

The Power Network

Jesus, the heretic, developed an extensive power network in the 'God movement,' a term used extensively by Greek scholar, Dr. Clarence Jordan, in his writings. Steven B. Sample, in *The Contrarian's Guide to Leadership*, describes Jesus' practical networking genius: "Jesus was extraordinarily effective in achieving leadership leverage through people chains. He recruited a dozen principal followers, who in turn recruited hundreds of others, who in turn recruited thousands of others, and so forth to a cumulative total of billions of followers over the past two thousand years." Heretics need to establish a power network to reach their impossible dreams.

Heretics can learn a lot about networking from a seemingly unlikely source: fire ants. The cohesive genius of fire ants, marvels of engineering teamwork, informs heretics to establish and develop a power network. Researchers from the Georgia Institute of Technology have discovered that fire ants are teamwork gurus that form a power network for productivity and protection. When a colony is washed out by flood, thousands of the insects quickly assemble into a tightly woven pancake-shaped raft that can float for months without a single ant drowning.

The influence of the Internet on our capacity to make use of networking with our colleagues and customers, suppliers, and competitors is phenomenally powerful. Virginia Heffernan, National Correspondent for Yahoo! News, points out a new reality: "Network computing and digital experience has decentralized the self. It has found the hallucinatory splendor in the present moment. It has underscored our fundamental interdependence."

At the WorldFuture2015 conference of the World Future Society in San Francisco, I heard Silicon Valley entrepreneur Gina Bianchini, the founder and CEO of Mightybell, give a keynote address, "The Road Ahead": "Our strong belief is that as technology gets better and better at surfacing the most relevant people to each other, then the probability of making new relationships goes up significantly. It's not a guarantee. But it goes up significantly. These are the 'modern guilds' for the 21st century. At Mightybell, we want to be that infrastructure for creating the kind of innovation that is happening in these pockets. We want to bring it to as many people around the world as possible."

Heretics believe that their power network includes everyone. Margaret Thatcher made this point clearly: "It pays to know the enemy—not least because at some time you may have the opportunity to turn him [or her] into a friend."

The Power Play

"It had long since come to my attention that people of accomplishment rarely sat back and let things happen to them," observed Leonardo da Vinci. "They went out and happened to things."

Heretics go out and happen to things. They inspire members of their movements to combine collaboratively all their energy, the foundation of all exceptional performance, to achieve their impossible dreams. They work and play together with a common core and a common connection for a common cause.

The *Fast Company* cover article, "The League of Extraordinary Women: How an inspiring alliance is saving lives and changing the world," by Ellen McGirt, caught my attention. On the cover stand three high-achieving women of power: Leila Janah of Samasource, Alicia Keys of Keep a Child Alive, and Maria Eitel of Nike. They are all part of The League of Extraordinary Women who have engaged in a significant power play: "The untold story of how an unprecedented network of high-achieving women from the largest companies, innovative startups, philanthropic organizations, government and the arts, combined forces to change the lives of girls and women everywhere." This story particularly resonated with me because I have coached remarkable women like those profiled in the article. What's really exciting about this League of Extraordinary Women power play is that it presents the opportunity for pockets of women to exert their influence together anywhere on the planet. The League brings a distinct set of power priorities to the needs of women and girls in the world and truly means business.

Morten T. Hansen, in his book *Collaboration: How Leaders Avoid the Traps, Create Unity, and Reap Big Results*, "formulates the underlying management architecture of collaboration, and presents a set of principles for what he calls disciplined collaboration, the leadership practice of properly assessing when to collaborate (and when not to) and instilling in people both the willingness and the ability to collaborate when required." In a sample of 185 managers, only 16 percent exhibited a clear-cut collaborative leadership style. Hansen suggests that one reason there aren't more collaborative leaders is the existence of five powerful personal barriers that block the three collaborative behaviors from emerging: a hunger for power, arrogance, defensiveness, fear, and big egos.

But there's good news from Hansen. "Companies, nonprofits, and governmental agencies that embrace disciplined collaboration perform better than those with an exclusively decentralized approach, because disciplined collaboration combines the results of all the independent units and results based on collaboration." However, he offers a word of caution: "Good collaboration amplifies strength, but poor collaboration is worse than no collaboration at all."

I experienced a great example of disciplined collaboration when the June Nelson-Becky Sneller Piano Duo performed at the Grand Rapids Festival of the Arts on June 5, 2015. Nelson has a Master's in Music and Education, and Sneller, a Master's degree in piano performance. Together, they executed their wide variety of musical numbers that included Hungarian Dances by Johannes Brahms, Gazebo Dances by John Corigliano, The Teddy Bears' Picnic by John W. Bratton, the Waltz from Masquerade, Sabre Dance from Gayane by Aram Khachaturian, and Funky. They performed with an exciting spirit of disciplined collaboration that was both mesmerizing and refreshingly enjoyable. Brava!

Indra Nooyi, the CEO of PepsiCo, and her team refer to their power play as 'connected autonomy.' Nooyi contends, "Organizations can have it both ways—performance from decentralized work and performance from collaborative work."

10.2 SET POWER PARTNERSHIP PARAMETERS

"As we look ahead into the next century," predicts Bill Gates, "leaders will be those who empower others."

Heretics empower members of their movements by thoughtfully setting power partnership parameters to frame the future with freedom and responsibility. Parameters enable heretics to establish the foundation of a common culture that encourages a climate of engagement.

Joshua Cooper Ramo, in his book *The Age of the Unthinkable*, addresses the motivational influence of parameters: "What we need is a framework for the sort of change that fits our world—and that lays a foundation for the widespread personal involvement of millions of people that will make such change useful, durable, and sustainable. Without these two elements, hope for change will dissolve quickly into lethargic frustration at best and, at worst, panic." This kind of future is tailor-made for heretics with its parameters for a flexible framework and extensive personal involvement on a global scale—two major operating principles of successful movements. Education at every level for every age will be dramatically disrupted. Unlearning will be required in order to make room for new concepts that will guide our creative thinking in the age of the unthinkable. My prediction is that heretics will lead the way doing their happy dance.

Since success is a moving target, heretics must necessarily be flexible to restrict or expand their parameters. Inflexible parameters kill creativity and transparent boundaries provide an essential safety mechanism. Let's explore how heretics set power parameters that empower others with expectations, boundaries, and support.

Expectations

"Few things can help an individual more than to place responsibility on him," observed Booker T. Washington, an American educator, orator, and advisor to presidents of the United States, "and to let him know that you trust him." Bennis and Nanus see expectations from another perspective: "Leadership, by communicating meaning, creates a common-wealth of learning, and that, in turn, is what effective organizations are."

Expectations provide the operating capital for change, especially systemic change. For example, expectations for me as a speaker on the circuit can make or break a presentation. When audience members come to an event with high expectations, they form a coalition with the speaker to work together toward a common goal. Both speaker and audience members take responsibility to motivate or inspire with a collaborative effort. When the audience comes with low expectations, the weight of the presentation rests with me as the speaker to persuade them to choose to be engaged.

Heretics empower others to translate intention into reality and sustain it by setting clear, high, and achievable expectations.

Clear Expectations

Desmond Mpilo Tutu highlights the need for *clear* expectations: "This is a great mercy, because in times such as our own—times of change when many familiar landmarks have shifted or disappeared—people are bewildered; they hanker after unambiguous, straightforward answers." When leading people from a wide range of generations, it requires an adaptive clarity.

In his article, "7 Tough Leadership Lessons from a Navy SEAL Commander: Taking tactics from the war room to the boardroom," Shawn Parr identifies the critical nature of clear instructions: "Navy SEALs focus on a very clear set of objectives, where significant importance is placed on defining the goal and motivating the team to follow. Even with highly complex operations, each SEAL has a clearly defined role, and expectations can be recited by each team member."

A president of a large company asked me as his coach to give him some fresh ideas to provide outstanding customer service. Customer complaints had piled up and he wanted to address the issue. I recommended that we look for an opportunity where he could experience first-hand the emotional dimension of what great customer service feels like and he agreed. I arranged for us to scoop and serve ice cream at a local dairy where I had experienced great service. With the permission of the owner, we put on the ice cream company uniforms complete with the appropriate hat and went to work. I reminded the president that he focus on playing the role of ice creamer server and not the role of a president. About a half hour into our shift, a person who works for his company came into the dairy. To his credit, the president maintained his composure. His employee said, "You look just like our company's president." The president responded, "I do have a twin brother." That three-hour hands-on experience clarified the president's expectations for revitalized customer service.

At the House of Flavors Restaurant and Dairy in Ludington, Michigan, the wait staff wear T-shirts with this clear message printed on the back: "This is a happy place. If you're grumpy, go home." Another T-shirt reads: "There will be a $5.00 charge for whining."

High Expectations

Heretics set clear and *high* expectations. Sam Walton, the founder of Walmart, claimed: "High expectations are the key to everything." He adds this leadership responsibility: "Outstanding leaders go out of their way to boost the self-esteem of their personnel. If people believe in themselves, it's amazing what they can accomplish."

Harvard professor, Robert Rosenthal, who coined the term "Pygmalion effect," affirms Walton's belief that if we expect others to succeed, they probably will. If we expect them to fail, they probably will. Sometimes my MBA students perceive me as being somewhat heretical. Some probably just think I'm a little weird because I begin a course by giving everyone an 'A.' If a student does 'A' work, he or she keeps the mark. If a student does less than 'A' work, he or she gets the appropriate grade. One student, after realizing he got an 'A,' promptly left the classroom. When he returned, I enquired what had happened to him. He replied: "Professor, that's the first time in my life I got an 'A,' and I didn't know how long it would last. So I went and called my wife and shared the good news."

Here's how Kouzes and Posner affirm positivity: "Positive expectations yield positive results. They also begin to create positive images in our minds, which yield other positive possibilities. Positive futures for self and others are first constructed in our minds." Case Western Reserve University professor David Cooperrider describes the phenomenon this way: "We see what our imaginative horizon allows us to see. Seeing is believing, and the results can be life-affirming and life-enhancing." If people believe they can perform, do the job, or live up to the expectations, they'll extend every effort to do so.

Achievable Expectations

Heretics pay particular attention when setting high *achievable* performance expectations. They ask members of their movements if they have the competence and education and mindset to accomplish tasks, and whether they have the necessary skill set. A cooperative discussion about achievability can prove to be invaluable. I've witnessed misguided leaders with a cruel mindset purposely set people up for certain failure. Setting the bar too high can be counterproductive and demoralizing, but providing a reasonable stretch can be rewarding for everyone.

At a Chamber of Commerce event, I met a life insurance salesperson. During our conversation, he shared with me his frustration of not being able to perform adequately for his boss and feared he wouldn't be able to keep his job. "From your name tag," he said, "I see you're a motivator. Maybe you can help me." I responded that I'd be glad to listen and learn about the current situation at his agency. He told me about the extremely high monthly quotas that were set by the agency and that at the end of every month they met and had, as he put it, a "come-to-Jesus moment." That was the moment when the production of each of the fifteen agents was put up on the screen and the reality that the lowest two producers were fired. No questions asked. With a degree of anger and sadness, he remarked, "If you're at the bottom, you're toast." I felt badly for his predicament, suggested that maybe that particular insurance company was a bad fit for him, and that I'd be happy to talk to him at another time. About a year later, I received a note from him expressing his thanks for my suggestion and that he changed companies and it had made a world of difference. Heretics set achievable expectations.

"Everybody is a genius," reflected Albert Einstein. "But if you judge a fish by its ability to climb a tree, it will live its whole life believing that it is stupid." Russell Ewing, a British journalist, offers guidance to differentiate a boss and a leader: "A boss creates fear; a leader, confidence. A boss fixes blame; a leader corrects mistakes. A boss knows all; a leader asks questions. A boss makes work drudgery; a leader makes it interesting. A boss is interested in himself or herself; a leader is interested in the group."

Let's continue our exploration of how heretics set power partnership parameters by setting boundaries.

Boundaries

Bennis and Nanus focus on the following four dimensions of empowerment: significance—making a difference in the organization and the world, competence—development and learning on the job, community—joined to a common purpose, and enjoyment—fun. Heretics establish boundaries that are developed with these four dimensions of empowerment in mind in order to guide, protect, and liberate members of their movements.

In their book *Three Keys to Empowerment*, Ken Blanchard, John Carlos, and Alan Randolph state: "In a hierarchy, structure is created to inhibit the behavior of people. Rules, procedures, policies, and management relationships inform people what they cannot do and how they must do a task. In empowerment, the structures have a different purpose and take different forms. Now, the structure is intended to inform team members about the ranges within which they can act with autonomy."

Heretics resonate with the empowerment model of boundaries with its attendant expectations, responsibilities, and restrictions. Boundaries provide that essential element of freedom that in my experience as a corporate consultant can increase creativity, productivity, and morale. Having the freedom to act without having to ask permission, a sign of trust that whatever happens you're supported, liberates associates to use their power within the set boundaries with a sense of ownership. Associates become fully engaged to use their own strengths effectively to propose new ways of improving the workplace and have the initiative and confidence to solve problems. They act as authentic heretics.

Boundaries Guide

To be empowered, associates must know what their specific responsibilities, authority, decision-making powers are to operate within the new boundaries to be created. Psychologist Ellen J. Langer highlights a pivotal concept regarding boundaries: "Rules are best to guide, not to dictate." Rules act as a GPS for organizational behavior.

"A dynamic system, whether a single organization or an entire civilization, requires rules," contends Virginia Postrel. "But those must be compatible with knowledge, with learning, and with surprise. Finding those rules is the greatest challenge a dynamic civilization confronts." In coaching senior executives, I usually begin by asking what one has to do to be recognized and praised in the organization, and what does one have to do to get in big trouble? The answers to those two key questions, in my experience, tell me volumes about their organization's boundaries.

Jeff Bezos, the CEO of Amazon, uses a guide for making six-page presentations with this rationale: "The traditional kind of corporate meeting starts with a presentation. Somebody gets up in front of the room and presents a PowerPoint presentation, some type of slide show. In your view you get very little information, you get bullets. This is easy for the presenter, but difficult for the audience. And so instead, all of our meetings are structured around a 6-page narrative memo. If you read the whole 6-page memo, on page 2 you have a question but on page 4 that question is answered.

"But that preparation does two things. First, it requires the team writing the document to really deeply understand their own space, gather ideas, gather data, understand the operating tenets and be able to communicate them clearly. The second thing it does is enable our senior executives to internalize a whole new space they may not be familiar with in 3 minutes of reading thus greatly optimizing how quickly and how many different initiatives these leaders can review."

Boundaries Protect

Boundaries guide and protect movement members especially when taking significant risks. They provide a framework for stability and creativity so necessary for imaginative, rapid, and competitive innovation in every field of endeavor including science, education, economics, and the arts. Heretics allow their movements the freedom to risk, fail, and succeed for the well-being of the organization and the people they serve. I met a CEO recently who disclosed that he wouldn't hire anybody who hasn't failed at least once. What a smart, progressive CEO. He's setting up a protective boundary regarding appropriate risk-taking as a determining factor in selecting a person to join his organization and fit in with the organization's culture.

Former U.S. Army lieutenant colonel, Fred Krawchuck, urges leaders: Don't wish for obedient employees. "Obedience is just too simple," he argues. "In a highly complex situation, anything too simple doesn't work. And it is a misservice to sit back and wait to be told what to do. There is something about moral courage, about standing up for what is right. It might mean you assume risk and write a position paper or schedule a briefing to help solve some of these difficult problems we're facing right now. I think we need more than just people doing what they're told or waiting to be told."

Boundaries Liberate

"You have to have the discipline," claims Peter Hall, former director of the National Theatre of England, "and then you'll be liberated by it."

Martha Graham, an American modern dancer and choreographer, whose influence on dance has been compared with the influence of Picasso on modern visual arts, or the influence of Stravinsky on music, agrees with Hall, and encourages liberating the body to interpret the music as the person perceives it.

Joshua Cooper Ramo points out this dangerous paradox: "The more closely we're bound, the less resilient we all become." When heretics set realistic and meaningful boundaries, their movements feel the absolute freedom to create within those boundaries. I discovered this reality in my military officer training. Within the established boundaries, I had the freedom to perform my duties and serve the organization with my best heart, mind, and soul. And if I had an audacious off-the-wall idea, my senior officers gave my idea consideration and gave me feedback on their decision. In fact, unlike other military training I have studied, we were encouraged to approach conflict with an open mind to design creative solutions.

When persons have well-established flexible boundaries, people act with passion and confidence. How refreshing to witness a front desk clerk at a Hilton Hotel who changed my room efficiently and personably without question. When he said, "No problem, sir," he really meant it. I asked him how empowered he felt in his job. He answered, "My manager trusts me to do whatever it takes to make our guests feel like they're at home."

Pirelli, the performance tire company, expresses and practices a philosophy of boundaries: "Power is nothing without control."

Support

Heretics set power partnership parameters with expectations, boundaries, and perhaps most important, support. They support their movements by giving referent power and loving unconditionally.

In 1959, social psychologists John French and Bertram Raven identified five bases of power: legitimate, reward, expert, referent, and coercive. To support their movements, heretics particularly give referent power, defined as the ability of a leader to influence a follower because of the follower's loyalty, respect, friendship, admiration, affection, or a desire to gain approval.

What a privilege for heretics who have earned the trust of their followers to support them with a variety of forms of referent power! I have witnessed these perceptive leaders affirm persons they want to encourage with one simple sentence of affirmation like, "You're particularly suited for that challenge," that can be worth its weight in gold. Sometimes leaders are surprised and even shocked at the power of their words of encouragement to influence the behavior of others. In addition, leaders use exploratory questions to engage their followers to clarify a problem, caution about a possible roadblock to achieving their goals, or offer the best form of referent power a leader can give by asking, "How can I help you?"

Alan Weiss, author of *Million Dollar Maverick*, comments, "Leadership is seldom about hierarchical position, expertise, or the ability to reward and punish. It's about 'referent power': I admire you, believe in you, and intend to follow you. That results in commitment and not mere compliance." Maya Angelou encourages referent power when she said: "Try to be a rainbow in someone's cloud." My mother, Mary Anne Sawyer Johnson, who believed that the future is as bright as the promises of God, daily assured me: "You can be anything. God created you to be anywhere in the world."

In the article, "Blank Checks: Unleashing the Potential of People and Businesses: How an unusual management technique inspires business teams to envision—and achieve—breakthrough," the authors Sanjay Khosia and Mohanbir Sawhney relate how, in 2007, Kraft Foods Inc. faced a major challenge with Tang, the powdered breakfast drink that had long been one of its iconic brands. The brand was caught in a cycle of underperformance. The unusual strategy Kraft used was to give Tang leaders in key countries, such as Brazil, a 'blank check' urging them to dream big and not worry about resources.

The secret of Tang's turnaround included freeing the team from resource constraints that could limit their imagination, and inspiring them to achieve unprecedented results. The authors conclude: "The key insight is that business leaders, instead of defining budgets and resources, should focus on defining ambitious goals, while leaving it to their managers and their team to ask for whatever resources they need to achieve these goals."

I know personally the immense freedom and humility I felt when I received a card that read: "May God bless you in your new adventure. We pray you'll never be restricted by lack of resources to change the world." My generous friends enclosed a gift of referent power: a signed blank check.

Heretics give referent power, and love members of their movements and the people they serve unconditionally. Mahatma Gandhi suggested that there are two kinds of power: "One is obtained by the fear of punishment and the other by acts of love. Power based on love is a thousand times more effective and permanent than the one derived from fear of punishment." Betsy Myers, advisor to two U.S. Presidents, observed, "Leadership creates a feeling. When people feel supported, listened to, appreciated, valued, respected ... they do their best work."

Heretics raise up the members of their movements by giving referent power and loving unconditionally.

10.3 PRACTICE THE STEWARDSHIP OF POWER

Gary Hamel describes a key role of the heretic: "If you are a leader at any level in any organization, you are a steward—of careers, capabilities, resources, the environment, and organizational values."

Heretics practice the stewardship of power as trustees. They agree with Benjamin Disraeli, a British politician who twice served as Prime Minister: "All power is a trust and we are accountable for its exercise." Leaders act as hosts, stewards of other people's creativity and intelligence for the advancement of the human family.

Peter Block, an American consultant in the areas of organizational development, community building, and civic engagement, and author of *Stewardship: Choosing Service over Self-Interest,* offers a very empowering definition of stewardship: "Stewardship is the set of principles and practices which have the potential to make dramatic changes in our governance system. It is concerned with creating a way of governing ourselves that creates a strong sense of ownership and responsibility for outcomes at the bottom of the organization. It means giving control to customers and creating self-reliance on the part of all who are touched by the institution. Stewardship can most simply be defined as giving order to the dispersion of power."

Block's definition of stewardship as "giving order to the dispersion of power" makes good business sense especially in situations where organizational restructuring or a merger are being considered. From a consultative point of view, I've found that asking three purposeful interrelated questions can be helpful in the process. The first asks about the nature of the task for which power is being directed. The second explores whether there is sufficient trust in the entity to grant power. And the third enquires if the prospective candidate has the talent to adequately address and complete the task. For a full sense of empowerment, all three questions deserve thoughtful attention.

"As we let our light shine," reflected Nelson Mandela, "we unconsciously give other people permission to do the same." Heretics practice the stewardship of power. They empower by example, get out of the way, and provide feedforward.

Empower By Example

"Do something wonderful," recommends Albert Schweitzer, a French-German theologian, organist, philosopher, and physician, "people may imitate it."

"If you want to change the world, who do you begin with, yourself or others?" enquired Russian novelist, Alexander Solzhenitsyn. "I believe if we begin with ourselves and do the things that we need to do and become the best person we can be we have a much better chance of changing the world for the better."

"We've consistently found that when getting extraordinary things done," reflect Kouzes and Posner, "leaders challenge the process, inspire a shared vision, enable others to act, model the way, and encourage the heart."

The most influential way in which a leader can empower by example involves encouraging the heart. The word 'encourage' derives from the French "*coeur,*" which means "heart." For leaders with a well-developed sense of their own heart, encouraging the heart of others may come naturally, but for those leaders who don't have that sense, they must first align themselves with a discipline of the heart in order to be effective at encouraging the hearts of their associates. That discipline includes cultivating a heart-to-heart relationship, a mutuality of heart connecting them soul to soul with empathy and love. When hearts in an organization beat as one, they can do the impossible.

Here's another image of empowering by example written in the enduring parable of Aesop's Fable of the Two Crabs, the crab and his mother.

One fine day two crabs came out from their home to take a stroll on the sand.

"Child," said the mother, "you are walking very ungracefully. You should accustom yourself to walking straight forward without twisting from side to side."

"Pray, mother," said the young one, "do but set the example yourself, and I will follow you."

The mother said, "Example is the best precept."

Heretics empower by example by being calm, caring, and consistent.

Be Calm

Remain calm, even if all hell breaks loose. Psychologist Daniel Goleman, reporting on the brain and behavioral sciences, offers his characteristic wisdom in his article, "Self-Regulation: A Star Leader's Secret Weapon."

He indicates that self-regulation is the quality of emotional intelligence that liberates us from living like hostages to our impulses.

A self-regulated person possesses an inclination toward reflection and thoughtfulness, and accepts uncertainty and change. Self-regulation is so imperative for leaders, he points out, because reasonable people, the ones who maintain control over their emotions, are the people who can sustain safe, fair environments. Goleman highlights as well that self-regulation has a ripple effect. It's a competitive asset that enhances integrity, which is not just an individual virtue but also an incredible asset for an organization.

Be Caring

Heretics lead by example by being caring. I recommend Ellen J. Langer's *Mindfulness: 25th Anniversary Edition* as the best resource for understanding and practicing caring or mindfulness. In *Mindfulness*, she reminds readers: "A mindful CEO can be mindful on two levels: by simply resolving the crisis in a mindful manner, or by using it as an opportunity for innovation. The most important function task for any CEO, and for the rest of us, is choosing what to be mindful about …

"The successful leader may be the person who recognizes that we all have talents and who thus sees her or his main job as encouraging mindfulness in those being led … Mindfulness can encourage creativity when the focus is on the process and not on the product. Mindful awareness of different options gives us greater control. This feeling of greater control, in turn, encourages us to be more mindful. Rather than being a chore, mindfulness engages us in a continuing momentum."

Heretics who care share. They mutually share life with their followers and create a strong bond that transcends ordinary relationships. My friend and colleague the late Rev. Earl Leard exemplifies this kind of caring connection. Earl was present whether he was right beside you enjoying a cup of tea or a thousand miles away on assignment. He always remembered birthdays and other significant days in the life of our family. You could count on Earl come rain or shine to be there when you needed a friend to talk to or a word of advice or encouragement in a difficult circumstance. He really was mindfulness in motion. God rest his soul.

Be Consistent

Heretics lead by example by being calm, caring, and consistent where their words and actions complement one another. What you see is what you get. They model the desired behavior in the organization. Mohandas Gandhi expressed the leadership responsibility to act consistently with this analogy: "Nonviolence is not a garment to be put on and off at will. Its seat is in the heart, and it must be an inseparable part of our being."

Actions, even seemingly inconsequential ones, certainly do speak louder than words. For example, when an employee of Timberland, a company that has a no-hero culture, encountered a man without boots, that employee took off his own boots, gave them to the stranger, and started a compassionate movement in his organization.

A university invited me to speak to its stakeholders including faculty, staff, and administrators at their annual retreat. At a preparatory meeting with three of the representatives who would be attending the retreat, I learned that the institution's president always arrived late to meetings, and harshly judged those who did the same. So when I met with the president, I shared what I had gleaned from my interviews, and he shrugged and indicated that he was a very busy person with heavy demands. In response, I told him that at the retreat I would be starting on time and would urge him to set an example. He agreed, but didn't follow through. When he did arrive, he discovered that the doors had been locked and he went bananas. The more he pounded on the doors, the more the audience applauded. He complained bitterly to his wife about my decision and she said, "Well, Mr. University President, you ought to hire the good doctor."

Empowerment by example releases employees' knowledge, expertise, experience, intuition, initiative, and wisdom. Theodore Roosevelt spoke to the influence of empowering by example: "Great thoughts speak only to the thoughtful mind, but great actions speak to all mankind."

Get Out Of The Way

"The best executive," observed Theodore Roosevelt, "is the one who recruits the most competent men around, tells them what he wants done, and then gets out of their way so they can do it."

Heretics lead by example by indicating the destination of the movement, and then by getting out of the way so members of the movement can fulfill their role. In her article, "Still Crazy After All These Years," Jennifer Reingold reports on her interview with Herbert "Herb" David Kelleher, the founder of Southwest Airlines. Reingold asked, "You've always talked about how important committed employees are to the success of a company. How did you make that work at Southwest?" Kelleher responded, "Well, the people did it. I just stayed out of their way. Be there when they're having problems, and stay out of their way when things are going well."

Leaders who micromanage like helicopter parents fail to bring out the best in their followers. "Never tell people how to do things," maintained General George S. Patton, a senior officer of the United States Army. "Tell them what to do and they will surprise you with their ingenuity." A CEO of a Fortune 100 company followed Patton's advice when he instructed his international executive team: "That's where we're going. Now get us there."

Rosabeth Moss Kanter, author of *Confidence: How Winning Streaks and Losing Streaks Begin and End*, stresses the importance of empowerment: "Confidence is enhanced when it is clear that people are empowered to take action, to solve problems, to voice their ideas, to create innovations. Accountability keeps people focused on the details of execution, while initiative keeps their heads above the fray so they can make split-second decisions about responding to the twists and turns of the play or search new ways to create the future."

I'm committed in my leadership coaching practice to model this principle of empowerment articulated by Kanter. To borrow a phrase from my pastoral role, I make every effort to practice what I preach. I usually schedule to meet with a CEO regularly for a half-day a month. Not wanting to risk the slippery slope of codependency, I get out of the way for the rest of the month. I do make it clear, however, that I'm available 24/7 for emergency consultation and if necessary to meet in person. Although none of my clients has ever abused this availability benefit of our working arrangement, every CEO I've coached has called early in our relationship in the middle of the night just to check if I'm really available 24/7.

"One of the first things required in movements," indicates Max De Pree, "is spirit-lifting leadership, leadership that enables, enriches, holds the organization accountable, and in the end lets go."

Provide Feedforward

Merwyn A. Hayes and Michael D. Comer, authors of *Start with Humility: Lessons from America's Quiet CEOs on How to Build Trust and Inspire Followers*, explain that training the brain requires four distinctive steps: assessment, motivation, practice, and feedback. In practicing the stewardship of power, let's begin by considering how heretics provide "feedforward."

You might ask, why feedforward? You're probably familiar with the term "feedback," which takes the learning from the past to inform our action in the future. Good feedback includes the following characteristics: timely, constructive, brief, focused on correctable issues, and helpful. Feedforward builds on the solid foundation of feedback, but emphasizes a more proactive approach to applying those learnings to future possibilities. The reality is that the future will probably not be like the past, and bring challenges never experienced or dreamt before.

FeedForward influences an organization's future performance by providing members with the benefits of a PHD: FeedForward that's Positive, Honest, and Direct.

Positive

Heretics frame feedforward positively. An anonymous author stated, "The positive thinker sees the invisible, feels the intangible, and achieves the impossible."

Jack Zenger and Joseph Folkman, in their Harvard Business Review article, "The Ideal Praise-to-Criticism Ratio," suggest that a little negative feedback goes a long way. Their research shows: "Negative feedback helps leaders overcome serious weaknesses. Our firm provides 360-degree feedback to leaders. We have observed among 50,000 or so leaders we have in our database that those who've received the most negative comments were the ones who, in absolute terms, improved the most … Only positive feedback can motivate people to continue doing what they're doing well, and do it with more vigor, determination, and creativity." Heretics need to find a flexible balance between positive and negative feedforward that matches the needs of a particular situation and the personalities involved. For me personally, I consider negative feedback as negative encouragement.

Heretics act as compassionate trusted coaches with a non-anxious presence to provide positive feedforward for members of their movements. Boyatzis and McKee explain the process of coaching: "The nature of the coaching relationship is complicated. At its best, coaching is a combination of deep understanding of the other person's hopes and dreams as well as the reality of their current situation. In this context, and with the support of clear ethical boundaries, the coach can provide support and advice, share expertise, and enable a person to engage in a process that will result in significant personal and professional development."

Honest

"However beautiful the strategy," recommended Winston Churchill, "you should occasionally look at the results."

Leaders have a responsibility to frame and express the truth in an artful way that encourages improvement. Novelist and playwright, Elias Canetti, commented, "I hate judgments that only crush and don't transform." Harry S. Truman confessed: "I never did give anybody hell. I just told the truth and they thought it was hell."

Heifetz and Linsky confirm, "Almost every person we know with difficult experiences of leadership has relied on a confidant to help them get through. Confidants can do something that allies can't do. They can provide you with a place where you can say everything that's in your heart, everything that's on your mind, without being predigested or well packaged." Heretics who value themselves and their followers often reach out to a coach in good and challenging times to ensure they perform in the best way possible. In leadership there are very few do-overs. Proactive coaches prepare heretics to act confidently in the most likely scenarios.

Bennis and Nanus, in their book *Leaders: Strategies for Taking Charge*, include this appropriate African-American church prayer: "Lord, we're not what we want to be, we're not what we need to be, we're not what we're going to be, but thank God Almighty, we're not what we used to be."

Direct

Nineteenth-century orator Robert C. Ingersoll observed, "In nature there are neither rewards nor punishments—there are consequences."

Heretics provide positive, honest, and direct feedforward as they communicate 'the consequences.' Mother Teresa encouraged kindness in the art of dealing with others in the short- and long-term: "Kind words can be short and easy to speak, but their echoes are truly endless." Mary Poppins sang good advice as well: "A spoonful of sugar makes the medicine go down in a most delightful way."

Ludo Van der Heyden, in the article, "The Problem with the CEO's Job Title," in the Harvard Business Review, remarked, "CEOs do not so much execute as influence execution through framing, decision-making, and evaluation. The best leaders operate from influence not coercion."

Effectively influencing the decision-making process of others often proves difficult especially when there are major consequences including the loss of income or the loss of employment.

A President I coached sought my counsel about an annual performance review she was going to conduct with one of her five Senior Vice-Presidents. She informed me about the VP's history including her efforts over the course of three years to help him improve his record of performance and how he had not shown appreciable positive change. She also shared with me that she was trying to be as objective as possible even though they grew up together since childhood and graduated from the same university. The President invited me to sit in on the review and listen to the conversation. Wisely, the President welcomed the VP and asked a couple of reflective questions that opened a calm and direct dialogue. To her surprise, when she asked him, "How can I help you going forward?" he answered: "Help me get a job that's a better fit." The President agreed and the meeting adjourned. Direct feedforward isn't always this easy but most of the time it does lead to favorable results.

Brené Brown informs us about the need to rehumanize work: "The most significant problems that everyone from the C-level executives to the front-line folks talk to me about stem from disengagement, the lack of feedback, the fear of staying relevant amid rapid change, and the need for clarity of purpose. If we want to reignite innovation and passion, we have to rehumanize work. When shame becomes a management style, engagement dies. When failure is not an option we can forget about learning, creativity, and innovation."

Lao-tzu, an ancient Chinese philosopher and writer, offered wise feedforward counsel:

Fail to honor people,
They fail to honor you;
But of a good leader, who talks little,
When his work is done, his aim fulfilled,
They will all say, "We did this ourselves."

CHAPTER 11

Resonate With Risk

"What you can do, or dream you can, begin it," wrote Johann Wolfgang Goethe, a German writer and statesman. "Boldness has genius, power and magic in it."

Heretics resonate with risk and enable their followers to do the same. The word resonance derives from the Latin *resonare*, which means "to resound, the reinforcement or prolongation of sound by reflection, or more specifically, by synchronous vibration." Heretics, in pursuing their impossible dreams, desire and anticipate a 'resounding success.'

For heretics, resonance with risk has its roots in their inner personhood. Goleman, Boyatzis, and McKee claim, "The fundamental task of leaders, we argue, is to prime good feeling in those they lead. That occurs when a leader creates resonance—a reservoir of positivity that frees the best in people. At its root, then, the primal job of leadership is emotional." The authors add an important assumption for heretics: "Each of the four domains of emotional intelligence—self-awareness, self-management, social awareness, and relationship management—adds a crucial set of skills for resonant leadership."

In another insightful book, *Resonant Leadership: Renewing Yourself and Connecting with Others through Mindfulness, Hope and Compassion*, the authors Richard Boyatzis and Annie McKee articulate for heretics the critical nature and scope of emotional intelligence: "Great leaders are awake, aware, and attuned to themselves, to others, and to the world around them. They commit to their beliefs, stand strong in their values, and live full, passionate lives. Great leaders are emotionally intelligent and they are mindful: they seek to live in full consciousness of self, others, nature and society.

"Great leaders face the uncertainty of today's world with hope: they inspire clarity of vision, optimism, and a profound belief in their- and their peoples'- ability to turn dreams into reality. Great leaders face sacrifice, difficulties, and challenges, as well as opportunities, with empathy and compassion for the people they lead and those they serve. Most important, we have found that leaders who sustain their resonance understand that renewing oneself is a holistic process that involves the mind, body, heart and spirit."

Perhaps you've seen the famous advertisement that, as the story goes, Sir Ernest Shackleton, an Antarctic explorer, ran in the newspaper to try to recruit men for his Endurance expedition: "Men wanted for hazardous journey. Low wages, bitter cold, long hours of complete darkness. Safe return doubtful. Honor and recognition in event of success." *Leading at the Edge: Leadership Lessons from the Extraordinary Saga of Shackleton's Antarctic Expedition* chronicles Shackleton's journey in detail. Shackleton issued an invitation to embrace a substantial risk for the sake of a big audacious goal. Many applied because they resonated with the idea of a bold adventure.

Heretics recognize that timing is an essential ingredient in the success of their movements. In addition, they know that there's probably no perfect time. In the leadership experiment, heretics accept risk as a given. Like the adventurous Shackleton, heretics resonate with risk through a process where they acknowledge, assess, and take risk.

11.1 ACKNOWLEDGE RISK

Jean Vanier observed, "We are very fragile in front of the future." Heretics agree and acknowledge risk as the first step toward taking action. Don Normans, author of *Emotional Design: Why We Love (or Hate) Everyday Things*, reflects, "In the world of 'design thinking,' acknowledging risk is the first step toward taking action, and with action comes insight, evidence, and real options."

Heretics acknowledge risk. They respect fear, assume vulnerability, and adopt courage.

Respect Fear

One Halloween, a young man dressed up as the devil for a masquerade ball complete with red suit, horns, and pitchfork. Unfortunately, the man mistakenly walked through the door of a church instead of the hotel door to the masquerade ball. A worship service was in progress. When the worshippers realized that the devil in person was there, they scattered. They all ran in every direction, except one elderly lady who was sitting midway in the sanctuary. She stayed put. Feeling especially empowered now by his new role as the devil, the man walked up to the lady and asked, "Aren't you afraid of me?" The woman snapped, "Why should I be? I've been living with your brother for fifty years."

Heretics nurture a healthy respect for fear, an integral dimension of our existence, a warning system built into our DNA to alert us to possible danger ahead and to take the measures to preserve our safety. Without an active early warning system, we'd be completely vulnerable. Heretics agree with Albert Einstein, who observed: "The world is a dangerous place to live; not because of the people who are evil, but because of the people who don't do anything about it."

The untoward actions of a few prompt us to scratch our heads and ask why. Sometimes we get clues to understanding the behavior of these individuals and groups, but we still face a mystery. The search for why continues. For example, why did James Eagan Holmes, at twenty-four, put on head-to-toe black body armor and methodically open fire on a sold out showing of the movie *The Dark Knight Rises* in suburban Denver, killing twelve people and injuring fifty-eight?

Sophocles, one of three ancient Greek tragedians whose plays have survived, accurately describes the ongoing struggle many experience with fear: "To him who is in fear, everything rustles." The proverb, "Once burned, twice shy," expresses the same sentiment that when something or someone has hurt you once, you tend to avoid that thing or person, and to be careful to avoid similar experiences in the future. If you've ever been burned in a business deal, you know personally how it feels.

A healthy respect for fear provides the foundation from which we can think, feel and act with confident awareness.

Assume Vulnerability

"When we were children, we used to think that when we were grown up we would no longer be vulnerable," reflected Madeleine L'Engle, an American writer best known for young-adult fiction. "But to grow up is to accept vulnerability. To be alive is to be vulnerable."

Vulnerability derives from the Latin *vulnerare*, which means "to wound." Heretics assume vulnerability as a major part of leading a movement, and the likely possibility of being wounded in the course of their adventure. Psychiatrist Dr. Scott Peck, in his best-selling book *The Road Less Traveled*, begins with this perceptive statement: "Life is difficult." He's right. Life is difficult and often unfair. There's no level playing field, no risk-free zone, and no guarantee. Absolute safety constitutes a grand illusion.

"Reflecting Absence," a 9/11 memorial, stands as a reminder of how vulnerable we are on a daily basis. In an article, "The remains of that day— What makes a successful memorial to 9/11?", *Financial Times* contributing editor Simon Schama writes that the project of architect Michael Arad and landscape designer Peter Walker is a model of moral tact and poetic indirection. A play of dialogues lies at the heart of their design: between the deep granite well of sorrow and the animated plaza filled with the living, between the fugitive quality of the waters and the regenerative growth of the hundreds of swamp oaks planted about at the upper level.

I vicariously experienced vulnerability when I visited "Titanic: The Artifact Exhibition" to mark the 100th anniversary of the sinking of the world's largest ship after colliding with an iceberg, and claiming more than 1,500 lives. Upon entry to the exhibit, I received a White Star Line Boarding Pass for the *Titanic*, a second-class ticket number 28133 assigned to Mr. Frederick Giles, age twenty-one, from Cornwall, England. Frederick and his brother Edgar were traveling to Camden, New Jersey, where their older brother John had found work as a professional horse trainer. The two brothers planned to stay with John and find work as well. Frederick was one of nine brothers, and was trained as a carpenter. He and Edgar had booked passage aboard *Oceanic* but had changed their tickets to *Titanic* because of the coal strike. Going through the exhibit through the heart and mind of Frederick reminded me of how vulnerable he was and we all are.

Sometimes, heretics face extreme vulnerability like the 'Hotshots,' whose primary duty involves the suppression of wildland fires on assignments throughout the United States and Canada. Firefighting involves working under very hazardous conditions for long periods of time and Hotshot crews are expected to accept the most difficult and hazardous tasks. A typical shift is sixteen hours and working for thirty-two hours without relief often occurs. Firefighters often endure hot, smoky, dirty, dusty working conditions with little sleep and poor food.

Brené Brown offers these words of purpose and hope: "Vulnerability is the birthplace of love, belonging, joy, courage, empathy, and creativity. It is the source of hope, empathy, accountability, and authenticity. If we want greater clarity in our purpose or deeper and more meaningful spiritual lives, vulnerability is the path."

Adopt Courage

Spanish poet Antonio Machado advised, *Caminante, no hay camino, se hace camino al andar,* which means, "Traveler, there is no path, the path must be forged as you walk." Fear often restrains us like a straightjacket. But don't let it. Adopt courage. Babe Ruth, the professional baseball homerun slugger, advised, "Don't let the fear of striking out hold you back." I came across the following anecdote on Jokes Gallery, taking a more humorous approach:

A couple on their honeymoon stayed at the Watergate Hotel, made famous by White House shenanigans during the Nixon administration. Remembering what happened in that dark time, the new bride was concerned and asked, "What if the place is still bugged?"

The groom looked for a bug. He looked behind the drapes, behind the pictures, under the rug. "Aha!" he shouted. Sure enough, under the rug was a small disc-shaped plate, with four screws. He got out his Swiss army knife, unscrewed the screws, and threw the screws and the plate out the window.

The next morning, the hotel manager asked the newlyweds how their stay was at the Watergate Hotel.

Curious, the groom said, "Why, sir, are you asking me?"

The hotel manager replied, "Well, the room under yours complained of the chandelier falling on them!"

How do heretics or movements adopt courage to travel where there is no path, or deal with the inevitable vulnerability in an unknown future? They look fear in the face, let go of fear, and then press on with courage to fulfill their impossible dreams.

"You gain strength, courage, and confidence by every experience in which you really stop to look fear in the face," noted Eleanor Roosevelt, an American politician, diplomat, activist, and the longest-serving First Lady of the United States. "You are able to say to yourself, 'I lived through this horror. I can take the next thing that comes along.'"

When one confronts fear head on, it unlocks and makes it possible to realize one's potential. I've discovered that fear and courage live as close neighbors. One of my challenges with university students involves building trust among us so that they can adopt courage and participate without the fear of giving a wrong answer or of being embarrassed or feeling stupid. Addressing this concern openly and sensitively provides a start on the process of building the necessary trust to move forward so that students fully engage in their academic enquiry. Once trust is established, learning becomes a satisfying experience that can last a lifetime.

Be assured that no perfect formula exists for acknowledging risk. Heretics acknowledge risk. They look fear in the face, let go of fear, and press on with courage. Then, they responsibly assess risk.

11.2 ASSESS RISK

Madeline K. Albright, the sixty-fourth Secretary of State of the United States, and now chair of Albright Stonebridge Group, reminds us: "Nothing is inevitable."

In his article, "The traits that separate CEOs from other leaders," Neil Amato revealed the findings of new research. Russell Reynolds Associates, an executive search firm which examined survey responses from more than 3,700 executives, including 134 chief executives at large companies in North America and Europe, found that a willingness to take calculated risks, a bias toward thoughtful action, and the ability to efficiently read people, are the three attributes that separate CEOs from other leaders. The next six traits were forward thinking, optimistic, constructively tough-minded, measured emotion, pragmatically inclusive, and a willingness to trust. Note that all three of the major traits the study revealed provide a firm foundation for assessing risk.

You may feel the urge as a heretic to go where angels fear to tread, but first, assess the risk. I learned a poignant lesson about assessing risk on my first visit to a Maasai tribe in Kenya. Our group arrived at a small village on the mountain in the early afternoon, enjoyed a warm welcome, a delicious dinner, and went to bed. Because my inner time clock was a few hours off local time, I woke up just before sunrise and decided to go for a walk.

I set out and walked for about an hour and as I came back close to the village, Maasai Chief Joseph came out to greet me. We chatted briefly and then Joseph called me over to the edge of the path and asked me what I saw. I looked and only saw tall grass as far as the eye could see. "Jump up like a Maasai herdsman," he said, "and tell me what you see." I still only saw grass. We went into the grass about twenty-five feet and jumped again. I could hardly believe my eyes. There, about a hundred yards directly in front of me, I saw a pride of lions. Chief Joseph said, "You're lucky, my friend. They already had breakfast."

Heretics, like surfers, wisely assess the risk of catching the giant waves at the Titans of Mavericks, the world's premier, high adrenaline, big wave surfing event. This one-day, invitation-only surfing competition is held at the legendary Mavericks surf break located near Half Moon Bay, twenty minutes south of San Francisco. The twenty-four Titans compete at the highest level of skill, risk, and athleticism to challenge these massive swells. The name "Mavericks" comes from a white-haired German Shepherd named Maverick that in the early days would follow surfers into the water. Waves reach up to sixty feet, exploding with such ferocity that it can be recorded on the Richter scale. Being touted as one of the most hazardous events in the world, these surfers assess the substantial risk in the full knowledge that others have lost their lives or been seriously injured challenging these gigantic waves.

In order to assess risk, heretics put on their *skepticles*, and ask whether it's worth the risk, and what price they're willing to pay.

Put On Your *Skepticles*

"Be bold in what you stand for," advises writer and poet Ruth Boorstin, "and careful what you fall for."

That's why heretics put on their *skepticles*, a term I heard while watching with my grandchildren a movie on Disney Channel. In a similar vein, the Disney movie *The Good Dinosaur*, an epic journey into the world of dinosaurs where an Apatosaurus named Arlo makes an unlikely human friend, the character Pet Collector introduces his "skeptical" pet: "And this is Dream Crusher. He keeps me from having unrealistic dreams." Don't you think every heretic should have one?

Dr. Michael Brown, Senior Minister at Marble Collegiate Church in New York City, includes in his book *Bottom Line Beliefs*, a story about a little girl who was curled up in her bed after her grandmother read her a fairy tale. Before drifting off to sleep, she asked, "Grandma, do all fairy tales begin with the words, 'Once upon a time'?"

Her grandmother answered, "No sweetheart. Most fairy tales begin with the words, 'If elected, I promise …'"

Businessman Bernard Baruch, with his *skepticles* on, identifies the same sentiment candidly: "Vote for the one who promises least; they'll be the least disappointing."

William Parsons, in 1844, comprehensively described the good merchant as "an enterprising man willing to run some risks, yet not willing to risk in hazardous enterprises the property of others entrusted to his keeping, careful to indulge no extravagance and to be simple in his manner and unostentatious in his habits, not merely a merchant, but a man, with a mind to improve, a heart to cultivate, and a character to form." That sounds like an excellent definition of a heretic at the top of his or her game.

Put on your *skepticles* and identify the pros and especially the cons of any proposed action wisely and thoughtfully. German writer and statesman Johann Wolfgang von Goethe cautioned, "It is much easier to recognize error than to find truth; the former lies on the surface, this is quite manageable. The latter resides in depth, and this quest is not everyone's business." Ask penetrating questions with the vigor of classical Greek philosopher Socrates. Specifically enquire about the context of an anticipated action and the possible negative consequences. If it looks too good to be true, readjust your *skepticles*, hit pause, and read the fine print carefully.

Keep in mind, *caveat emptor*, a Latin term that means "let the buyer beware," similar to the phrase "sold as is," a term used to indicate that the buyer assumes the risk that a product may fail to meet expectations or have defects. Trusting your gut for insight and intuition may not be the most reliable source for decision-making, because our intuition is often wrong especially when we're searching for patterns and causes. Daniel Goleman, psychologist and author of *Leadership: The Power of Emotional Intelligence*, issues this warning: "The brain's perceptual misalignment in recognizing dangers has reached a historic danger point." I can confirm Goleman's assessment having witnessed over three hundred people running to get in line to pay a thousand dollars to get rich quick at an Internet sales seminar.

Keep your *skepticles* on as we move on to ask whether the action you're considering is worth the risk.

Is It Worth The Risk?

"Know your strengths—and weaknesses," advise Matt Goldman, Phil Stanton, and Chris Wink, co-founders of the Blue Man Group. "Assess the risk, and bite off what you can chew. No one person has to have all the skill sets, but you have to hire people who have them. It's about collaboration, quiet leadership, and having fun."

Nicolaus Copernicus (1473-1543), a Renaissance Polish mathematician and astronomer, is one of my favorite heretics of all time. In the early 1500s, when virtually everyone believed Earth was the center of the universe, Copernicus proposed that the planets instead revolved around the sun. But Copernicus faced one high hurdle. At that time, the Church stated that the Earth was the center of the universe, and as a priest, Copernicus felt he could not go against its teaching. It was only on his deathbed, in 1543, that Copernicus agreed to have his book, *On the Revolutions of the Celestial Spheres*, published. It was one of the most influential books ever written on astronomy, and had a deep impact on Western thought. For the heretic, timing can be a significant factor.

Sir Richard Branson relates the best advice his late father gave him:

"When I was 15 and wanted to leave school to start a national student magazine, I remember him telling me that I couldn't do so until I had sold £4,000 worth of advertising to cover the printing and paper costs of the first edition of the magazine, so we knew the sales would be all upside. I worked out of the phone box with even more determination to try to get advertisers to support us. Once I'd got the advertising sold I went to see the headmaster and told him I was leaving school. He told me I would either go to prison or become a millionaire! While it was a big risk to leave school, I knew I had a good idea and knew I had the downside covered, so I was confident I was making the right decision. The truth is rules are made to be broken. However, the theory is sound: trust your instincts, but protect the downside."

In 1984, after much prayerful consideration, I decided to take a big risk by leaving my pastoral responsibilities and starting a speaking, coaching, and consulting business. I thoroughly enjoyed my role in the church, but felt called to use my gifts in a wider ministry in the world. So I left the relative safety of the parish and with the support of family and friends made the leap that included a steep learning curve. And I have never regretted my decision to become a social entrepreneur.

"The biggest risk is not taking any risk," remarked Mark Zuckerberg, co-founder of the social networking website Facebook. "In a world that's changing really quickly, the only strategy that is guaranteed to fail is not taking risks."

Playwright Pierre Comeille offers a closing thought about risk: "To win without risk is to triumph without glory."

What Price Are You Willing To Pay?

"Live as if you were to die tomorrow," advised Mahatma Gandhi. "Learn as if you were to live forever."

In life, love, and work, real risks require asking: What price are you willing to pay, or how much are you willing to invest or lose? Heretics, who generally have a high tolerance for risk, take big risks to achieve their highest reward, their impossible dreams. And if they should fail in their endeavor, consider it an opportunity to learn and grow.

Note the delicate balance between the two questions: "Is It Worth the Risk?" and "What Price Are You Willing to Pay?" Mike Figliuolo, in his article, "Everyone Needs a Little Revolution," issues caution when discerning the real cost of taking action: "Realize that being a revolutionary comes with a price tag. You could become an outcast. People will call you names. In extreme cases, you'll get shot. The pile of crap you seek to tackle must be worth the price you're willing to pay (and that you ask members of the mob to pay)."

"Real adventure," says Yvon Chouinard, a rock climber, environmentalist, and outdoor industry businessman whose company, Patagonia, is known for its environmental focus, "is defined best as a journey from which you may not come back alive, and certainly not as the same person." Heretics sometimes will risk at all costs and throw caution to the wind, willing to pay the ultimate price. Some who risk it all lose it all.

Many heretics through the years have responded to a sacred or secular call to risk themselves for the sake of others. Cheryl Beckett answered such a call to do humanitarian work in Afghanistan. A native of Owensville, Ohio, the thirty-two-year-old graduate of the agricultural intern program at Educational Concerns for Hunger Organization (ECHO) volunteered to help feed the Afghan people by introducing nutritional gardening projects. She also spoke Pashto and worked with women and children who sought medical care from International Assistance Mission.

As a single woman, Beckett knew she was potentially in danger, but she also knew God called her to the work. "I have never doubted that this, for whatever reason, is where God has intended me to be," Beckett wrote in an e-mail to a friend at her home church. Regrettably, on August 5, 2010, armed forces in Kuran wa Munjan District of Badakhshan Province in Afghanistan attacked and killed Beckett and nine of her colleagues, members of the International Assistance Mission (IAM) Nuristan Eye

Camp team. I thought about Beckett's compassionate service and sacrifice as I watched the movie *Frozen*, when Snowman Olaf said, "Some people are worth melting for."

Like Cheryl Beckett, as a passionate follower of Jesus, I identify with her commitment and desire to serve God's purposes in the world. Both of us were willing to pay the ultimate price. The difference was that Cheryl paid that price before I did. I committed myself to children in Kibera Slum in Nairobi, Kenya. I believed they were worth melting for and followed my commitment to establish a feeding program in the heart of Kibera. In preparation for my trip to Africa in June 2005, I took all the required precautions and took my daily medication to prevent malaria. In spite of my diligence, a tick bit me and I contracted malaria. I shook uncontrollably for seven hours with severe alternating chills and fever. I fainted while lying down in bed. Of the four strains of malaria, I got the one that comes with a lifetime guarantee. That means for a couple of hours every month, I feel like I have the flu and my temperature sometimes reaches 105 degrees. To complicate matters, I contracted typhoid fever as well. If you're looking for a quick weight-loss program, this really works. I lost thirty pounds in less than two weeks.

Heretics resonate with risk. They acknowledge, assess, and take risk.

11.3 TAKE RISK

Christopher Columbus, the Italian explorer and citizen of the Republic of Genoa, completed under the auspices of the Catholic Monarchs of Spain four voyages across the Atlantic Ocean. This legendary navigator and risk-taker advised, "You can never cross the ocean until you have the courage to lose sight of the shore." A heretic must take risk to pursue his or her impossible dream with all the implications that would have for their movement and for the world in which they live.

In our rapidly changing world, the most successful employers will be those who can find, recruit, engage, support, and retain the needed top talent. Senior executives are competitively hunting for people who can think creatively, take initiative, and eagerly accept accountability for results. But the hunt is not going well. In a recent survey of recruiters, both in-house and independent professionals, they discovered that it has become much more difficult to find people who have the background, skills, and experience to perform as high achievers. Employers admit privately that they are limping along with an insufficient team of leaders at the senior and middle management levels.

What's missing? The shortage seems to be in highly competent leaders who inspire people to follow them into bold ventures that differentiate their companies from their competition. This elusive quality might be described as an "entrepreneurial spirit." This perspective, and the courage that goes with it, has not been taught by enough schools, including highly touted business schools. Employers, more concerned with fiscal conservatism than risky new ventures, have certainly promoted this drive. The lack of brave, inspired, calculated risk-takers in leadership roles depresses stimulation and development of followers with similar traits.

So why take risks? Joshua Cooper Ramo, in his book *The Age of the Unthinkable*, provides these clues to answer why we should take risk: "It's tempting to feel that forces at work now are so big that there is no point in action at all. But in fact the opposite is true. Even small changes can have an impact on our future and this is why we must all get involved. We are at the start of a profound crisis that is going to demand radical changes. It is a struggle that, as Immanuel Wallerstein has written from his perspective as an historian, may continue for twenty, thirty, fifty years and the outcome is intrinsically uncertain. History is on no one's side. It depends on what we do."

Ramo is right. It does depend on each one of us to do what we can do to impact the course of history. The collective impact of our small risks can be phenomenal. I asked myself whether it was worth all the time, money, and energy to write a book about leadership, and made a conscious choice to risk getting my message out to leaders everywhere in the world. The greater risk is getting noticed in an economy flooded with an explosion of new titles. According to the latest Bowker Report (September 7, 2016), more than 700,000 books were self-published in the U.S. in 2015, which is an incredible increase of 375 percent since 2010. And the number of traditionally published books had climbed to over 300,000 by 2013 according to the latest Bowker figures (August 5, 2014). The net effect is that the number of new books published each year in the U.S. has exploded by more than 600,000 since 2007, to well over 1 million annually. At the same time, more than 13 million previously published books are still available through many sources. Here's the miracle: we're connecting because I took a risk to write and you to read. Together, we can make a world of difference.

One could take the inaction of what Steven B. Sample calls "artful procrastination," but as global consultant Alan Weiss points out: "Procrastination is about fear. Egocentric people fear losing. Insecure people fear winning. Depressed people fear both."

The American philosopher and psychologist William James believed, "It's only by risking our persons from one hour to the next that we live at all." Let's explore how heretics take risk fearlessly, boldly, and adaptively.

Fearlessly

"We are all afraid—for our confidence—for the future, for the world," wrote Jacob Bronowski in *The Ascent of Man*. "This is the nature of the human imagination. Yet every man, every civilization, has gone forward because of its engagement with what it has set itself to do. The personal commitment of a man to his skill, the intellectual commitment and the emotional commitment working together as one, has made the Ascent of Man."

After acknowledging and assessing risk, heretics take risks fearlessly. They endorse what Katherine Anne "Katie" Couric, the American journalist who currently serves as Yahoo! Global News Anchor, encouraged: "Be fearless. Have the courage to take risks. Go where there are no guarantees. Get out of your comfort zone even if it means being uncomfortable. The road less traveled is sometimes fraught with barricades, bumps, and uncharted terrain. But it is on that road where your character is truly tested. Have the courage to accept that you're not perfect, nothing is and no one is—and that's OK."

This following story inspires me every time I read it. Two tribes in the Andes were at war. One tribe lived in the lowlands and the other high in the mountains. The mountain people invaded the lowlanders one day, and as part of their plundering, they kidnapped a baby of one of the lowlander families and took the infant with them back up into the mountains. The lowlanders didn't know how to climb the mountain. They didn't know any of the trails that the mountain people used, and they didn't know where to find the mountain people or how to track them in the steep terrain. Even so, they sent out their best party of fighting men to climb the mountain and bring the baby home.

The men tried first one method of climbing and then another. They tried one trail and then another. After several days of effort, however, they had climbed only several hundred feet. Feeling hopeless and helpless, the lowlander men decided that the cause was lost, and they prepared to return to their village below. As they were packing their gear for the descent, they saw the baby's mother walking toward them. They realized that she was coming down the mountain that they hadn't figured out how to climb. And then they saw that she had the baby strapped to her back. How could that be?

One man greeted her, "We couldn't climb this mountain. How did you do this when we, the strongest and the ablest men in the village, couldn't do it?"

She shrugged her shoulders and said, "It wasn't your baby."

The city of Grand Rapids (GR), Michigan, was Kurt Kimball's baby. He loved GR and for twenty-two years served fearlessly as its City Manager overseeing the city's day-to-day operations and its preparation for the future. As the GR's top executive, he provided exceptional leadership to an organization with 1700 employees and an annual budget of $350 million. During his tenure, he received numerous awards and accolades for his distinguished service and leadership. His education prepared him to lead fearlessly. He received a B.A. in Contemporary Diplomatic Studies from the University of Michigan and an M.P.P. in Public Policy at U of M's Gerald R. Ford School of Public Policy. Kurt handled the complaints of citizens fairly and firmly and when threatened with a suit, his fearless response was: "Take a number and get in line." He now consults in the area of leadership with Pondera Advisors based in Grand Rapids.

John Heider, in *The Tao of Leadership*, gives this intriguing percentage perspective about risk-taking: "Thirty percent of the people love life and fear death. Thirty percent of the people prefer death and avoid life. Thirty percent of the people fear both life and death. Only ten percent of the people have the wisdom to accept both life and death as facts, and simply enjoy the dance of existence."

Heretics comprise part of the 10 percent who choose to take risks fearlessly.

Boldly

"I believe that the most important single thing, beyond discipline and creativity," claimed Maya Angelou, "is daring to dare."

Adam Bryant, author of *The Corner Office: Indispensable and Unexpected Lessons from CEOs on How to Lead and Succeed*, found that superb CEOs consistently demonstrate these characteristics: passionate curiosity, battle-hardened confidence, team smarts, an ability to be concise, and a willingness to take risks when it is most difficult. Consider, for example, the risk that these heretics took in the field of aviation. In 1903, Wilbur and Orville Wright achieved the first powered, sustained, and controlled airplane flight. The Wright brothers surpassed their own milestone two years later when they built and flew the first fully practical airplane, and earned the designation "First in Flight." Charles Lindbergh, an American aviator, made the first solo nonstop flight across the Atlantic Ocean on May 20 to 21, 1927. Like Lindbergh, Amelia Mary Earhart became the first female aviator to fly solo across the Atlantic Ocean on June 17, 1928, for which she received the U.S. Distinguished Flying Cross. Finally, Sally Kristen Ride, an American physicist and astronaut who joined NASA in 1978, became the first American woman in space in 1983.

Chris Albrecht, in his book, *Mavericks at Work,* urges leaders everywhere to take risks boldly: "We have to be more aggressive and take bigger risks than before. We're actively looking for new cliffs to jump off. We're doing things nobody else will do, because they can't chase us into those spaces. We didn't get here by playing by the rules of the game. We got here by setting the rules of the game." Walt Disney maintained a similar perspective: "All our dreams can come true if we have the courage to pursue them."

Jonathan Eig, a former reporter at the *Wall Street Journal* and best-selling author of *The Birth of the Pill: How Four Crusaders Reinvented Sex and Launched a Revolution,* tells the remarkable story of how four heretics challenged the status quo by taking substantial risks boldly to achieve their impossible dream: "In the 1950s, four people—the founder of the birth control movement, a controversial scientist, a Catholic obstetrician and a wealthy feminist—got together to create a revolutionary little pill the world had never seen before. They were sneaky about what they were doing—skirting the law, lying to women about the test they performed and fibbing to the public about their motivations."

Heretics must wrestle with whether "the ends" of their impossible dreams they've conceived, and to which they have passionately committed themselves, justify "the means" to fulfill them. From an ethical perspective, one could find ample evidence that the "Four Crusaders" acted illegally and didn't tell the whole truth to the public and their female subjects whose lives they may have put in danger. We can presume that the obstetrician lived up to his physician's oath to "Do no harm." Would it have been possible to invent the pill in some other way? In any case, millions of men and women around the world, myself included, applaud their work and thank them for their contribution to global health and happiness.

What an incredibly exciting period to be a heretic! "Life is no 'brief candle' to me," wrote playwright George Bernard Shaw. "It is a sort of splendid torch which I have got a hold of for the moment, and I want to make it burn as brightly as possible before handing it on to future generations."

The phrase, "Daring Greatly," comes from Theodore Roosevelt's speech "Citizenship in a Republic," sometimes referred to as "The Man in the Arena," delivered at the Sorbonne in Paris, France, on April 23, 1910:

> "It is not the critic who counts; not the man who points out how the strong man stumbles, or where the doer of deeds could have done them better. The credit belongs to the man who is actually in the arena, whose face is marred by dust and sweat and blood; who strives valiantly; who errs, who comes short again and again, because there is no effort without error and shortcoming; but who does actually strive to do the deeds; who knows great enthusiasms, the great devotions; who spends himself in a worthy cause; who at the best knows in the end the triumph of high achievement, and who at the worst, if he fails, at least fails while daring greatly, so that his place shall never be with those cold and timid souls who neither know victory nor defeat."

Adaptively

Charles Darwin observed, "It is not the strongest of the species that survives; nor the most intelligent that survives. It is the one that is most adaptable to change."

Heifetz, Linsky, and Grashow define adaptive leadership as "the practice of mobilizing people to tackle tough challenges and thrive … Adaptive challenges can only be addressed through changes in people's priorities, beliefs, habits, and loyalties. You have three core responsibilities to provide: direction, protection, and order." They maintain that what people resist is not change *per se*, but loss. And when change involves real or potential loss, people hold on to what they have and resist the change: "Practically speaking, the leader must find a way to disappoint people without pushing them completely over the edge. Exercising leadership might be understood as disappointing people at a rate they can absorb." Or, as Winston Churchill advised, "If you are going through hell, keep going."

Organizationally, adaptation occurs through experimentation. And for most organizations, that presents some difficult challenges. Human health professionals point out that as many as one-third of all pregnancies spontaneously miscarry, usually within the first weeks of conception, because the embryo's genetic variation is too radical to support life. A part of taking risk adaptively involves awareness of one's present reality. Consider this tongue-in-cheek story about Sherlock Holmes and Dr. Watson, Holmes' friend and assistant, on a camping trip, created by British author, Sir Arthur Conan Doyle.

After dinner and a bottle of wine, they lay down for the night, and go to sleep. Some hours later, Holmes awoke and nudged his faithful friend. "Watson, look up at the sky and tell me what you see."

Watson replied, "I see millions of stars."

Holmes continued: "What does that tell you?"

Watson pondered for a minute.

"Astronomically, it tells me that there are millions of galaxies and potentially billions of planets.

"Astrologically, I observe that Saturn is in Leo.

"Horologically, I deduce that the time is approximately a quarter past three.

"Theologically, I can see that God is all powerful and that we are small and insignificant.

"Meteorologically, I suspect that we will have a beautiful day tomorrow.

"What does it tell you, Holmes?"

Holmes was silent for a minute, then spoke: "Watson, you idiot.

Someone has stolen our tent!"

In a *Fast Company* cover story, "The Secrets of Generation Flux: Modern business is pure chaos. But those who adapt will succeed," writer Robert Safian relates the findings of D. J. Patil at the University of Maryland. Patil, who has researched weather patterns, explains, "There are some times when you can predict weather well for the next fifteen days. Other times, you can only really forecast a couple of days. Sometimes, you can't predict the next two hours. The business climate, it turns out, is a lot like the weather. And we've entered a next-two-hours era. The most important insight is identifying when things are chaotic and when they're not."

Safian concludes his article: "You don't need to be a jack-of-all-trades to flourish now. But you do need to be open-minded."

For me, these are exciting adventurous times to embrace uncertainty and confidently contribute to the welfare of our global human family. I've learned that I'm the only person I can control and willingly accept that responsibility as a work of adaptability in progress. Chaos aptly describes this period in our history and heretics particularly will have to sharpen their adaptability skills and be open-minded in order to survive and thrive.

Reinhold Niebuhr, an American theologian, ethicist, and professor at Union Theological Seminary for more than thirty years, stated, "God grant me the serenity to accept the things I cannot change, the courage to change the things I can, and the wisdom to know the difference."

CHAPTER 12

Champion Change

Heretics take change personally. They agree with Gandhi who reflected: "We cannot change the world but I can change." From the heretic's perspective, change starts with them. They accept the role of change agents by beginning the change with themselves.

Heretics are the champions of change. They are primarily change agents who identify a pressing need, possess a deep commitment to their impossible dream that satisfies that need, and an intense determination to achieve that dream—all of which require an appreciation of change. Then, they take a leap of faith to create and model a path for others to change as well.

The future described by the National Intelligence Council (NIC) in the United States' report, "Global Trends in Alternative Worlds 2030," which outlines the major trends and technological developments we can expect in the next twenty years, beckons us. "Change is the law of life," remarked John F. Kennedy. "Those who look only to the past or the present are certain to miss the future."

Let's explore how heretics champion change by adopting a triple-A approach: Appreciate, Anticipate, and Acclimate change.

12.1 APPRECIATE CHANGE

Heretics appreciate the nature of historical and contemporary change, and find inspiration in the wise words of Chuang Tzu, a fourth-century B.C.E. Chinese philosopher.

She who wants to have right without wrong,
Order without disorder,
Does not understand the principles
Of heaven and earth.
She does not know how
Things hang together.

How things have changed. Where would you get a watch in 1880? You could buy a watch at a store, or if you wanted one that was cheaper and a bit better, you'd go to one of the 500 train stations across the northern United States. Richard, a telegraph operator on duty in the North Redwood, Minnesota, train station, received a huge crate of watches. When no one claimed the crate, Richard sent a telegram to the manufacturer and asked what they wanted to do with the watches. The manufacturer didn't want to pay to return the freight, so it wired Richard to see if he could sell them. Richard agreed to sell the watches, and sent a wire to all the telegraph operators in the system asking them if they wanted a good cheap pocket watch.

He sold the entire case in less than two days, ordered more watches, and encouraged the telegraph operators across the country to set up a display case in their stations offering to all the travelers high quality watches for a cheap price. Richard became so busy that he hired Alvah, a professional watchmaker, to help him with the orders. Their business took off and soon expanded to include many other lines of dry goods. Richard Sears and his partner, Alvah Roebuck, retired from the train station, and moved their company to Chicago. And the rest, as they say, is history.

Heretics would agree with Edgar Henry Schein, a former professor at the MIT Sloan School of Management, who made a notable mark on the field of organizational development when he advised, "If you want to try to understand something, try to change it." They'd also affirm with Max De Pree that change is a gift, even when we operate in a volatile, uncertain, complex, and ambiguous (VUCA) world.

One resource, *FutureThink: How to Think Clearly in a Time of Change* by Edie Weiner and the late Arnold Brown, I've found particularly insightful and practical to inform my own appreciation of change, and to help other entities invent their future. It also contributes to a clear understanding of change-drivers, those dynamic forces that alter or intensify change today and tomorrow.

By now in the book, you're probably aware that I'm a heretic, a change-agent who's committed to helping leaders create and adapt to change to stay ahead of the curve. I view change as a natural phenomenon and approach change from an active perspective. I'm wired for change and have the capacity to change quickly with my 97 percent fast-twitch muscles. People have two general types of skeletal muscle fibers: slow-twitch (type I) and fast-twitch (type II). Slow-twitch muscles help enable long-endurance feats such as distance running, while fast-twitch muscles fatigue faster but are used in powerful bursts of movements like sprinting. That partially explains why I gained a reputation as a hurdler—clearing obstacles on the track. I also feel comfortable around and in water with its constant motion, and find inspiration sitting beside or sailing on lakes or oceans.

Let's discover how heretics appreciate contemporary change that is constant, complex, and convulsive, and the change-drivers impacting each of these dimensions.

Constant

Classic change may be described as normal, natural, and of the everyday variety. However, today we're experiencing a new normal of constant change: accelerating, relentless, pervasive, and persistent. This quadruple whammy leaders face expects them to do more with less, faster with fewer, better than ever, now!

The major change-driver for the new normal of constant change is accelerating constant mobile connectivity. My impression is that the majority of leaders at every level don't understand the staggering speed of contemporary change and its mind-bending implications for the future of all organizations. They confidently confide in me as their leadership coach that they feel overwhelmed with the constant nature of change, and when speed and mobility are added to the equation, they feel powerless to maintain the status quo let alone move forward. Unfortunately, some even deny that it's happening and as a result put themselves and their organizations at greater risk.

One of the key resources that has helped my understanding of the changing world of change is *The Mobile Wave: How Mobile Intelligence Will Change Everything* by Michael Saylor. He states his premise: "Technology is acid. Unleash it and it burns away accumulated inefficiencies in economics, in industries, and in products. It dissolves extraneous links in production chains, shortening them, eliminating costs and time. It cuts away layers of middlemen and exposes corruption so that everyone can see it … The acid of technology etches away the unnecessary, reshaping things and leaving behind only the core that is durable enough to withstand it. Mobile technology is very powerful acid. It has been unleashed and it will change everything." Note that Saylor uses the past perfect tense of the verb. If heretics don't get with the program today, their learning curve in the future will go straight up.

Saylor offers the following guideposts for heretics to help them understand the mobile wave and take advantage of substantial benefits of mobile intelligence:

- "Understand the wave, you can ride it. Refuse to adjust, you will be swallowed."
- "The technological wave marking this second decade of the twenty-first century is indeed radical. It is disruptive and transformational. But there is no need to fear."

- "What amplifies the transformational power ahead is the confluence of two major technological currents today: the universal access to mobile computing and the pervasive use of social networks."
- "By 2015, we're going to have 4.5 billion devices connecting people worldwide."
- "Mobile computing will be the most disruptive technology of our generation, and the revolution it leads is happening fast."

Heretics celebrate the new normal of constant change. They fasten their seatbelts and enjoy the mobile wave.

Complex

The leadership challenge for heretics requires dealing with the unknown, the perplexing, and the bewildering. "The skills required by a business executive today are many, varied, and not found in combination," observed Michael Novak in his book *Business as a Calling: Work and the Examined Life*. "Among them are the ability to grasp the possibilities of new technologies, to understand complex market forces, to master financial questions complicated by instantaneous international transactions, and to provide moral and intellectual leadership for a large (and often widely dispersed) corporation, while attending to the crucial matters of personnel."

One of my perceptive MBA students complained that there are so many factors to consider when preparing for the future. She told me she had followed my advice to 'identify the dots' and then connect them, but discovered, "The dots keep moving!" I asked, "Is it like trying to put socks on an octopus?" She quickly responded, "Oh yeah! They never stop moving for a second."

A Herman Trend Alert article titled, "Creativity: The Most Crucial Factor for Leadership Success," points out the need for leaders who can creatively deal with complexity. According to the 1,541 CEOs, general managers, and senior public sector leaders polled around the world, creativity is the number one leadership competency going forward. Top talent practices and encourages experimentation and innovation throughout their organizations.

This new kind of creative leader will be capable of tweaking systems to come up with new answers on how you run, organize, and develop businesses. In fact, creative leaders will have to make deeper business model changes just to keep up. To succeed, they will have to take more calculated risks, find new ideas, and keep innovating in how they lead and communicate. Seventy-nine percent of CEOs anticipate even greater complexity ahead and more than half of the CEOs doubt their ability to manage it. This is a cause for pause on leadership development.

In 1970, British cyberneticist Stafford Beer forecast that the great challenge of the Information Age would be "managing modern complexity." He posed two interrelated questions. The first asked how do people learn to cope with the complexity of the future? The second asked whether we even have the capacity to manage and understand the complexity? Certainly for public policy decisions, mastering the complexity and making informed decisions presents a challenge. Enter David Pearce Snyder, who addressed these questions at the World Future Society's conference in July 2009. Snyder introduced "complexipacity," a term he coined that refers to one's capacity to deal with complexity.

The change-driver that's stretching complexity is innovation. "One moment the world is as it is," reflects author Anne Rice. "The next, it is something entirely different. Something it has never been before." For many that's anxiety-producing, but for heretics, increasing complexity marks the possibility of a renaissance, a new age of creativity.

Convulsive

Heretics appreciate convulsive change and subscribe to the description of change offered by Bennis and Nanus in their book, *Leaders*, that "nothing is more central to modern organizations than their capacity to cope with complexity, ambiguity, uncertainty—in short, with spastic change." Spastic, spasmodic change may be described as disruptive, disorienting, and destructive. Paroxysmal attacks or paroxysms, from the Greek *paroxusmos*, are sudden recurrences or intensification of symptoms, such as spasm or seizure.

Convulsive, spasmodic change happens often without warning and demands astute leaders deal immediately with the circumstances with a view to the future. The list of these changes continues to grow: 9/11, stock market crash, Charlie Ebdo, missing airliner, Ebola, Katrina, mass shootings, and tsunami, to name a few. Joshua Cooper Ramo indicates that in a rather short period of time our world has undergone dramatic economic, social, and political transformations. This kind of convulsive change, he contends, will not slow down. For the foreseeable future, instability and unpredictability will become the new normal. Ramo believes that we should accept and embrace this new reality and capitalize on the many opportunities that this fast-paced world will bring us. Note that Ramo frames the future as an opportunity and not as a threat.

Competition and social unrest constitute two of the major change-drivers of convulsive change. The first, competition, derives from the Latin *competere*, which means "to strive together." Futurist Raymond Kurzweil, in his book *The Singularity Is Near*, highlights the impact of competition: "The product of a paradigm-shift such as the printing press took about a century to be widely deployed. Today, the products of major paradigm shifts, such as cell phones and the World Wide Web, are widely adopted in only a few years' time."

The second change-driver of convulsive change, global social unrest, adds another dimension to our worldwide situation and prospects for the future. The Millennium Project, in its latest State of the Future Report, recognizes humanity's momentous strides forward in health, literacy, and many other critical areas, but warns of stalling or moving backward on many other fronts.

So, how does a heretic lead in these uncertain times? Joshua Ramo makes the following recommendations:

- People or organizations need to be more anchored than ever in purpose;
- Business is no longer just about profit but about enhancing every life and community that we touch;
- We need to have a holistic view of the world, one that combines economic, political, social, consumer, and technological trends;
- Leaders need to live in both global and local worlds;
- Caring is the new selling in the age of transparency;
- Leaders need to develop structures along the principle of "centralized decentralization";
- Leaders must acknowledge that the most important leadership characteristic to thrive in this ever-changing world is resilience.

Heretics appreciate the constant, complex, and convulsive nature of change today and tomorrow, and embrace the challenges it brings to them and to humankind. In my experience, heretics intuitively recognize the need for thoughtful reflection and engage others in disciplined discernment regarding change. They view change not as a threat, but as an opportunity worth seizing. To do that, and to champion change, they will have to expand their capacity to anticipate change.

12.2 ANTICIPATE CHANGE

"It's what you do before the storm comes that most determines how well you'll do when the storm comes," contends Art Petty, in his book *Leadership Caffeine-Ideas to Energize Your Professional Development: Slightly More than 80 Power-Packed Essays on Improving Your Effectiveness as a Leader*. "Those who fail to plan and prepare for instability, disruption, and chaos in advance tend to suffer more when their environments shift from stability to turbulence."

Mike Figliuolo, managing director of ThoughtLeaders and author of *One Piece of Paper*, reports on a study that asked: Have you resolved to lead differently next year? Here are their responses: 44.6 percent said a little, I've made some small resolutions for how I'll lead differently; 29.89 percent reported somewhat, I've made a few big, focused leadership resolutions; 17.24 percent indicated not at all, I'm going to keep going with the way I do things now; 8.28 percent affirmed absolutely, I've made many resolutions to change my leadership. In Figliuolo's opinion, 60 percent of leaders don't get it. More than 60 percent of them aren't planning to change much of anything. It appears that the majority plan to continue to do the same thing with undetermined results.

For heretics, anticipating change fuels their impossible dreams and their perseverance to realize them often with great sacrifice. This idea of anticipating change drew me to join The World Future Society more than thirty years ago. As a Boy Scout, I memorized and have practiced to the best of my ability its motto: "Be prepared." One can't predict the future, but one can prepare for it. To be sure, one cannot prepare for every possible outcome because to do so would result in terminal fatigue. Leaders need to be selective in what they prepare for. When I saw the trend of corporations using social media, I encouraged a CEO I was coaching to get acquainted with this development and learn how to use it effectively internally and externally.I find it curious that most business schools still use the case study model as a primary means to learn the lessons to lead. Forward thinking institutions recognize that one can learn valuable lessons from the past, but because the future will in all likelihood be different from the past, educators must also engage students in a vigorous exercise to anticipate and create the future. In my experience, university students welcome the opportunity to proactively create the future including clarifying their dreams to meet the societal needs they might fulfil profitably.

As a visiting professor at Daystar University in Nairobi, Kenya, I divided my leadership class into groups of four students each and challenged them to create a new product or service that would benefit the global family and make a profit. One group of highly motivated entrepreneurial students proposed establishing a medical tourism business dedicated to providing specific surgeries at a local medical facility with high-tech capacity at a reasonable cost, a small fraction of the cost of the same procedure in United States. Imaginatively, they proposed an experiential benefit: an opportunity after the surgery to go with an attendant physician on a once-in-a-lifetime African Safari at The Maasai Mara National Reserve, a large game reserve in Kenya. Today, these future-oriented social entrepreneurs lead a thriving business that saves lives and provides a pleasurable visit to Kenya.

Eudora Welty's 1944 essay, "Some Notes on River Country," begins with this memorable line: "A place that ever was lived in is like a fire that never goes out." Heretics resonate with the spark of "original ignition" that having been struck once, lives on: "Sometimes it gives out glory, sometimes its little light must be sought out to be seen, small and tender as a candle flame, but as certain … When we live outside ourselves with sufficient intensity of feeling, we in turn have a chance to be changed."

Heretics carry this fire of anticipation in their hearts, minds, and souls, and imagine their impossible dream of a compelling future and the challenges and opportunities they may face on the way to the dream's fulfillment. They anticipate change as an ally, not an enemy. They prepare for the future proactively in the same way Olympic athletes prepare for their event(s) by integrating strength, flexibility, and endurance in their training program.

Heretics anticipate change. They build change-steadiness, maintain change-readiness, and develop change-hardiness.

Build Change-Steadiness

Inspired by the paintings of Japanese artist Katsushika Hokusai, poet Roger Keyes reflected: "Practice as if your life depended on it, as in many ways, it surely does. For then you will be able to live the life you have—and live it as if it truly mattered."

Sharon Daloz Parks, Director of Leadership for the New Commons, an initiative of the Whidbey Institute in Clinton, WA, in an article, "Leadership Can Be Taught: A Bold Approach for a Complex World," points out that "conventional power, meaning authority over people and budget, is less important than 'presence,' and that the mysterious quality of 'presence' rests less on innate personality than on a style of interacting with others in an organization." Parks defines presence as "the ability to hold steady and to improvise in the midst of the conflict and tumult of adaptive work."

Heretics build change-steadiness, or a sense of presence as Parks described it, first in themselves, and then in the culture of their movements. Emergency Room physicians provide an excellent model of acting with calm intentionality in life and death situations. And heretics, by the very nature of the change they promote, will face intense responses from those affected by change.

Lanny Vincent, one of the authors of *The Maverick Way: Profiting from the Power of the Corporate Misfit*, found that "new ideas in companies threaten the existing order. They activate the company's 'autoimmune system,' which protects the existing corporate structures against products that are 'not invented here' or 'not sold here.'" In Vincent's view, innovative ideas and the groups who come up with them have to be insulated and protected from the corporate structure.

In a Money Watch article, "Great leaders aren't smug," Margaret Heffernan indicates that executives who underestimate themselves perform better than those who overestimate themselves, that "a certain modesty, humility, or even perhaps anxiety makes better leaders," and "a modicum of self-doubt improves performance … The key advantage that self-belief bestows is that it encourages individuals to aim higher. Expectations drive (even if they don't determine) outcomes, so those who think they can go farther are more likely to do so. But the same confidence that gets them to the top may be exactly what makes them fail when they arrive. What this means for managers is they shouldn't be seduced by the smug and the brash but should look out for the smart leaders who don't quite know how good they are. I'd bet the bank on those people."

I've observed what Heffernan describes in my executive coaching practice. Leaders who engage a coach tend to have a healthy strategic balance of humility and hutzpah. They don't profess to know it all and are willing to listen and learn. They approach novelty with respect and discipline themselves to make wise decisions.

Heretics weave change-readiness into the fabric of their movement's culture for the singular purpose of championing change.

Maintain Change-Readiness

"Automatically, spontaneously, reflexively—these aren't the words we use to describe how our organizations change, but they should be," claims Gary Hamel, in his book *What Matters Now: How to Win in a World of Relentless Change, Ferocious Competition, and Unstoppable Innovation.* "That's the holy grail—change without trauma."

Heretics realize that they've got to be change-ready, or "get their ducks in a row," a phrase derived from seeing a mother duck taking her brood from nest to water with her ducklings waddling in a line behind her. Maintaining change-readiness means being prepared, equipped, organized, and standing by at the ready, to take advantage of opportunities that arise.

My dear friend, Vince Radzik, tells of living in a community where the expression, "Are You Ready for Freddie?" referred to being ready for the services of a local funeral home operated by Freddie. Are your things in order if you should die? Simon Sinek, in his book, *Start with Why*, refers to the "School Bus Test" that asks the leadership succession question: What if the leader was killed by a school bus?

Heretics often perform as quick-change artists with swiftness, flexibility, and nimbility, a measure of the capacity to be nimble. We're all familiar with the English language nursery rhyme, "Jack be nimble, Jack be quick, Jack jumped over the candlestick." The rhyme was first recorded in a manuscript around 1815. Jumping candlesticks provided a form of fortune telling and clearing a candle without extinguishing the flame signaled good luck.

Heretics can learn about maintaining change-readiness from U.S.

swimmer Michael Phelps who broke the all-time record for most medals won by an Olympian in the 2012 Olympic Summer Games in London. One of the best lessons came from winning a medal in the Olympics in Beijing in 2008 while swimming with his goggles full of water. He couldn't see a thing and still won gold. After that race, Phelps said that while he had never competed before with water in his goggles, he had practiced that way.

A week before I travelled to Kenya to coordinate our feeding program in Kibera Slum, I received a courtesy call from the Red Cross to participate in its refresher course for Cardiopulmonary resuscitation (CPR), a lifesaving technique useful in many emergencies. So I signed up in order to maintain my change-readiness. During the training, the instructor called on me to demonstrate to the class how to perform CPR on an infant. Immediately, it became obvious that I was rusty and not ready. With the instructor's help, however, I mastered the steps I needed to take if that circumstance should arise.

Two weeks later, as I walked through Kibera on a sweltering afternoon, a distraught young woman ran up to me and screamed, "Help! Help my baby! He choked and stopped breathing!" Then she thrust her infant into my arms. I put my CPR training to work as I called for medical help. I laid the six-month-old on the ground and confirmed that he wasn't breathing. I opened his mouth to see if I could locate any obstruction and discovered a small bone lodged in his throat. With my little finger, I gently removed the bone and gave him two quick rescue breaths. He began to breathe. I sighed and gave the little boy back to his grateful mother. In fewer than thirty seconds, I saved a child's life, thanks to my CPR training.

Heretics anticipate change. They build change-steadiness, maintain change-readiness, and develop change-hardiness.

Develop Change-Hardiness

"Good business leaders," noted Jack Welch, former CEO of General

Electric, "create a vision, articulate a vision, passionately own the vision, and relentlessly drive it to completion."

Heretics, in order to achieve change, must develop change-hardiness, the ability to endure difficult conditions, to keep on keeping on until they realize their impossible dream. The nature of change evolves as a dynamic process. Change as we have noted before changes and the work of adapting to change never ends. The context and conditions for the initial dream may have changed, altering or adjusting the original dream, requiring one to create a completely new one.

Developing change-hardiness takes effort and a willingness to stretch one's capacity. Heretics consider it a privilege to lead a movement toward a higher cause or an odyssey, a long wandering and eventful journey, a long adventurous voyage, or an intellectual or spiritual quest. "A journey of a thousand miles," noted Chinese philosopher Lao Tzu, "begins with a single step." And then reality sets in. It's one step after another for over 999 miles. If an average person has a stride length of approximately 2.1 to 2.5 feet, then that means that it takes over 2,000 steps to walk one mile. Another Chinese philosopher, teacher, and politician believed, "It does not matter how slowly you go, so long as you do not stop."

In the darkest days of World War II, families in England huddled around their radios to listen to the inspiring words of Winston Churchill. Britain stood virtually alone against the powerful Luftwaffe that dropped thousands of bombs during the night raids of the Blitz. On June 4, 1940, after the Dunkirk Evacuation, which removed over 338,000 British, French, and Belgian soldiers from the threat of the German army, Churchill delivered perhaps his most famous and stirring speech: "We shall go on to the end, we shall fight in France, we shall fight on the seas and oceans, we shall fight with growing confidence and growing strength in the air, we shall defend our Island, whatever the cost may be, we shall fight on the beaches, we shall fight on the landing grounds, we shall fight in the fields and in the streets, we shall fight in the hills; we shall never surrender ..."

Thomas Edison, an American inventor and businessman, who developed many devices that greatly influenced life around the world, including the phonograph, the motion picture camera, and the long-lasting, practical electric light bulb, reminds us, "Many of life's failures are men who did not realize how close they were to success when they gave up."

Heretics not only champion change, but they appreciate, anticipate, and acclimate change.

12.3 ACCLIMATE CHANGE

Thích Nhat Hanh, a Vietnamese Buddhist monk, teacher, and peace activist advocates, "Let us enjoy breathing together."

Heretics consciously breathe together or acclimate, where they become accustomed to a new climate or a new condition with all its challenges. I experienced how challenging acclimating could be when, after arriving from mid-America at the U.S. Track and Field Training Center in Colorado Springs, Colorado, I tried valiantly to catch my breath in the high altitude air.

Heretics guide the process of acclimating change, inviting and inspiring their followers to adopt and internalize their story. Annette Simmons, in her book *The Story Factor: Inspiration, Influence, and Persuasion through the Art of Storytelling*, recommends, "A strategy of successful influence requires that you understand the stories that compete with your new ideas." People will hold on to their current stories that are near and dear to them and that provide a sense of stability. A new story upsets the apple cart and triggers resistance to hearing a new story. Heretics appreciate that their followers need time to process proposed changes in order to consider letting go of the old story. And then and only then, will they be able to begin internalizing the new story and making it their own.

Heretics need to be sensitive to the emotions and attitudes that change sparks. Acclimating change can be very difficult for some, like Queen Victoria, who refused to budge. In the movie *Mrs. Brown*, Queen Victoria sank into a deep depression after the death of her husband Albert. Her advisers came up with an idea to lessen the effects of her psychological condition. They sent for her pony to be brought to Balmoral, accompanied by a handsome Scot named John Brown. She is not interested in being cheered up, and is infuriated when she looks out in the royal courtyard to see John Brown standing at attention beside her saddled pony. Day after day, she refuses to go down. Day after day, he returns. Finally, she sends someone to tell him that she is not now and may never be interested in riding. Unmoved, John Brown responds, "When her majesty does wish to ride, I shall be ready."

"Failure is not fatal," observed John Wooden, head coach at UCLA, "but failure to change might be."

To acclimate change, heretics focus on the future, tweak the tempo, and control the temperature.

Focus On The Future

"All who have accomplished great things have had a great aim, have fixed their gaze on a goal which was high, one which sometimes seemed impossible," claimed Orison Swett Marden, an American inspirational author who wrote about achieving success in life and founded Success Magazine in 1897.

Martin Luther King, Jr. encouraged his followers in the civil rights movement to focus on the future in his 1968 "I've Been to the Mountaintop" speech: "I just want to do God's will. And He's allowed me to go up to the mountain. And I've looked over. And I've seen the Promised Land. I may not get there with you. But I want you to know tonight, that we, as a people, will get to the Promised Land. So I'm happy, tonight. I'm not worried about anything. I'm not fearing any man. Mine eyes have seen the glory of the coming of the Lord."

The contemporary context of global leadership today leaves a lot to be desired: lack of vision, corruption, civil disruption, self-serving, distrusted, inability to resolve conflict, old thinking and habits, outdated processes, resistance to change (loss), closed to new ideas, organization dying, changing markets, lack of resources, and dwindling sales to name a few. This is a perfect time for heretics to focus on the future, initiate movements, and change the world for the better. In an age of distractions, however, keeping one's focus on the future is difficult. Warren Bennis calls this diversion "the Unconscious Conspiracy to take you off your game plan." Henry Ford noted, "Obstacles are those frightful things you see when you take your eyes off your goal."

On a personal note, I focus on the future in a variety of ways including learning from the past, anticipating the future, and living fully now. I'm also an active member of the World Future Society, the world's premier community of future-minded citizens who are dedicated to uniting the architects of the future. Its membership, united by a shared desire to tackle the world's biggest challenges, comprises futurists of all types; entrepreneurs, executives, forecasters, economists, scientists, students, parents, and conscious citizens. The conferences sponsored by the Society help me stay connected with fellow futurists and track the trends especially in the areas of the big three Is: Identity, Intimacy, and Integration. In addition, I speed read voraciously and keep in touch with contemporary cultural developments through movies, theater, and music.

German philosopher, Arthur Schopenhauer, hit the nail on the head for heretics when he observed, "Talent hits a target no one else can hit; genius hits a target no one else can see."

Tweak The Tempo

Heretics recognize the importance of purposefully tweaking the tempo or varying the speed of organizational change effectively.

An article, "The creed of speed: Is the pace of business really getting quicker?" in *The Economist*, begins with this reality: "A customer downloads an app from Apple every millisecond. The firm sells 1,000 iPhones, iPads or Macs every couple of minutes. It whips through its inventories in four days and launches a new product every four weeks. Manic trading by computers and speculators means the average Apple share changes hands every five months."

"Such hyperactivity in the world's biggest company by market value makes it easy to believe that 21ˢᵗ-century business is pushing its pedals ever harder to the metal. On Apple's home turf in Silicon Valley, the idea that things are continually speeding up is a commonplace. The pace of change is accelerating," Eric Schmidt and Jonathan Rosenberg of Google assert in their book *How Google Works*. "For evidence, look no further than the 'unicorns'—highflying startups—which can win billion-dollar valuations within a year or two of coming into being. In a few years they can erode the profits of industries that took many decades to build."

The article, "The creed of speed," also reveals, "America's executives worry that they won't keep up with this quickening world," and concludes with this enlightened sentence: "Forget frantic acceleration. Mastering the clock of business is about choosing when to be fast and when to be slow."

For the past twenty-five years, I've had the opportunity to assess the tempo of both profit and non-profit organizations and to recommend how these institutions could tweak their tempo for maximum results. *Tempo*, Italian for time, is the speed at which a passage of music is or should be played, and is measured according to beats per minute. It's not rocket science, but organizations, according to their context, need to appropriately speed up or slow down.

When accelerating, it's important not to speed up too quickly. I've witnessed leaders directing what I would call a "Corporate Chicken Dance" where the music gets faster and faster with unfortunate results. John Kotter, the Konosuke Matsushita Professor of Leadership, Emeritus at Harvard Business School, and the Chief Innovation Officer at Kotter International, a firm that helps leaders accelerate strategy implementation, describes the current state of leadership: "The old ways of setting and implementing strategy are failing us in part because we can no longer keep up with the pace of change ... We can't keep up with the pace of change, let alone get ahead of it. At the same time, the stakes—financial, social, environmental, political—are rising."

Decelerating the tempo usually helps leaders gain or regain control of operations by establishing "organizational speed bumps" to slow down the action. When a leader takes the organizational pulse and finds that there's one or a combination of "No Factors"—no purpose, no meaning, no laughter, or no fun—it's time to cut the speed to get a close look at the spirit of the entity.

Control The Temperature

One of the major responsibilities of the heretic in championing change involves accurately assessing the temperature of a movement and then appropriately controlling the temperature.

Let me express my appreciation for the insightful work of Dr. Ron Heifetz as well as his colleagues in this particular dimension of leadership. Heifetz and Linsky, in their book *Leadership on the Line*, provide a developmental process for championing change: "First, create a holding environment for the work; second, control the temperature; third, set the pace; and fourth, show them the future." The second phase, controlling the temperature, requires heretics to be attentive and adaptive in order for their movements to thrive. If the temperature is too hot, movements fizzle. If the temperature is too cold, movements freeze to death.

Heifetz, Linsky, and Alexander Grashow, in their practical book *The Practice of Adaptive Leadership: Tools and Tactics for Changing Your Organization and the World*, offer guidance for the novice and experienced leader: "If you try to stimulate deep change within an organization, you have to control the temperature. There are really two tasks here. The first is to raise the temperature enough that people sit up, pay attention, and deal with the real threats and challenges facing them. Without some distress, there is no incentive for them to change anything. The second is to lower the temperature when necessary to reduce a counterproductive level of tension … We call this span the productive range of distress.

"To orchestrate conflict effectively, think of yourself as having your hand on the thermostat and always watching for signals that you need to raise or lower the temperature in the room. Your goal is to keep the temperature—that is, the intensity of the disequilibrium created by discussion of the conflict—high enough to motivate people to arrive at creative next steps and potentially useful solutions, but not so high that it drives them away or makes it impossible for them to function."

Heretics should aim to keep the temperature at a level where the movement can move forward and be productive, but also provide safeguards so the movement doesn't explode or you are not harmed. In my experience, taking the heat of others' anger without undermining your work is probably one of the toughest tasks of leadership. Monitoring your movement's tolerance for taking heat is critical. I can attest as a corporate leadership coach, the temperature of leadership at the top determines in large measure the temperature of the entire organization. Part of my coaching responsibility is to help the leader use his or her strength of temperament to effectively control the temperature of the organization. On occasion, I've advised a leader to take a step back and reduce their heat in order to alter the organization's temperature. Of course, movements need some heat in order to advance, but too much heat can have disastrous consequences.

Heretics champion change: they appreciate, anticipate, and acclimate change. And with T. S. Eliot, they experience a new beginning:

And the end of all our exploring
Will be to arrive where we started
and know the place for the first time.

CONCLUSION

Thanks for joining me on this journey of discovery in *Lead Like a Heretic: How to Challenge the Status Quo—and Thrive.*

Here's an adapted question from the book's introduction: What do Pope Francis, Florence Nightingale, Steve Jobs, and perhaps you have in common? You're all heretics—courageous souls who don't conform to an established attitude, doctrine, or principle.

We've covered a lot of ground. We first considered the profile of the heretic as servant, dreamer, and challenger. Then we examined the integrated process heretics use to fully engage, energize, and empower their followers to do the impossible.

"When the effective leader is finished with his work," believed Lao Tse, "the people say it happened naturally." I hope you now have enough leadership theory and practice to confidently start your own movement and with purpose and passion address the needs in the world you've uncovered and want to fulfill.

In his book *Tribes: We Need You to Lead Us*, marketing guru Seth Godin writes, "Heretics are the new leaders. The ones who challenge the status quo, who get out in front of their tribes, who create movements … Suddenly, heretics, troublemakers, and change agents aren't merely thorns in our side—they are the keys to our success."

The Greeks appreciated the distinction between two kinds of time. *Chronos*, from which we get the word 'chronology,' signifies ordinary measured time on a watch. *Kairos* means 'opportunity time,' the right season, the right time for action, the critical moment. As a civilization, I'm convinced we're facing a *Kairos* and need heretics who will boldly swim against the current to bring hope, health, and harmony to our global family.

Heretics lead from the inside out. "If a man loses pace with his companions," reflected American philosopher Henry David Thoreau, "perhaps it is because he hears a different drummer. Let him step to the music which he hears, however measured, or far away." So get out there and shake up the establishment. Raise a ruckus. Color outside the lines. Push the envelope.

The global family calls out for heretics like you and me who will challenge the status quo, and in the words of poet Robert Frost, choose to take the road "less traveled."

> *Two roads diverged in a yellow wood,*
> *And sorry I could not travel both*
> *And be one traveler, long I stood*
> *And looked down one as far as I could*
> *To where it bent in the undergrowth;*
>
> *Then took the other, as just as fair,*
> *And having perhaps the better claim,*
> *Because it was grassy and wanted wear;*
> *Though as for that the passing there*
> *Had worn them really about the same,*
>
> *And both that morning equally lay*
> *In leaves no step had trodden black.*
> *Oh, I kept the first for another day!*
> *Yet knowing how way leads on to way,*

I doubted if I should ever come back.

I shall be telling this with a sigh
Somewhere ages and ages hence:
Two roads diverged in a wood, and I—
I took the one less traveled by,
And that has made all the difference.

Let's stay in touch and keep our conversation going to support each other to make a world of difference.

ABOUT THE AUTHOR

 Dr. Phil Johnson is an accomplished life coach to diplomats, major CEO's and celebrities, as well as an ordained minister and practicing pastor at the New Day Community Church. He has spent many years overseas working in slums from Africa to Southeast Asia to South America and he has participated in major international events such as the United Nations World Peace Conference in Israel in 1999.

He has four decades of experience helping organizations including corporate (Ford, IBM, DuPont), professional (National Retail Federation, Million Dollar Round Table, Auto Dealer Associations), and charitable (Juvenile Diabetes Research Foundation, Eden Church, Daystar University in Nairobi, United Way), to focus on their future, develop practical strategies, and act purposefully and profitably.

Dr. Johnson has published eight previous books, as well as three commissioned musicals and over a hundred articles. He makes his home in Grand Rapids, Michigan.

OTHER BOOKS BY DR. PHIL JOHNSON

The Compassionate Conspiracy
(Promontory Press, 2015)

Soulwise: How to Create a Conspiracy of Hope, Health and Harmony
(NanoHouse Press, 2010)

Time-Out! Restoring Your Passion for Life, Love and Work
(Stoddart, 1992)

Goodbye Mom, Goodbye
(Welch Publishing, 1987)

And More Celebrating the Seasons with Children
(Pilgrim Press, 1986)

More Celebrating the Seasons with Children
(Pilgrim Press, 1985)

Celebrating the Seasons with Children
(Pilgrim Press, 1984)

The Great Canadian Alphabet Book
(Hounslow Press, 1981)